A Celebration of
Young Poets

Illinois and Indiana – Spring 2007

Creative Communication, Inc.

A Celebration of Young Poets
Illinois and Indiana – Spring 2007

An anthology compiled by Creative Communication, Inc.

Published by:

CREATIVE COMMUNICATION, INC.
1488 NORTH 200 WEST
LOGAN, UT 84341

ISBN: 978-1-60050-121-0

Foreword

I am often asked, "What is the criteria used in selecting poems for your anthologies?" I feel that poetry should create images, make the reader think, or just be entertaining. This is a broad definition. Poetry itself is difficult to define. From the beginning of the written word, poetry has existed. However, from this beginning the complexity and styles have evolved over the years.

The poets in this anthology represent the best that our youth have to offer. For many it may be their first attempt at writing poetry, for others it may reflect many hours of instruction and learning. For all the poets who were chosen to be published, it reflects a level of writing that eluded most of the entries to the contest. Only forty-five percent of the entries were selected to be published.

We congratulate these young writers. There is no success without effort and trying. Taking the risk of failure, the poets who are included between these pages are on the road to success.

Enjoy these young poets and what they have to offer us. They offer us hope in their future and in ours.

Sincerely,
Thomas Kenne Worthen, Ph.D.
Editor
Creative Communication

WRITING CONTESTS!

Enter our next POETRY contest!
Enter our next ESSAY contest!

Why should I enter?

Win prizes and get published! Each year thousands of dollars in prizes are awarded in each region and tens of thousands of dollars in prizes are awarded throughout North America. The top writers in each division receive a monetary award and a free book that includes their published poem or essay. Entries of merit are also selected to be published in our anthology.

Who may enter?

There are four divisions in the poetry contest. The poetry divisions are grades K-3, 4-6, 7-9, and 10-12. There are three divisions in the essay contest. The essay division are grades 4-6, 7-9, and 10-12.

What is needed to enter the contest?

To enter the poetry contest send in one original poem, 21 lines or less. To enter the essay contest send in one original essay, 250 words or less, on any topic. Each entry must include the student's name, grade, address, city, state, and zip code, and the student's school name and school address. Students who include their teacher's name may help the teacher qualify for a free copy of the anthology.

How do I enter?

Enter a poem online at:
www.poeticpower.com

or

Mail your poem to:
  Poetry Contest
  1488 North 200 West
  Logan, UT 84341

Enter an essay online at:
www.studentessaycontest.com

or

Mail your essay to:
  Essay Contest
  1488 North 200 West
  Logan, UT 84341

When is the deadline?

Poetry contest deadlines are December 5th, April 5th, and August 15th. Essay contest deadlines are October 17th, February 15th, and July 18th. You can enter each contest, however, send only one poem or essay for each contest deadline.

Are there benefits for my school?

Yes. We award $15,000 each year in grants to help with Language Arts programs. Schools qualify to apply for a grant by having a large number of entries of which over fifty percent are accepted for publication. This typically tends to be about 15 accepted entries.

Are there benefits for my teacher?

Yes. Teachers with five or more students accepted to be published receive a free anthology that includes their students' writing.

For more information please go to our website at **www.poeticpower.com**, email us at editor@poeticpower.com or call 435-713-4411.

Table of Contents

Spring 2007
Poetic Achievement
Honor Schools

* Teachers who had fifteen or more poets accepted to be published

The following schools are recognized as receiving a "Poetic Achievement Award." This award is given to schools who have a large number of entries of which over fifty percent are accepted for publication. With hundreds of schools entering our contest, only a small percent of these schools are honored with this award. The purpose of this award is to recognize schools with excellent Language Arts programs. This award qualifies these schools to receive a complimentary copy of this anthology. In addition, these schools are eligible to apply for a Creative Communication Language Arts Grant. Grants of two hundred and fifty dollars each are awarded to further develop writing in our schools.

Adams Central Elementary School
Monroe, IN
Judy Minger*
Kathleen Schwartz

Arlington Elementary School
Arlington, IN
Stephanie Ward
Mary Wilkinson

Battle Ground Middle School
Battle Ground, IN
Jeremy Bloyd
Richard Fudge*
Mrs. Zeh

Bell-Graham School
Saint Charles, IL
Scott Etters
Janet Hornbostel*
Eileen Lubrano*
Mrs. Saylors
Mrs. Thomas

Belzer Middle School
Indianapolis, IN
Lorna Curtis*

Bright Elementary School
Lawrenceburg, IN
Linda Schmidt*
Deborah Whitacre

British School of Chicago
Chicago, IL
Victoria Bleathman*

Center Street Elementary School
Fairfield, IL
Jane Best
Debbie Dallas
Brenda Rush
Marjorie Simpson*

Christian Life Schools
Rockford, IL
Patricia Vespa*

Churubusco Elementary School
Churubusco, IN
Mrs. Bartlett
Julie Leedy*
Mrs. O'Connor

Cloverdale Middle School
Cloverdale, IN
Mrs. Allee*

Country Meadow Elementary School
Ashley, IN
Mrs. Griffin
Dawn Passwater*
Christy Tingley
Sally Wilson*

Countryside School
Champaign, IL
Kathy Eckstein
Sharon Henson

Creekside Elementary School
Elgin, IL
Nancy Shaffer*

Cynthia Heights Elementary School
Evansville, IN
Susan Yarbor*

Dixie Bee Elementary School
Terre Haute, IN
Diana Zwerner*

East Elementary School
Pendleton, IN
Donna Hutton*

Elwood C C School
Elwood, IL
Mrs. Jones*

Emmanuel-St Michael Lutheran School
Fort Wayne, IN
Connie Hoyer*

Floyds Knobs Elementary School
Floyds Knobs, IN
Mr. Lang
Kelly Robertson*

Francis Granger Middle School
Aurora, IL
Carla Axt-Pilon
Mrs. Grapenthein*
Robyn Winters*

Frank H Hammond Elementary School
Munster, IN
Bonnie Gardner*

GCMS Elementary School
Gibson City, IL
Jennifer Allen
Rosemary Brill
Mrs. Cox
Ms. Crowley
Betty Goembel
Mrs. Seneca

GCMS Middle School
Gibson City, IL
Jill Gibson*
Joan Ricks*
Mrs. Warren

Goodfield Elementary School
Goodfield, IL
Mrs. Mickna*

Haubstadt Community School
Haubstadt, IN
Cindy Motz*

Hiawatha Elementary School
Kirkland, IL
Mrs. Mecklenburg*

James R Watson Elementary School
Auburn, IN
Tina Bassett*
Diane Dean*
Ellen Eberling
Candace Post
Lisa Pyck*
Susie Samuelson
Tammy Smith
Pam Warner*

Laketon Elementary School
Laketon, IN
Dennis Craft*

Levan Scott Academy
Fort Wayne, IN
John Chowning
Jacqueline Howard*
Robin Peterman
Mrs. Raypole
Mrs. C. Smith
Ms. Starks
Michelle Woolf

Linton-Stockton Elementary School
Linton, IN
Kelly Lannan*
Pam Puckett*

Marine Elementary School
Marine, IL
Sharon Logan*

McHenry Middle School
McHenry, IL
Kay Collins
Mrs. Stern

McKenney-Harrison Elementary School
Auburn, IN
Midge Kelham
Dixie Minnich
N. Pinnington*

Mentone Elementary School
Mentone, IN
Mr. Early
M. Nellans
Mrs. Revere
Mrs. Sanders
Mrs. Sellers
Mrs. Shriver

Morgan Elementary School
Palmyra, IN
Laurie M. Grubb*

Norman Bridge Elementary School
Chicago, IL
Siohban Bermeo
Peggy Bowen
Tracey Cutler
Jane Harrison
Catherine McGuire
Aida Liz Quintana*

North Intermediate Center of Education
Mount Carmel, IL
Mrs. Merritt*

Oak Hill Elementary School
Lowell, IN
Audrey Retzlaff*

Our Lady of Peace School
Darien, IL
Mrs. Calomino*

Peck Elementary School
Chicago, IL
Ms. Ali
Ms. Hausknecht
Mr. Hossin
Ms. Marrero
Mrs. Meyer
Mrs. O'Connor
Consuelo Rodriguez
Ms. Russo
Ms. Zayed*
Ms. Zygadlo

Peoria Academy
Peoria, IL
Susan Diggle
Ali Saucier*

Perry Central Elementary School
Leopold, IN
Darlene Davis*
Becky Hubert
Dawn M. Lynch

Robein Elementary School
East Peoria, IL
Lisa Carroll*

Rochester Middle School
Rochester, IL
Mrs. Morgan*
Kellie Morrisey*
Nancy Schrenk
Ginger Shelato*

ROWVA East Elementary School
Altona, IL
Heidi Libby
Ms. Oldeen

Sacred Heart School
Winnetka, IL
Amy J. Cattapan*

Seton Catholic School
Moline, IL
Michelle Melin*

Smithton Community Consolidated School
Smithton, IL
Ms. Toenjes*

St Agnes School
Chicago Heights, IL
Mary Ann Olley*
Odessa Simich*

St Anthony's School
Streator, IL
Ann Deobler*

St Barbara School
Brookfield, IL
Ms. Miller*

St Colette School
Rolling Meadows, IL
Victoria Pepe*

St Jacob Elementary School
Saint Jacob, IL
Shirley Schmitt*

St John Evangelist School
Saint John, IN
Connie Hass*

St John of the Cross Parish School
Western Springs, IL
Virginia Grecco*
Mrs. Udovich

St Joseph School
Addison, IL
Regina Costas
Yvonne Marler*
Mrs. Stafford

St Mary Elementary School
Avilla, IN
Cindy Stahl*

St Mary School
DeKalb, IL
Mrs. Dobie*

St Matthew School
Champaign, IL
Kathleen Marietta
Karen Pickard*
Mary Wurth*

St Pius X Catholic School
Indianapolis, IN
Kathy Taber*

St Robert Bellarmine School
Chicago, IL
Sr. Ann Fanella
Linda Hoffman*
Donna Jaconetti
Elizabeth LaBonte

St Theresa School
Evansville, IN
Linda E. Jacobs*

Stanley Clark School
South Bend, IN
Kylea Asher*
Mary Dickerson*
Doris E. Smith*

Staunton Elementary School
Brazil, IN
Denise Brush*
Viviane Edwards*

Thayer J Hill Middle School
Naperville, IL
Debra Crews
Mrs. Cronin
Alexa Wagner

Tremont Elementary School
Tremont, IL
Tracey Harrell*

Universal School
Bridgeview, IL
Mrs. Hamoud
Mrs. Hasan
Mrs. Jarad
Ms. Khan
Mrs. Mashni
Mrs. Moukaddem
Ms. Mujahid
Mrs. Senalan*
Mrs. Syed

Language Arts Grant Recipients 2006-2007

After receiving a "Poetic Achievement Award" schools are encouraged to apply for a Creative Communication Language Arts Grant. The following is a list of schools who received a two hundred and fifty dollar grant for the 2006-2007 school year.

Aaron Parker Elementary School, Powderly, TX
All City Elementary at Jane Addams, Sioux Falls, SD
Barstow Intermediate School, Barstow, CA
Benton Central Jr/Sr High School, Oxford, IN
Broome High School, Spartanburg, SC
Carver Jr High School, Spartanburg, SC
Clarksville Elementary School, Clarksville, VA
Dunlap Middle School, Dunlap, IL
Edward Bleeker Jr High School, Flushing, NY
Emmanuel-St Michael Lutheran School, Fort Wayne, IN
Florida Youth Challenge Academy, Starke, FL
Fort Towson Jr/Sr High School, Fort Towson, OK
Fox Creek Jr High School, Bullhead City, AZ
Galena Primary School, Galena, IL
Hancock County Middle/High School, Sneedville, TN
Harrison County High School, Cynthiana, KY
Lehi High School, Lehi, UT
Lester B Pearson Catholic High School, Gloucester, ON
Lincoln Jr/Sr High School, Alma Center, WI
Little Flower Day Care Center & Prep School, Brooklyn, NY
Madison Park Technical Vocational High School, Boston, MA
Marsh Grammar School, Methuen, MA
Miller City-New Cleveland School, Miller City, OH
Northeast Baptist School, West Monroe, LA
Onsted High School, Onsted, MI
Roselle Park Middle School, Roselle Park, NJ
South Nodaway Elementary/High School, Barnard, MO
Spring Creek Elementary School, Laramie, WY
Springfield Local High School, New Middletown, OH
St James Catholic School, Abbotsford, BC
St John the Baptist School, Silver Spring, MD

Language Arts Grant Winners cont.

St Thomas More Academy, Burton, MI
Tahoka Middle School, Tahoka, TX
Thomas Lake Elementary School, Eagan, MN
Turner Middle School, Kansas City, KS
Virginia A Boone Highland Oaks Elementary School, North Miami Beach, FL
Washington School, Greenville, MS
Willamette Christian School, Eugene, OR
Woodcliff Middle School, Woodcliff Lake, NJ
Woodcrest School, Tarzana, CA

Young Poets
Grades 4-5-6

Note: The Top Ten poems were finalized through an online voting system. Creative Communication's judges first picked out the top poems. These poems were then posted online. The final step involved thousands of students and teachers who registered as online judges and voted for the Top Ten poems. We hope you enjoy these selections.

Top Poem Grades 4-5-6

American

Streaming colors,
Red, white, and blue.
Proud, graceful,
Fighting for you.
Our flag is bright,
With stars and stripes.
It lights the night,
When there is fright.
We put our hearts,
In red, white, and blue.
I'm proud to be an American,
And so should you,
Standing for freedom,
Truth, justice
And responsibility.

Alec Beeve, Grade 6
Rochester Middle School, IL

Top Poem Grades 4-5-6

Angel

February 15th 1999, you came to us in the mix of time…
You were born the day after Valentine's.
We all loved to call you mine.
After months and weeks, grew a disease…
A poor little baby grew so very weak.
The doctors all looked to see what could be,
But every time, came up with nothing.
Even though the sickness had grown, you were the happiest baby I had ever known.
And the thing I still miss the most, was on that special video.
Showed you laughing happily as can be, although handicapped you were.
Could never match our deepest fear.
However this fear had came to us face to face.
On a beautiful fall day, October 20th 2001
Trees' leaves were red.
Your favorite color on your worst day…parents and sisters waking up.
To hear the sirens in your yard.
Your sisters go out and see others crying.
Too young to understand the meaning of the word dying.
And now today, I'm now grateful.
For having a sister that was like you.
Rest in peace little angel.

Jacey Daniels, Grade 6
Three Rivers School, IL

Top Poem Grades 4-5-6

Brutus

So far away
But yet so near
In my memory
Your image so clear
I miss your whining song
I used to hear at night
Your warm fuzzy fur
Cuddling next to me tight
In a better place now
Your spirit free
I miss you boy,
Do you miss me?

Jessica Drake, Grade 6
GCMS Middle School, IL

Top Poem Grades 4-5-6

Invisibility

No one really sees me,
They don't know me either.
I live behind a mask,
A mask of invisibility.
Nobody talks to me at all.
But I have one friend
She is kindhearted and brave.
We will be friends forever.
And when I'm near her
I don't feel like I'm
INVISIBLE.

Katharine Hafner, Grade 4
Bell-Graham School, IL

Top Poem Grades 4-5-6

I Remember

Papa, I remember…
when you were 4 feet taller than me
when you would sit in your special chair and I would crawl up your legs just to sit with you
when we would visit the first thing I would do was run into your arms
when I dipped my hands and feet into cement so you would remember how little I once was
the train ride to the football game with many "Are we there yets?"

Grandma, I remember…
when I was a *very* independent two year old
when we got our nails done and it was the first time for both of us
the anticipation I always felt when we pulled into your driveway
the excitement I felt when I saw you in the audience at my play
playing *Monopoly* for three hours
doing puzzles that just never seemed to fit together

But most of all, Papa and Grandma, I remember your love.

Allison Hutchinson, Grade 6
Immaculate Conception School, IL

Top Poem Grades 4-5-6

Mystical Creature

I think that there's a mystical creature under my bed.
He's got orange hair, brown teeth, purple eyes, and a huge red head.
He eats everyone's favorite toys,
And worst of all — he eats girls and boys!
Mom says, "There isn't a creature there!"
But I'm no fool, I can see its spiky blue hair.
Dad said, "It doesn't exist, so it won't eat you."
But I can hear its awkward moo.
I wanted to prove them wrong, so I got the courage to look under my bed,
It was a bunch of clothes, two purple balls, and a toy cow head!

Kaitlin Kralj, Grade 5
Lincoln Trail Elementary School, IN

Top Poem Grades 4-5-6

My Wish

I pray every night
Hoping my dad
Is in the right place.

My grandma describes
The things he did
When he was younger.
He did
The same things I do now.

Sometimes when I glance
At a picture of him…
I cry.

I always wish
He was here right now
But that wish
Will never come true
I love my dad
I wish that he was here,
Just for me.

Auston Moronez, Grade 6
Linton-Stockton Elementary School, IN

Top Poem Grades 4-5-6

Snowflakes

Snowflakes dancing in the sky,
Precious to the human eye.
Kisses on your pure white skin,
Flowing on the rapid wind.
Twinkling like chandeliers,
Filling heart with winter cheer.

Taylor Payne, Grade 5
Tremont Elementary School, IL

Top Poem Grades 4-5-6

Confusion

Confusion is when you can't figure it out
When every answer you get seems to have doubt
You can't think about anything, nothing at all
Your brain just stops like your mind's hit a wall
When all the letters and words become unclear
And all the digits and numbers disappear
When your mind and brain refuse to expand
Confusion is when you don't understand

Elane Stephenson, Grade 5
East Elementary School, IN

Top Poem Grades 4-5-6

The Stars

The stars glisten in the pitch black night
They speak to me with their glorious light
The stars may disappear during the day
But I'll always remember what they say

Stars slowly begin their majestic shine
In the afternoon
The stars begin their wondrous words
Under the nighttime moon

Stars are like luminous white flowers
With tremendous black leaves and stems
And a big, white, lighted rose
Right in the middle of all of them

Nova Sturchio, Grade 5
Beebe Elementary School, IL

Drip Drop

Drip
  Drop
    Drip
      Drop
The rain says on top of my head.
Drip
  Drop
    Drip
      Drop
And then I know it's spring.
Drip
  Drop
    Drip
      Drop
I hear the flowers blossom.
Drip
  Drop
    Drip
      Drop
Now I'm sure it's spring.

Jack Oberkiser, Grade 4
Country Meadow Elementary School, IN

When Donkeynators Attack

There once was a farm
That bred lots of donkeys.
One day aliens appeared,
But the donkeys weren't affeered!

Ah, out came the donkeynators.
They were invaders.
They were dictators.
They were assassinators.

Their armies came.
They lost, for shame.
The donkeys ate the aliens so hasty!
You see, they really were quite tasty!

Then they heard a loud thump, thump,
And saw a spaceship go bump, bump,
As it climbed up and up and away,
Leaving the donkeys to eat their hay.

Kyle Knox, Grade 4
Countryside School, IL

Freak the Mighty

Freak
small, weak
dying, choking, joking
smart, weird, huge, slow
helping, crying, sleeping
eats, fights
Max

Greg Coultas, Grade 6
Perry Central Elementary School, IN

Christmas

Christmas
Jolly, happy
Snowing, laughing, living
Fun, exciting
That's what Christmas is.

Garrett Brackin, Grade 5
Cloverdale Middle School, IN

The Playground

The playground is the best,
Kids are always playing games,
Catching the ball as they fall,
Everyone is having fun,
Everyone goes inside.

Taylor Welch, Grade 6
Rochester Middle School, IL

Tristan

T rue
R ight
I ntelligent
S mart
T rustworthy
A wesome
N ice

Tristan Lehnert, Grade 4
Coal City Intermediate School, IL

Basketball

Basketball is my favorite sport,
I love to play it on the court
Some people play on the street
but I think that the standards don't meet
Playing some teams can be challenging,
but when you hear the scoreboard ring
that might mean you won the game
then everybody knows your name.

Kelsey Brune, Grade 6
Rochester Middle School, IL

Tumble Weed

Tumble weed rolling
Down the hill searching for a
Place to stay tonight

Isabella Gau, Grade 6
Thayer J Hill Middle School, IL

Drums

I love my Dad!
He is so cool
He loves to play drums!
I love to play drums!
We have so much fun.
We have lots in common.

Nick Todd, Grade 6
Rochester Middle School, IL

Spring

S weet smelling flowers are near
P retty flowers
R ainbows and more
I see fun all around
N ever sad
G lad glad glad

Alaina Putman, Grade 6
Elwood C C School, IL

Horse

Horse, horse, wild and free
Horse, horse, listen to me
Horse, horse, let me be

Stephan Kinder, Grade 4
Coal City Intermediate School, IL

Mountaintops

Tall and pointy rocks
Cool and breezy mountaintops
High up in the sky

Margaret Hartnagel, Grade 5
Stanley Clark School, IN

Yellow Highlighter

Part of the bright sun,
Yellow rays across a page,
Like smacking lips when I open it,
Ready to give my page kisses.

Kimberly Heitz, Grade 5
James R Watson Elementary School, IN

The Great Senses

I hear birds chirping
I see the sun shine brightly
I touch the sharp grass
I smell the fragrant flowers
I taste the clean oxygen

Holly Kavanaugh, Grade 6
Elwood C C School, IL

My Name Is Jay

My name is Jay
I live in a bay
I play with hay
Me and my friend Ray!

Josh Watson, Grade 5
Gard Elementary School, IL

Basketball

Basketball
Tricky, fun
Running, passing, shooting
At the buzzer, it is shot
Score!

Ryan Kennedy, Grade 5
Floyds Knobs Elementary School, IN

Angry/Calm

Angry
Red, fiery
Irritating, peeving, storming
Bitter, sullen, placid, civil
Resting, hushing, boring
Cool, quiet
Calm

Elaina Etter, Grade 5
Frank H Hammond Elementary School, IN

I Remember When…

I remember when we went to Disney World
We saw all the Disney characters
I waved and got their autographs

I remember when we went up in Cinderella's castle
We went on the Snow White ride
I was terrified of the evil witch

I remember when we ate breakfast with Mickey and Minnie
We ate delicious food shaped like Disney characters

I remember when we had to leave
I said good-bye to all my Disney friends
I said good-bye to Cinderella's castle
I felt like a magical Disney movie when the movie was over.

Madison Dillon, Grade 6
Haubstadt Community School, IN

Memory

When I was five.
I wanted to dunk the basketball.
I had pulled a plastic slide by the basketball goal.
I set the goal on six feet.
I climbed to the top of the slide.
With a basketball in my hand.
Then it happened.
I jumped and tried to dunk it.
I missed and fell on my face.
Mom came and cleaned the blood off my face.
I never did it again.

Garrett Elpers, Grade 6
Haubstadt Community School, IN

Illini

Illini came out to play on Friday night,
Things looked very good at first.
A lively crowd of orange, oh what a sight,
But, they were saddened by Tech's last burst.

It was the last game for Carter and McBride,
They really knew how to play basketball.
The young men with a lot of pride,
To the very end, they gave it their all.

Ross Royal, Grade 5
GCMS Elementary School, IL

I Am

I am a curious kid
I wonder if I will ever stop
I hear that I am curious
I see people laughing at me
I want to be the best I can be
I am a curious kid

I pretend I am anything
I feel sad that people laugh at me
I touch my heart
I worry that it might go away
I cry because my curiosity always gets me in trouble
I am a curious kid

I understand my curiosity
I say I'm curious
I dream I am more
I try to be better
I hope I am good
I am a curious kid

Devin Taylor, Grade 4
Levan Scott Academy, IN

Who Is My Little Sister?

Who is my little sister?
She makes me feel good.
She is very funny.
She is a cool gift.
She likes to throw food at me.
She always says my name every time she sees me.
She's crazy about cake.
Sometimes she drives me crazy.
She is a nice baby.
She is the thing that makes me smile.
That is my little sister!

Dustin Nevil, Grade 4
Morgan Elementary School, IN

Sunset

The sunset is calm
I can see all the colors
Of the sunset here
With the water far away
It is a peaceful feeling

Sam DeZeeuw, Grade 6
Smithton Community Consolidated School, IL

Rain Forest

The rain forest is filled with beautiful nature
Waterfalls,
Birds chirping a lovely melody
I could hear the sound of the ocean waving back and forth
I see the monkeys communicating with each other
The rain forest is filled with beautiful nature

Tejah Renne Johnson, Grade 4
Martin L King Elementary School, IL

Awesome Bands

Which bands do you like?
The Beatles, Dave Matthews, the Doors?
Or is it The Who or Guess Who?
Fleetwood Mac or the Rolling Stones?
Chicago, America, or Queen?
Eagles, Bob Seger, or Pink Floyd?
Led Zeppelin, or Lynard Skynard?
Is it Crosby, Stills, Nash, and Young?
Could it be Jefferson Airplane?
Do you like Buffalo Springfield?
CCR, Byrds, Animals, Cars?
Kansas or the Doobie Brothers?
Which bands do you like?
Rachel Gatwood, Grade 6
Perry Central Elementary School, IN

My Poems

I am a mermaid poet
Sitting on a rock
Of thought
Writing fishy poems
Quickly my poems swim down
On the ocean's floor
And hide in grains of cold sand

I am a dancing poet
Dancing on a stadium of beaming lights
Writing jazz poems
Quickly my poems dance down
On the ground
And jiggy back up for an applause

I am a famous poet
Riding in a limo
Quickly my poems shine like a star
And then hide in the crowds of people
Mariali Rodriguez, Grade 6
St Barbara School, IL

Rottwieler

Rottweiler
Humungous dog
Running, playing, growling
Biggest of them all.
Wild
Caitlynn Hile, Grade 4
Cynthia Heights Elementary School, IN

The School Dog

M akes me smile
A ctive
R ests
C hildren love him
O bey
Seth Sukraw, Grade 6
Rochester Middle School, IL

My Dreams

Images in my head
Not thinking, but dreaming,
Wishing, wondering.
Thoughts passing by,
And feelings too,
Loving, caring, missing,
Lots of new ideas.

Memories from before
Some good,
Some bad,
All are in my dreams.
Brittany Smiley, Grade 6
Laketon Elementary School, IN

Evil

Evil
Powerful, scary,
Crying, freezing, nothing,
I am scared by its evil intentions —
Non-feeling, tearing, pulsing,
Nightmarish, isolation
Shadow
Michael Sayre, Grade 6
Stanley Clark School, IN

My Poems

I am a star poet
Standing on a star
Writing shining poems
As they float away
Becoming a new star.

I am a fire poet
Sitting on a line of fire
Writing poems that burn in the air
They flow away in the breeze.

I am a cloud poet
Laying on a cloud
Writing fluffy poems
That seem like they are not even there.
They disappear right before my eyes.
Marisa Schwerin, Grade 6
St Barbara School, IL

Basketball

Basketball
Quick, aggressive
I love to shoot the ball
Throw, hit, shoot, run
It's fun to get a homerun
Tranquil, happy
Baseball
Rachael Utt, Grade 5
Tri Elementary School, IN

Family

D iligent
J ealous

J oyful
O utrageous
R eally nice to me
D oes me favors
A lways tells jokes
N ice
Toby Lambert, Grade 4
Morgan Elementary School, IN

Christmas

Fun, extravagant
Surprising, exciting, loving
White, fun
Christmas is awesome.
Taylor Mescall, Grade 5
Cloverdale Middle School, IN

Grandpa

When my mom said Gramps died
I couldn't help but to cry.
When we got in the car
I couldn't help but to cry.
When we stepped into the funeral home
I couldn't help but to cry.
When I saw his coffin
I couldn't help but to cry.
When I saw Gramps
I couldn't help but to cry.
When I looked at old pictures
I couldn't help but to cry.
When it was my turn to give a speech
I couldn't help but to cry.
When they buried him next to Granny
I couldn't help but to cry.
On the way home
I couldn't help but to cry.
Now if I think about him
I can't help but to smile!
Isabel Adams, Grade 5
Perry Central Elementary School, IN

Friends

Friends are people you rely on
and never let you down.
Friends are people you love
and go through bad times with.

Friends are people I have
and love so very much.
Friends are people I have
and will never have just one.
Ashley Saalman, Grade 5
Perry Central Elementary School, IN

Snowy Day

I wake up,
A snowy day I see.

Sparkling like diamonds,
Scattered so beautiful.
Soft as cotton,
Cold as ice.

I got to bed,
A snowy day I saw.

Alison Kennedy, Grade 4
Country Meadow Elementary School, IN

My Cats (Chance and Simon)

C ats
H ome where Chance lives
A lways wants out
N ever in one spot long
C an jump high
E ating his and her chicken and fish cat food

A nd don't forget they love to pounce each other
N ot hard to find Simon on account he is so plump
D isguised when Chance goes outside

S leeps every minute he can
I n winter he stays in my mom's bed
M an, Simon always thinks of his edibles
O ver over over weight
N ever leaving Chance alone

Falesha Frederick, Grade 6
Perry Central Elementary School, IN

I Wonder

I wonder why there are humans,
I wonder why people disagree with one another,
I wonder if there are people beyond the universe,
I wonder if there is a Heaven,
I wonder if there is a God,
I wonder if I will ever be famous,
I wonder why we are who we are,
I wonder when the world will end,
I wonder why people die,
And I wonder if Chicago will host the 2016 Summer Olympics.

Saul Zamora, Grade 6
Norman Bridge Elementary School, IL

Motocross

Motocross is my game
I hope to get all the fame
I'm usually in the zone
Because I want the golden cone
Jump by jump time passes by
Especially when you like to fly

Davis Uphoff, Grade 5
North Intermediate Center of Education, IL

Disneyland

Dancing lights outlining a fairy-tale castle
Sunscreen and popping corn
Rushing wind and stomach flutters
Cool creamy confections
Magical moments

Morgan Papesh, Grade 5
Frank H Hammond Elementary School, IN

Short Girl Big Dreams

There was this girl who was short.
She could work miracles on the basketball court.
This girl was named Tyra Buss.
She was so good they often made a fuss.
She practiced day and night.
On the court she put up a good fight.
She'd dribble through everyone even if they were tall.
Her dreams are to play professional basketball.
She has big dreams and she might be short
but she never shows it on the court.

Tyra Buss, Grade 5
North Intermediate Center of Education, IL

Why Did It Have to Be You?*

The breathtaking scent of your sweet-smelling perfume
Looking into your eyes of sadness
Listening to your comforting voice once more in my ears
The feeling of your wrinkly hand touching mine

The way your curly hair felt when I gently combed it
The sound of your favorite TV show playing
Smelling baby lotion on your skin
I will never forget you, Grandma

Jessica Kirkley, Grade 6
Linton-Stockton Elementary School, IN
*In loving memory of Mary Kirkley

Ray and His Friends

There was a boy named Ray
He was gray
His friend was a yellow fellow
He had a yellow cello
His other friend was blue, his name was Lou
He had a clue on his shoe!

Keaton Taylor, Grade 5
Gard Elementary School, IL

Him

He's gone, never see him again.
The thought of him leaving unbearable.
But it happened to him. He left us forever.
But no matter how much I think
Of the good times I will still miss him.
Him. It's a small word but it means that a lot.
It means Him.

Kristen Krill, Grade 4
Churubusco Elementary School, IN

My Dream Car

I'd feel I'm in seventh heaven
If only I owned a Corvette 2007.
I slide into the squishy seat
And find the pedals with my feet.
The engine starts with the turn of a key.
I hear the roar and I feel free.
Rt. 66 from east to west;
My Vette and me will stand the test.
The top is down, the wind in my hair;
Sometimes I feel I don't have a care.
The motor hums, the miles fly by
The summer sun moves across the sky.
The CD plays another country song.
I want to drive all night long.
Like a blue streak on ribbon of black.
Four chrome rims reflecting back.
The road ends but my dream will live
For I know my future has a lot to give.

Mark D. Hageman, Grade 6
Central Jr High School, IL

Meet Me by the River

Meet me by the river
Where the wolves cry
The wind whistles
And the fish are not shy

Meet me by the river
Where the cold, gray water flows
Sunlight makes it glisten
And the green grass grows

Meet me by the river
Where the bluebird flies
passing you by
And the moon will rise

Meet me by the river
Where we can stay
And have a good laugh
Until you move away

Meet me by the river
Where I'll say goodbye
I wanted you to stay
I really, really tried

Christina Gutierrez, Grade 5
Bell-Graham School, IL

Beef

B e mine
E very day
E ven
F orever

Shadow Hilton, Grade 4
Shoals Elementary School, IN

The Old Barn

The rusty hinges squeak as the door opens.
A child walks in and the rotting boards creak beneath her feet.
The barn has some sort of magic about it.
It has witnessed a colt's first shaky steps and
a cow drawing its last breath.
The barn has heard childrens' screams of delight as they played in the
bales of hay, stacked one on top of the other.
Then, all of a sudden, it was quiet.
The children had gone.

The barn remained quiet for many years, but
The girl breaks the spell of emptiness that the barn holds.
She can hear the children screaming and playing in the hay.
She understands the magic that awaits her.

Morgan Kaiser, Grade 5
Tremont Elementary School, IL

The Seasonal Tree

Autumn leaves drizzle down in a mystical rainbow of crimson, gold, and burnt apricot.
The sparkle and swirl in the harvest moon.
They dance in speckled, torn, and sweetly shaped costumes.
They change colors as the seasons end.
Soon, they crumble and crunch away.
Autumn is done, and the tree is bare.

Now the tree is icy and snow-covered, shimmering and twinkling on full moon nights.
It blows in snowstorms, looking so full of gloom.
The snow gradually melts away. Soon the robins will come to say, "Hey!"
Winter is done.

The tree is officially decorated for spring.
Ribbons of blossoms, ornaments of leaves, and a nest at the top
Symbolize that it is the chickadee's tree.
Bunnies come and hop beneath it.
The Easter bunny even knows to leave colorful eggs there.

Summer is here!
Children play and sing beneath the chickadee's tree, laughing and singing.
It looks so sweet.
It is camouflaged in lots of green; the perfect hiding place for children,
Or we can enjoy a quiet picnic in the shade.
The seasonal tree is a never-ending gift!

Kaitlyn Black, Grade 5
Tremont Elementary School, IL

Christmas Eve Night

The jingle and jangle of the sleigh bells ringing.
The beautiful sounds of carolers singing.
The rush in the stores from people buying last-minute presents.
The moon shining in a bright, and silver crescent.
The newest member of the family putting the star on top of the Christmas tree.
The friends sledding and screaming with glee.
The rush of Christmas makes everything bright.
I just can't believe that it's Christmas Eve night.

Courtney Burchfield, Grade 6
Dakota Elementary School, IL

Volcano

Something burst out in flames,
Taking out its madness on innocent people,
Crushing and exploding everywhere it goes,
Being with no sadness, only an evil smile on its face,
It makes people run for the lives in an aching, hot, fiery way,
From a heartbreaking turn from a beautiful landscape view,
Sweeping away people, pets, animals, and more,
With a non-tired gallop through the entire explosion,
With an awakening view of a hazardous morning,
With lava pouring into your window,
Your feet start to move in a speed-like way
Trying to run away from an evil eye on the horizon,
Blowing flames out of nowhere for houses to burn,
I hope that the children, adults, and pets
Get safely through that torturous raid!!!!

Michelle Wood, Grade 4
Oak Hill Elementary School, IN

Spectacular Spring

The spectacular colors that spring brings
The color of flowers, purple, pink, yellow, blue, and green
The bunnies dance
and the different birds sing in a perfect melody
The flowers bloom as they let their beauty shine
All the buds on the trees, one morning will bring leaves
once again we will see new life
What a spectacular spring this will be!

Alayna Henze, Grade 6
Dakota Elementary School, IL

Summertime

Summer time
is a time for laughter and joy
to have carefree fun with your friends
to watch movies over and over with a big bowl
of popcorn
to play outside all day and night
a time for worriless days
time to turn off all alarm clocks
to wake up with the sunshine in your face
and the best part of the free two months is
NO HOMEWORK

Andrea Estes, Grade 6
Rochester Middle School, IL

Owl

Owl owl in the sky.
Nothing escapes your watchful eye.

In the sky you fly so high.
Then you swoop down on mice that you make die.

Last you look upon the sky.
You see the moon and wonder why.

Grant Saldivar, Grade 4
Creekside Elementary School, IL

Books

You never know what to expect
You never know what will happen next
Sometimes you can't put it down
Sometimes is might be as scary as a clown.
Always imagining pictures in your head
Always not listening when your mom tells you to go to bed
Feeling always special or sad
Feeling always something funny or really bad
All the excitement, emotions, feelings, and images
Are all the amazing things books have!

Brynne Doherty, Grade 6
Rochester Middle School, IL

Slavery

Day by day we were taken
Day by day we were raided
By those whom we hated
They took us and left us there to die
They gave us disease and epidemics, but why?
There we lay in the middle deck
There we lay chained and sitting back
With no lights and a sign of death
And all they did was watch us die
Watch us cry
Watch us pray
No space to move or say
No lights to read or find the way
And today we're no longer slaves, but free
We're free to say as we please
We're free to follow our dreams
We're free because we believed
Believed that we'd be free one day
Now is the time to say we're free at last, today!!

Safia Siddiqui, Grade 5
Universal School, IL

Ode to My Dog

My dog is cute and cuddly, soft and fuzzy
He is cool and funny.
When you go to school he will be sad
But when you get home he'll be glad you're back.
He will play with you all day while you're on a bay.

Marcus Payton, Grade 5
Morgan Elementary School, IN

Flying

Flying is soaring through the air.
Some people choose to fly in a plane.
When you fly the sky feels near.
Don't go too high or you'll feel the pain.
If you go way up you'll start to freeze.
Take caution when you're way up there.
There may be a hurricane or just a strong breeze.
Just make sure you share the air.

Thomas Woods, Grade 5
Perry Central Elementary School, IN

Tractor

Tractor
Enormous, powerful
Pulling, digging, plowing
Works in the fields
Case
Corbin Fretz, Grade 5
Staunton Elementary School, IN

The Hawkeye

We see him eye the rough lake,
circling higher than the twirling trees.

Turning his head,
   a glare from his eye,
      he swoops
down,
   down,
      down.

In a split second
he's up again,
   a fighting fish in his clenched claws.

A flap of his wings,
   he flies at lightning speed,
far,
   far,
      far,
         out of sight.
Kira Bolos, Grade 4
Pleasant Hill Elementary School, IL

2-1-95

Two one nine five is my day
in that day I just want to play
in that day I'm really happy
because I get really snappy
Jimena Villagómez, Grade 6
San Miguel School, IL

Josh

J ust fine
O utstanding
S o cool
H ottie
Krysta Braiman, Grade 4
Morgan Elementary School, IN

Good Books

Good books
Fun, exciting
Twisting, reading, plotting
Read until you fall asleep
Fun books
Caleb R. Harper, Grade 5
GCMS Elementary School, IL

My Woods

White tails, great flails
As the deer go trampling by

Blue skies, birds fly
As the coyotes race by

Moon glares in the eyes of strangers
As I walk back to my bike

Leaves fall, they shock us all
As the world passes by.
Renae Blocher, Grade 6
Laketon Elementary School, IN

Ode to My Parents

I love my parents, yes I do.
I love my parents.
They love me too.
My mom is sweet.
She is as sweet as a bird tweet tweet.
My dad is nice.
He is nice as mice.
My parents laugh when I say words
Like tode or pode.
I love my parents.
My parents say when I cry
What's wrong sweetie pie.
My parents are the best.
My dad can be funny
As funny as a bunny.
My mom is nice
As nice as a piece of spice.
My dad can be mean
As mean as a big bean.
My parents are great
As great as a plate.
Skylyn Howell, Grade 4
Morgan Elementary School, IN

Jen's Pen

Jen went to her den,
There she got her pen.
She wrote some words,
And drew some birds,
Then took it back to her den!
Sarah Johnston, Grade 6
ROWVA East Elementary School, IL

Nature

Nature is pretty
Nature can be beautiful
The winds are so cold
The mountains are really tall
Nature can touch the spirit
Nicholas J. Etzkorn, Grade 6
Elwood C C School, IL

Fire

I am sitting by the fire
Watching flame after flame
Melting away into a new one

After a while, the fire is slowly dying
And I can see
The next day up ahead
In my bright future

As the night passes
One minute at a time
That I can count before
I gently fall into a dream

With deep thoughts waiting to
Come alive to surround me,
To paint a picture and
Show me when
The next fire is.
Alexa Gallione, Grade 5
Maplebrook Elementary School, IL

Life

Life is a cherished thing
You have one
Not two
Not three
But one and only one
Live it up
You don't know what happens tomorrow
Love what you have
Know
And see
Life is a cherished thing
And it should stay that way
Jimmy Crotty, Grade 6
St Joseph School, IL

Cardinals

Cardinals
Red, black,
Singing, nesting, feeding
State bird for seven
Flying, chirping, pecking
Pretty, common
Bird
Sara Krock, Grade 4
Dixie Bee Elementary School, IN

Basketball Pass

A basketball, basketball
dribbling down the court
pass it to each player
Back and Forth
Aaron Lloyd, Grade 5
Hendry Park Elementary School, IN

Spring Is Near

Spring is near,
Hurry and get here,
Animals meet and greet,
Flowers come out and about,
Trees come out and sprout,
The sun is shining without a doubt,
Snow melts,
Farmers strap on their belts.

Dwyene Harris, Grade 6
Emmett Louis Till Math & Science School, IL

What Happened to the Earth

Our earth is supposed to be neat.
It should smell good,
But instead it smells like feet
And is littered with food.
God created this place
To be beautiful,
But instead it's a disgrace.
It looks like a home for a bull.
Our water is polluted.
Lake Michigan's green.
Our bushes are dead instead of fruited.
This isn't a pretty scene.
I am only eleven, but I know
Our Earth was clean long, long ago.

Mark Carrillo, Grade 6
St Matthias/Transfiguration School, IL

Sam and Jack

We are 2 children going to the same preschool,
We are 2 kids playing on the same little league team,
We are 2 teenagers going to the same High School,
We are 2 young adults going to different colleges,
We are 2 adults, one is a senator and one is in the MLB,
We are 2 elderly men watching the same TV show,
We are 2 friends,
We are 2 lives,
We are 2 stories,
Our stories intertwine.

Daniel Friedman, Grade 6
Alexander G Bell Elementary School, IL

Be Yourself

Be yourself
There's nothing else that's better than you.
Jewelry, clothes, and shoes,
Those are some things to impress you.
That's not yourself,
That's you being someone else.
When you try to impress someone else
That just means you hate yourself.
Popular isn't about being shown,
It's about you being you on your own.

Lexes O'Hara, Grade 6
Rochester Middle School, IL

I Wonder

I wonder why some people smoke,
I wonder why living costs so much,
I wonder why people take things so seriously,
I wonder why there is war,
I wonder why our soldiers aren't coming back for good,
I wonder why we sleep,
I wonder why things we care about suddenly get destroyed,
I wonder if there is really a Heaven,
I wonder why people yell instead of just talking,
And I wonder why we hide from fake fears.

Kamarie Bostic, Grade 6
Norman Bridge Elementary School, IL

Silent Thunder

Silent thunder, we all have one.
A spark inside everyone, a desire.
A will we cannot seem to ignore, silent thunder.
For some, it feels like a rumble, some a pleasant ache.
Silent thunder, we all have one.

Silent thunder, we all have one.
Some cannot find theirs for a while, but it's there.
For those that can't find theirs,
They'll grow older and be exposed to new ideas.
Maybe suddenly, maybe gradually, it will show itself.
Silent thunder, we all have one.

Silent thunder, we all have one.
Sometimes, silent thunders are replaced by others, then others.
Sometimes, past silent thunders come back.
Sometimes, people only have one their whole life.
Silent thunder, we all have one.

Silent thunder, we all have one.
People may have many silent thunders at once,
No individual one greater than the other.
That's okay, maybe your silent thunders are to help the world.
Silent thunder, we all have one.

Megan Angell, Grade 4
Ranch View Elementary School, IL

German Shepherd

German Shepherd big and strong,
Loud and howling all night long;
German Shepherd with your big sharp teeth,
Who would know your soft and playful underneath;
German Shepherd barks and chews,
Scares the cat and ruins my shoes;
German Shepherd fast and quick,
Chasing things to give a lick;
German Shepherd with pointy ears,
Annoying me throughout the years;
German Shepherd loyal and true,
Man's best friend and I love you!

Andrew Ridder, Grade 6
St John Evangelist School, IN

Winter

Winter is snowy.
The weather is very weird.
The snow is falling.
Chris August, Grade 4
St Joseph School, IL

Cleaning

I have to clean
The house today,
I want to
Go out and play.

I have to clean
The house today.
Now,
Can I play croquette?
Allison Brown, Grade 4
Creekside Elementary School, IL

The Red Rose

Rose, rose, rose,
there it goes.
In the wind — Oh!
It blows. It's going to
bloom soon.
I hope it's not
a broom.
Brooke Martin, Grade 4
Marine Elementary School, IL

Witch

Witch
Tired, unearthly
Rasping, worrying, cackling
The good children must be warned!
Calling, envying, slumping
Old, funny
Mystery
Haley Luck, Grade 6
Stanley Clark School, IN

House

A house
busy place
crowded and shouting
dinner at the table
home sweet home
Josh Womack, Grade 6
Rochester Middle School, IL

Panther

Panthers, wild and free
Running as swift as the wind
Dangerous but sweet!
Justin Lee, Grade 5
Stanley Clark School, IN

A Little Cub

Something told the cub,
He just had to grow.
Though he liked being small,
He was as small as dough.

He was young and tiny,
and he liked it.
But although his age wasn't a problem,
his problem was his size.

He took out a book about size,
from his old little shelf.
He never thought of growing up,
because he just wants to be himself.

Something told the cub,
he doesn't have to be an adult.
So he had no choice but to be tiny,
and leave him alone it's not his fault.
Zbigniew Pasierbek, Grade 6
Norman Bridge Elementary School, IL

The Blue Bird

The blue bird says
"Come follow me!
I can fly you over the sea!
Over the mountains, through the woods,
It looks windy,
Put up your hood,
When we return, you will be,
In a world of fancy free!"
Ashley Lantz, Grade 4
Oak Hill Elementary School, IN

Summer Is Here

Summer is here, summer is here
The hottest time of the year.
Summer is here, summer is here
The cold is not here.
Summer is here, summer is here
My birthday is near.
Summer is here, summer is here
The best time of the year.
Brandon Smith, Grade 4
Oak Hill Elementary School, IN

Lonely Me

I seem to have a problem.
My friend has vanished.
My boyfriend has left.
Everyone around me seems
to be taking me out of the picture.
Now I have no one around.
I'm so lonely.
Destinie Kuhn, Grade 6
Laketon Elementary School, IN

Spring

Spring is here! Spring is here!
Things are changing everywhere.
Birds are singing,
Bells are ringing,
I can feel it in the air.

I'm feeling stronger,
The days are longer,
Flowers are growing,
Faces are showing.

People are starting to open their doors,
To get out and do some outside chores.
Spring fever has hit me,
And I'm ready to play.
It's hard to sit still
All through the day.

Spring makes me happy,
As you can see,
But I'm not the only one:
IT'S NOT JUST ME!
Ryan Jackson, Grade 4
Butterfield School, IL

Tick Tock

Tick, tock
we have
a clock.
It goes
by time.
"O" look!
Midnight! We go fast asleep
just in a blink.
David Daiber, Grade 4
Marine Elementary School, IL

Monkey

M onkeys swing from trees
O r wild jungle vines
N ever boring any day
K eep on going in the rain
E xciting as can be
Y et they are fascinating
Jay Vanderhyden, Grade 6
Elwood C C School, IL

Summer

S pring is gone,
U ntil next year,
M other's picking flowers.
M y sisters play
E verywhere they go,
R oses bloom.
Anna Brookens, Grade 5
First Baptist Christian Academy, IL

Over You

I'm over your hair, I'm over your smile,
I'm over your laugh, over your style.
The eyes that you could get lost in,
The laugh that would make anyone near join in.
I can tell you that I don't like you anymore,
The process of getting over you was very sore.
When you left me I thought I'd never get over you,
I guess when you said you loved me, it wasn't true.
So these are the reasons why I'm so over you

Megan Freveletti, Grade 6
Rochester Middle School, IL

Basketball Dreams

D are to dream about basketball
R emembering every move you make on the court
E very swish you hear
A lways staying focused on the court
M any screaming fans cheering you on
S ome nights we all dream

Bria Walker, Grade 6
Thayer J Hill Middle School, IL

Flowers

F ly little flower far far away
L ittle flower come back home
O ther flowers won't replace you
W hen will you come back home to me
E veryone misses you
R ed orange, blue, and purple flower so beautiful
S o won't you come home!!

Siera Mills, Grade 4
Shoals Elementary School, IN

Believe

Believe
Believe in your dreams
Believe in today
Believe that we can build a better world
Believe that there is light at the end of the tunnel
Believe that the best is yet to come
Believe in yourself

Ryan Rompola, Grade 6
St Joseph Elementary School, IN

Troublesome Mornings

In the morning
Argue with my siblings
Get out of the bathroom
Can't find something to wear
Does this match
Are my jeans clean
One second I need to do my hair
Thanks, now my hair is going to be a mess
Hurry we are going to miss the bus

Courtney Shields, Grade 6
GCMS Middle School, IL

Mind

Mind
Disembodied, scary
Walking, talking, scaring
Torture, brainwash, sad, ominous, creepy
Kidnapping, speaking, hurting
Mastermind, intelligence
Brain

Dan True, Grade 6
Stanley Clark School, IN

King George the Third

King George the third
Was really absurd
He got the colonists mad
From the taxes that were bad
The Boston Tea Party was made
And the taxes weren't paid
The Revolution started
And in 500 days the British departed
Thus America was born
George Washington was sworn
As the first president of the United States of America.

Jake Lieske, Grade 5
Bell-Graham School, IL

Hope Is

If hope could be a color
it would be as red as the American flag

If hope could be a taste
it would taste like watermelon or apples

If hope could be a smell
it would be double chocolate chip fudge brownies

If hope could be a sound
it would be a soft beating of the heart

If hope could be a feeling
it would be the warm feeling of fire from the fireplace

If hope could be an animal
it would be a dog to love and play with

Matthew Gunby, Grade 4
St Agnes School, IL

Night and Day

Night
Dark, cold
Sleeping, snoring, turning
Bedroom, night-light, swimming, baseball
Playing, jumping, running
Warm, light
Day

Samuel A. Hayden, Grade 6
Rochester Middle School, IL

Bold Cat!

Roger! Roger!
Black and bold.
Wanting attention
Wanting someone to
Hold him.

Purring! Purring!
In my ear, trying
To get rest I guess
That won't happen
Here.

Cuddly! Cuddly!
Acting nice,
All of a sudden
He comes out with
A FIERCE
Bite!

Watch out! Watch out!
Here he comes,
A big bold cat
For everyone to
LOVE!
Sonya Mack, Grade 4
Creekside Elementary School, IL

Ode to Summer

Shades, ice cream, parties, and fun
What a wonderful summer has begun!
No more homework; no more tests
Plenty of secrets we will give our best.
Friends stop and play all through the day
Summer is finally on the way!
Ashley Hollinshead, Grade 6
Rochester Middle School, IL

Pink

Pink is the color of a baby girl.
It's a beautiful pink flamingo
In the calm waters of the meadow.
Could it be a flat, rectangular, metallic
Pink iPod?
Pink reminds me of a little
Girl with a satin pink bow in her hair.
Pink is sweet, sticky, fluffy, cotton candy
Bought at a local carnival.
I love to see shades of pink on a
Beautiful warm summer evening in the
Bright and colorful sunset.
Pop! goes the bubble made from
Pink bubble gum.
Pink is the sister of red
And the cousin to purple.
Mackenzie Brush, Grade 5
Staunton Elementary School, IN

The Wind

The wind blows on a current flow
The wind whispers but cannot cry
The wind flows in the sky
The wind can talk
but cannot walk
The wind can blow
Nicholas Armijo, Grade 5
Norman Bridge Elementary School, IL

Blue

Blue is the empty sky
Blue is the color of eyes
Blue is baked berry pies
Blue is cold frosty mountains
Blue is skiing down the slopes
Blue is the deep ocean.
Blue is frozen crystal clean.
Blue is the color of peace.
Diane Bendik, Grade 5
Norman Bridge Elementary School, IL

Baby Star

There once was a baby star.
She said, "Mom, will you get me a car?"
"Not for years."
She started with tears.
I promise I won't go very far.
MaryKate Polito, Grade 5
Seton Catholic School, IL

The Hammer

BANG, BANG, BANG

My nose may be
Solid and rock hard
I'm only a hammer
And all you're giving me
Is a headache

BOOM, BOOM, BOOM

My head is spinning
From this pain of
Beating on a giant nail
Stop
Please it hurts

Ding, Ding, Ding

Yes, I am safe
My bottom quietly
Hits the wall
As I sit here
Safely, in the garage
Charity Betts, Grade 6
Linton-Stockton Elementary School, IN

Love in a War

Love in a war
Is when you go all out
To fight for freedom
There is no doubt
You miss her so
As you can see
No no you cannot leave
She says as you go
Even though you don't want to show
That you are sad
For you are a man
that miss the love
It's okay to have a love in a war
Trenton Wood, Grade 6
North Middle School, IL

Snow

Coming from clouds
Down, down, down
Extremely cold
Falling in small pieces
Why, it's snow!
Meaghan Sharp, Grade 5
GCMS Elementary School, IL

What Is on My Farm

What is on my farm?
3 horses
A big tractor
A four-wheeler
A big go-cart
A big old barn
A horse trailer
3 acres of the finest
in the area
A gate
Two big stalls
A lot of food
That is my farm!
Cody E. Lewis, Grade 4
Morgan Elementary School, IN

Summer

Summer
My favorite season
There are many reasons
There is the sun
The cold, there is none
And most of all it is fun
There is camp
No need for a lamp
Because the light has been amped
Everyone cheer
Summer is here!!
Jimmy Mangan, Grade 6
Sacred Heart School, IL

What Is a Little Brother?*

A little brother is a cool little guy;
he helps you, plays with you, and goes with you.
The bad part is that he leaves his trash on the floor,
he leaves his clothes on the floor,
doesn't flush the toilet,
he yells at everyone,
he leaves without permission too.
But other than that he's peaceful.

Tyler Carr, Grade 4
Morgan Elementary School, IN
*Dedicated to Wayde Carr

My Poems

I am a mountain poet
I sit on the peak in the dark
Writing my poems
I look out into the cold and mysterious sky
As my poems carelessly glide away
Turning into stars and showing the way for lost climbers.

I am an ocean poet
Riding on an abandoned ship
My poems dive into the water finding a faraway magical land
They are the guards of the magical gates.

I am a sky poet
Writing my poems on white fluffy clouds.
My poems race away on them
Having fun and drifting of into the wonders of the sky.

I am a tree poet
Sitting on a branch looking up into the starlit sky
A pile of poems under me
But my poems are gold
Because they're the most special to me.

Jackie Sukacz, Grade 6
St Barbara School, IL

The Tracks

They say some people are from the wrong
        side of the tracks.
But what's on the right side that's not on
        the other?
Is it the train that separates them?
Is
  it
    from
      the
        hate
          in
            our
              world?
Or are they simply afraid to look in the mirror
        and see what they've become?

Nicole Sparks, Grade 5
East Elementary School, IN

The Song of Pyrite

Shiny yellow fool's gold
Is like the high sparkling stars
That are in the sky
This very night
As I walk under them and sing…
Adorable pyrite of light
Is like the big sweet full moon
Oh! How beautiful!
The never ending happiness in the lovely sun

Erika Brown, Grade 5
Beebe Elementary School, IL

What Is a Dog?

They bring a lot of trouble.
They make a lot of smelly things.
I really don't know why.
When I take my dog out all she does is bark.
I really don't know why.
Dogs are weird.
They come in every shape and size.
They are always sleepy.
That is a dog!

John David Fessel, Grade 4
Morgan Elementary School, IN

What Lies Ahead

No one really knows
What lies ahead.

You could get shot in the blink of an eye
Or find riches for a lifetime.

You could just find out that you're being stalked
Or find yourself at a family picnic at the park.

You could figure out you have a deadly disease
Or find out you're as healthy as ever.

Expect the unexpected
Because no one really knows
What lies ahead.

Alexis Gonzalez, Grade 6
St Anastasia School, IL

Harsh Words

Harsh words are like fire burning wood
People can get hurt.
Harsh words are like a snakebite
The poison is in you forever
Never leaving you
It's like the words are burning in your mind.
People need to be careful with harsh words
Their tongue is like a lake of fire
Burning everything in sight.

Aliecea Meredith, Grade 6
Laketon Elementary School, IN

Mom

Mom
comes in
furiously,
obviously
mad.
Becki Bolinger, Grade 6
Gray M Sanborn Elementary School, IL

Middle School

Middle school is fast,
I don't know how long I'll last?
Homework is flying at me,
It's becoming a catastrophe.
It's not fair,
My homework seems to disappear!
The teacher suspects I didn't do it,
It's not true! I won't admit to it!
Social studies, science, math too,
Is something I will not do!
Square root, division, pi,
Is something I will deny,
But if I push myself through,
School will have some value.
After all, to get into a good college,
You have to have a lot of knowledge.
Patrick Brady, Grade 6
St John Evangelist School, IN

What Is a Dog?

What is a dog?
His name is Shaggy.
He plays with you.
When you're sad
he makes you happy.
He is a poodle
but he does not look like it.
He loves you
and you love him.
He is funny.
He is cute.
He is a good dog.
That is my dog.
Seth Houglan, Grade 5
Morgan Elementary School, IN

Spring

Spring is near.
Spring is here.
Some people hate spring.
But I love spring.
Spring is when the birds chirp.
But my brother says they burp.
My family says that only west has spring.
But I say No! Everybody has spring.
Krystal Beckner, Grade 4
Chrisney Elementary School, IN

My Ferret

I had a ferret named Brandy.
She was really nice. She loved to play
And fight but that all ended when she got sick,
So we took her to the clinic and the doctor said,
"She has to stay overnight." The next day my mom came to camp and said
"We had to put her to sleep." I cried for a long time, but at the same time
I was telling myself at least she's in a better place, now I don't have to worry anymore
About her being sick forever. I also miss her all the time, but I sometimes
Forget about her because it's in the past.
Christopher K. White Jr., Grade 6
Christian Life Schools, IL

I Store Memories

I'm many different colors all around,
I can work up and down.
Big and small are my shapes,
I can be as confusing as a math equation.

I come in travel size with a string attached to me,
Anyone can use me, either a he or a she.
I take memories of things I look at.
Many stores sell me to everyone.

When you press a button, I say click,
Sometimes I have a clock in me, and it goes tick!
I'm like a computer because I need to be programmed,
Then again, you might be able to figure me out.

You may see me everywhere you go.
I may or may not work, you may never know.
Sometimes adults get mad because they left me at home.
Once in a while I will break, and you will need another one of me.
Rachel Kent, Grade 6
Our Lady of Peace School, IL

Winter Fairy

The winter fairy has come at last
She wakes from her long sleep
She's ready for her winter day
She spreads her wings and floats away
She takes her wand and casts away
Water freezes, snow falls, icicles grow
She waves her wand a second time
The water freezes faster, the snow falls faster, the icicles grow bigger
The snow turns into a blizzard
The snow twists and turns in the whistling wind
One last thrust of her wand
Water stops freezing, snow stops falling, icicles stop growing
She looks around at the blanket of snow she left
She throws her arms up and yawns
She floats back down
She lays down very weary
The day is over and the deed is done
She is ready for her long sleep
Cynthia Baker, Grade 6
Dakota Elementary School, IL

Just Remember

To me the things we remember
Are the things that mean the most
Your first baseball game
A funeral, a wedding
That one time at your friend's house
I don't think it matters
Just remember

Never forget your family
Because they're always there
Remember last Christmas
The presents under the tree
Not only are there toys
But symbols of your parent's love
It may seem little now but
Just remember

I live for the moments I'll always remember
With the friends I'll never forget
I can't wait to talk to them later
Laughing, talking, remembering
I won't forget the moments
I'll remember

Melissa Deatsch, Grade 6
Immaculate Conception School, IL

Jonathon T.

There once was a boy
Named Jonathon T.
He planned to take over the world
But I said better off you than me.

When he was a man
He actually did succeed
And I'm sorry I laughed
At Jonathon T.

He made me do pushups,
And sit-ups, and crunches
He made me serve him
Breakfasts, dinners and lunches

I hope that you liked
Jonathon T's story
I hope you know it was painful for me
And I hope that you thought it was not boring.

Brice Ahrens, Grade 5
Floyds Knobs Elementary School, IN

Bees

Bees, they whisper to you when they buzz,
Bees, they're like little airplanes,
Bees, they buzz busily, but they sting too!
People see them and go insane.

Maria Geise, Grade 5
Arlington Elementary School, IN

Bring Me Back

Take me back
Where I need to be
Bring me home
So I can sleep

Those who know
Where I may be
Please no longer hold
The secrets you keep

Hatred and anger
Matters no more
Help me return
To the family I adore

Take me back
Where I need to be
Bring me home
So I can sleep

Kohdee Hicks, Grade 6
Avilla Elementary and Middle School, IN

My Class

My class is very different I really have to say
You should have seen what Barney did just the other day
He coughed and spit upon my food
I said, "Hey that is very rude"
He looked at me and with a glare. He said, "I really do not care"
Then there is another girl we call her Fuzzy Bear
We call her that because she has the weirdest looking hair
It's really big and puffy. She thinks she's a big tuffy
But she wouldn't hurt a fly.
There is another guy. We call him Big Ty
He is so big and round that He makes a loud, loud sound
When he stomps on the ground
There is another girl named Frankey
She has a big bump on her knee
It was from a big bee. She named it Lilly
As you can see my class is very different
I really have to say
I wish I didn't have to go to school
Each and every day

Derek Greifzu, Grade 5
Center Street Elementary School, IL

Couplets

Couplets here couplets there
Couplets, couplets everywhere

I went to the library to take a look
And I found a couplet in a book

When I got home I went to sleep
To dream about couplets that make me weep.

Samantha Welz, Grade 4
St Robert Bellarmine School, IL

Bullies

Bullies
Selfish jerks
Teasing, laughing, punching
Stand up for yourself
Talking, confronting, shouting
Brave, proud
Anyone

Eddie Fiala, Grade 5
Bell-Graham School, IL

Give Me

Give me friendship.
Give me authority
And I will help those in need.
Give me love.
Give me trust.
Give me bravery
And I will embrace the human race.

Berenice Martinez, Grade 6
Norman Bridge Elementary School, IL

Mom

Mom
Loving, nice
Kissing, playing, hugging
Pretty, cute, kind, funny
Walking, cleaning, playing
Cutie, worker
Dad

McKenna Macklin, Grade 5
Adams Central Elementary School, IN

Dancing Lights

On a late dark night,
A swarm of pink dancing lights,
Flicker through the sky.

Kayla Everhart, Grade 5
Arlington Elementary School, IN

Baseball

Baseball is the bomb
When you hit the ball
You think it is going
Over the fence. Too short!

When you get on the field
You think the ball
Is coming at you
Going to hit you. Ouch!

When you make the winning run
The team in the dugout
Will explode
Jumping and yelling. Hooray!

Cole Smith, Grade 6
Perry Central Elementary School, IN

Virginia Beach

Hot sand
Cold water
Horizon line
Beautiful sight
Seashells everywhere
Atlantic Ocean
Crashing waves
Salty water
Bright sun
Clear air

Megan Martinez, Grade 5
Bell-Graham School, IL

Animals

A nteater	**N** ewt
B ison	**O** tter
C ockatoo	**P** iranha
D onkey	**Q** uail
E mu	**R** hinoceros
F ish	**S** kunk
G iraffe	**T** arantula
H ippopotamus	**U** nicorn
I guana	**V** ery slow turtle
J aguar	**W** alrus
K angaroo	**X** -ray fish
L emur	**Y** ak
M anatee	**Z** ebra

Kelsey Sellers, Grade 4
Shoals Elementary School, IN

Singing

It's my own world
Where melodies fly
And harmonies soar
My own beautiful place
Where words float
And notes rush by
A magical place
Where I'm lost
In myself
Singing high as the trees
Or low as the sea
The world's such a beautiful place
When I sing

Emily May, Grade 6
GCMS Middle School, IL

Dog

Big, brave
Hunting, barking, running
Tall, wagging tail, fluffy, cute
Pounce, meow, run
Lovable, playful
Cat

Shane Karner, Grade 5
Adams Central Elementary School, IN

Dancing Is Fun!

D oing air flairs.
A nyone can do it.
N othing can stop me.
C ouldn't take me away.
E ven you can do it too!

Tony Orlando, Grade 4
Norman Bridge Elementary School, IL

Wolves

Wolves
Gray, lively,
Mean, vicious, active,
Almost extinct,
Mean dogs

Shauna Maesch, Grade 5
Staunton Elementary School, IN

Friendship

Friendship is a priceless gift
That can't be bought or sold.
Boys come in life and go,
But friends always come and stay.

Shailea Anderson, Grade 6
Laketon Elementary School, IN

Cross Country Running

Can run more
Running non stop
Open road to run in
Side by side running
Sprint long
Congrats team
Others cheering
Up to others to help win
No sad days
Try to stay up
Running on the path
Younger kids running.

Andy VanHook, Grade 6
Rochester Middle School, IL

Pressure

To feel the pressure,
To feel your heart pump in you,
To hear the strange voice
Encourage you to do it,
And then to let it all go.

Kirsten Eissman, Grade 5
Gray M Sanborn Elementary School, IL

The Hatch

Chicken, chicken hatch!
Ducky ducky goes to hatch.
Alligator sleeps.

Jordan Bohnenstiehl, Grade 4
Marine Elementary School, IL

Blue

Calmness is a clear, pure blue
It smells like the sweet, new blooming flowers
It tastes like the salt water in the ocean
It sounds like the calm waves slashing all around
It feels like floating in the calm air.

Delilah Wright, Grade 5
East Elementary School, IN

Summer Fun in the Sun

Summer fun is as bright as the morning sun
The air is warm
You relax.

The time to play
Is every day
You pull out the old Slip 'n Slide
Get ready, get dressed and go outside!

Fireworks on the fourth of July,
Birds chirping as you walk by,
The flowers are as pink as little pigs.
I'm so happy,
I skip!
It's getting late, so I go inside
Tomorrow will be an ever better trip.

Summer fun to me is being filled with joy
And never sad
Because nothing could ever go bad!

Allyse Salamone, Grade 5
St John of the Cross Parish School, IL

Discipline/Pandemonium

Discipline
Conduct, concentration
Breathing, meditating, drilling
Willpower, control, berserk, ferocious
Rampaging, raging, stampeding
Crazy, hyper
Pandemonium

Rahul Agarwal, Grade 5
Frank H Hammond Elementary School, IN

Chocolate Chip Cookies

Chocolate chip cookies are
As hot as a beautiful fire about to burn
As delicious as your favorite food
As chocolatey as a cold, tasty Hershey's chocolate bar.
It can take your imagination to a place
You have always dreamed of visiting
Best when you take them fresh out of the hot oven.
When I think of chocolate chip cookies,
I think...
Mmmmmmmmmmm!

Tera Havey, Grade 5
St John of the Cross Parish School, IL

Pokagon, Pokagon

Pokagon, Pokagon,
It waits for me.
Pokagon, Pokagon,
Sam, Charlie, and me.

Visiting, swimming,
Having a ball.
Too bad it only comes,
Once every fall.

Ice cream and cousins,
Having a blast.
Making a scrapbook,
To look at the past.

Chipmunks and squirrels,
Stuffin' their cheeks.
Wish we could stay,
For many more weeks.

Pokagon, Pokagon,
It waits for me.
Pokagon, Pokagon,
Makes me happy!

Andrea Hockenberry, Grade 6
Emmanuel-St Michael Lutheran School, IN

Dogs

My dogs are wild.
They like to run and chase me.
Dogs are the best pets.

Rece Buckmaster, Grade 4
McKenney-Harrison Elementary School, IN

Tundra

Here in the Tundra, cold and bare
where nothing grows there.
I sit here alone in the snow
where the temperatures can be 40 below.

Here on this cold, hard ground
frozen extinct animals have been found.
The Caribou Moss spongy and green
is one of the few plants that are seen.

Polar bears, furry and white
capture the sun and reflect its light.
The summer sun shines 24 hours each day,
giving the wolves lots of time to play.

With 20% of the earth as its home
the Tundra is the newest, the youngest biome.
Tundra, the land of the midnight sun
here we have much fun.

Brina Lo Destro, Grade 6
Holy Angels Elementary School, IL

Mater

I have a friend named Mater.
I will not see him later.
He read a book,
About a cook.
Later he has to go cater.
Paige Hinthorne, Grade 6
ROWVA East Elementary School, IL

Chicago

C hicago cubs
H eartland
I llinois's biggest city
C hicago bears
A lot of history
G reat vacation spot
O ne of the biggest cities in America
Jarod Altadonna, Grade 6
Rochester Middle School, IL

Waiting

Slowly breathing
Waiting for the enemy to attack
Waiting in the trenches
When Sarge calls, "Move out!!!"
It looks like the enemy is the one waiting
I wonder what he's thinking.
Judson Huxtable, Grade 5
Bell-Graham School, IL

Zombies

Zombies
Ugly, weird
Biting, hating, running,
Zombies are always chasing.
Monsters
Ryan Ross, Grade 5
Staunton Elementary School, IN

Forest Autumn

Deep in the forest

Pinewood smell
And falling leaves

A peaceful autumn
William Walsh, Grade 5
Our Lady of Peace School, IL

Fat Pat

There once was an old man named Pat,
Who was incredibly fat.
"He's as big as a sow,
Or even a cow!",
Some people would say about Pat.
Keith King, Grade 6
ROWVA East Elementary School, IL

Animal

A living, breathing, creature
N o one seems to understand them
I love them, my friends
M y escape from daily life
A creature that I can rely on
L oving, thriving, moving, living
Courtney Walsh, Grade 6
Elwood C C School, IL

Leaves

Oh beautiful leaves
As they blow
In the warm summer breeze
As crisp as could be
Olivia Cripe, Grade 5
Stanley Clark School, IN

Nighttime

Late at night
The stars go by
You hear so many fights
You see a shooting star fly
You wish upon the star's light
Nighttime you will rest in peace
Nighttime you will close your eyes
Someone wakes you up at night
You will see it was just
At nighttime you dream
Cheyenne Welborn-Karlsen, Grade 6
GCMS Middle School, IL

Honorable Man

Martin Luther King Jr.
A strong man, brave
Leading, Protesting, speaking
And honorable man
He had a dream
Javier Mendoza, Grade 6
San Miguel School, IL

What Is a Dalmatian?

A cute ball of fur
A wagging tail
Polka-dotted friends
Keeps robbers away
Great to play with
Loves chew toys
Perfect pillow
Makes me happy
Best barks
Sometimes small
A nice welcome home
Best friend
That is a Dalmatian!
Emily Schroeder, Grade 5
Morgan Elementary School, IN

Summer

Summer is my favorite season,
but it's not a good reason
for wearing a winter coat,
but you can go on a boat,
and ride it all day,
but not all night, because every night
people sleep tight, and people don't
let the bed bugs bite, even though
there aren't any.
Kara Zeigler, Grade 6
Rochester Middle School, IL

My Room

Pink and green
I hate my room!
I want a light green room,
With a dance floor.
I love to dance!
I hate my room
The same colors since I was four
I hate my room
I'm older now
I want to make my room,
Well, MY ROOM!
Molly Gros, Grade 5
St John of the Cross Parish School, IL

Soaring Through the Sky

I wanted to fly
I jumped off a couch
Flying, Flying, Flying

Flew down the stairs
Showed my sisters
Gave them rides
Flying, Flying, Flying

After the rides
Flew through the garage
Past grandpa
Flying, Flying, Flying

Out outside
Up to the roof
Landing on the roof
Flying, Flying, Flying

Up in the air
High in the sky
Buildings small as cars
Flying, Flying, Flying

So happy, so excited
Flying all around
Liahona Axelson, Grade 5
Cumberland Elementary School, IL

You Make Me...

You make me laugh
You make me smile
You can make me mad
But you can always make me glad
You make me feel stunning
You make me feel glamorous
You make me feel hideous
But you can always make me feel gorgeous
You make me courteous
You make me humane
You make me obnoxious
But you can make me be respectful
You make me feel brilliant
You make me feel quick-witted
You make me feel dumb
But you can always make me feel intelligent
You make me feel enormous
You make me feel tremendous
You make me feel miniature
But you make me feel massive too
That's why I love you!

Renee Hinsey, Grade 6
St Theresa School, IN

Hope

If hope could be a color
it would be blue as the ocean water

If hope could be a taste
it would be a fresh apple

If hope could be a smell
it would be homemade apple pie

If hope could be a sound
it would sound like birds chirping in the summer

If hope could be a feeling
it would be like hugging a grandparent

If hope could be an animal
it would be a lion roaming through the grass

Kyle Pugh, Grade 4
St Agnes School, IL

Trees

Tall or short they're all trees.
Easy to climb or hard to climb they're all trees.
Straight or crooked they're all trees.
Ugly or pretty they're all trees.
Fat or skinny they're all trees.
Old or young they're all trees.
Brown or green they're all trees.
It don't matter to the tree they're all trees.

Austin LeClere, Grade 5
Perry Central Elementary School, IN

A Girl's World

A girl's world...

Doing your hair,
Painting your nails,
And most of all talking about BOYS.
Shopping with your friends,
Talking about how weird your mom is behind her back.

A girl's world...

Katie Elliott, Grade 6
Rochester Middle School, IL

Dog/Cat

Dogs are frolicking through the fresh snow
Night comes and they have to go
They go home and go to bed
Goodnight doggies all is said

Night comes and they have to go
Then the cats go through the snow
Goodnight doggies all is said
Cats have taken over the fields

Then the cats go through the snow
Dogs wake up it's morning now
Cats have taken over the fields
The dogs go out, cats run away

Dogs wake up it's morning now
Take your place in the fields to play
The dogs go out, cats run away
Dogs are frolicking through the fresh snow

Sarah Willging, Grade 4
Bell-Graham School, IL

The Waterproof Brain

Swimming over a world of knowledge;
Sprinting over a mathematical sea;
Paddling through the realm of reading and writing;
Treading in the waters of truth and lies;
I am the waterproof brain;
The living, breathing, swimming brain.

Tucker Arendsee, Grade 4
Arnett C Lines Elementary School, IL

Softball

S it. Sit on the bench not on the field!
O utfield. A place where the ball goes for some homeruns.
F riends. You can make friends when you play.
T rip. Oh no, don't trip!
B at. Swing the bat.
A t last. At last we won!
L ike. Like the game you're playing.
L ose. Oh no, we lost.

Jamie Timm, Grade 5
GCMS Elementary School, IL

Moms and Dads

Moms are always dressing up.
Dads are always messing up.
Moms are always so organized.
Even though dads never realize.
Moms are normally caring.
While dads are acting so daring.
Moms are up early in the morning.
While dads are still in bed snoring

Andrew Huber, Grade 5
Perry Central Elementary School, IN

Z. L. M. That's Me!

Zoe Leigh Minzenberger
I love to skate
I love to sing
                act
                        and play
I love to cartwheel
        flip and hang.
            Swim
                Jump
                    And have fun
Zoe Leigh Minzenberger
It's fun
to have fun!

Zoe Leigh Minzenberger, Grade 4
Lincoln Elementary School, IL

Taihjeem D.

T oo cool
A wesome
I nteresting
H as great ideas
J ack-a-roo cool
E xtra funny
E very bit CRAZY
M y best friend

D ouble trouble with me
    C
        O
            O
                L

Amber Leow, Grade 5
Morgan Elementary School, IN

The Winner

Winner:
Dedicated, hardworking,
Playing, singing, dancing,
Gives it their all.
Running, jumping, swimming,
Determined, successful,
Champion.

Jack Rushin, Grade 6
Sacred Heart School, IL

Beautiful

Such beauty the world holds before my eyes.
Such wonder, such power, I'm hypnotized.
With every splash and trickle of a waterfall,
With all the beauty and grace of a flower.
Such beauty the world holds before my eyes.
The world keeps spinning, as does my head when I see the Earth in front of me.
Such beauty the world holds before my eyes.

Sydney Goffinet, Grade 5
Perry Central Elementary School, IN

Chalk Dust

On a ledge I sleep,
I don't open my eyes to take a peep.
I am picked up, and up, up, up I go.
I'm now on a roller coaster, you know.
I swerve around, go up, and loop de loop!
It is too bad I haven't yet drawn a hoop.
Oh look, I've drawn a word and it's cool.
A child says "Oh! So that's how you spell pool."
An adult woman's footsteps are heard in the hall.
Children scramble, put things away, erase my beautiful work and all.
Chalk stick Luna is next to me.
She is longer, by an inch, you can see.
I am a race car fast and lean.
We are nice while other chalk sticks are mean.
We are like roller coaster test riders.
Every new word a new ride and we ride them because we aren't hiders.
But now I am a forgotten chalk stick unable to write,
I am almost chalk dust and can no longer put up a fight.

Mallory Clark, Grade 6
Our Lady of Peace School, IL

Maxey

bus driver Miss Kiki fun stories hilarious laughing seats music,
talking screaming arguing hats violins backpacks Miceala,
funny screeching humiliating color iPod Tyler bustling cell phones,
peaceful Caleigh bumping charging writing staring Kylie new clean,
horn noisy gossip helping exciting homework sharing Sarah,
annoying jumping exclaiming beautiful barbaric elbowing crowded,
humor newspapers reading rooting singing games comfy Maxey*!

*The name of our bus.

Amy Nealon, Grade 6
Thayer J Hill Middle School, IL

Singing

Singing is my passion.
I love to sing the classics, like the minuet.
I love to hear my voice dance and sore, like a bird young and light.
I hear the crowd clapping after a song you feel proud.
Proud of what you accomplished.
When I hit the right pitch or ace a song.
When people are amazed on how beautiful your voice is.
You feel proud of your gift.

Clara Burton, Grade 5
Floyds Knobs Elementary School, IN

Robbers (A Poem for Two Voices)

Sneaking.

                       Night is our camouflage.

Robbers,

                           Stealing,

Using night for protection.

                       Gunshots firing…

Tight metal cuffs on our hands…

                         Don't do it!

Crime never pays.

                       Crime never pays.

Inmates
Konnor O'Keefe and Michael Boyd, Grade 5
Tremont Elementary School, IL

Night Noises

Night noises oh so sweet
Waves crashing, wind howling, owls hooting
Noises of the night
Crickets chirping, and stairs creeping
Night noises oh so sweet
Annie Laudick, Grade 6
St Pius X Catholic School, IN

Spring

My family loves to play outside in the spring.
But they have to go in when the phone starts to ring.
We love to throw rocks in the creek.
We do it almost every week.
Sometimes we scare the little minnows.
And it scares them when the wind blows.
My family loves to play outside.
And we really love to play on the slide.
Bailee Kennedy, Grade 4
Chrisney Elementary School, IN

Dad

When you walk in the house every day
There's a smile on my face and yours

You always have fun
Wherever you go
Never stop trying to be
The best dad you know

When you walk in the house
There's always light wherever you go
You never stop loving the family you know

When you walk in the house
There's something new
You always teach us something new as we grow

Now you know the way you are
Keep on being that wonderful one
Brianne Fenton, Grade 6
Hannah Beardsley Middle School, IL

The Mouse, the Frog, and the Log

On one certain drizzly morn'
A frog saw a nice big log.
He stepped inside it — it suited him well.
He decided to inhabit it.
The next minute
He heard a LOUD knock.
Standing right there
Was a large fluffy mouse!

Then the mouse said,
In a high little voice,
"Oh, won't you, frog dear,
Let me come and live here?"

So the frog agreed with the cute little mouse,
And they both moved into his nice cozy house.
But later that night the frog started croaking,
And the mouse started shedding his long gray fur.
They both got angry and left in a hurry.
Now the old log is alone.
The log is happy,
But just a bit sappy.

And that's the story of the Mouse, the Frog, and the Log!
Valerie Makri, Grade 4
Countryside School, IL

If Hope Could Be…

If hope could be a color
it would be white, as fluffy as a cloud.

If hope could be a taste
it would be a strawberry.

If hope could be a smell
it would be a flower blooming in the summer.

If hope could be a sound
it would be a choir.

If hope could be a feeling
it would be my mom and dad hugging me.

If hope could be an animal
it would be a butterfly in the air.
Arielle Kelly, Grade 4
St Agnes School, IL

Winter

Winter is the best time of the year.
You get up and make snowmen, snow forts,
and snow balls to have a snowball war.
When you get cold you go inside
and have hot chocolate.
Ben Roesel, Grade 4
Oak Hill Elementary School, IN

My Instruments

A contrabass, a B flat flute,
A piccolo, and one big lute,
A piano and snare drums too,
A church choir that just sings "OOH."

A clarinet, a saxophone,
A castanet, a baritone,
A mandolin, an obeophone,
A violin, a cool French horn.

My instruments and me are soaring,
I can't figure out how they're boring.
Maciej Smusz, Grade 5
Cloverdale Elementary School, IL

My Garden

My garden
Sparkles in the sun
My garden
Makes me have fun
My garden
Sweet as can be
My garden
Is lucky for me
My garden
Puts me in the mood
My garden
Cooks really good food
My garden
Is never in a hurry
My garden
Never gives me a worry
My garden
Sings me good night
My garden
Shines in the moonlight
Melissa Norman, Grade 6
Francis Granger Middle School, IL

Baseball

Baseball is fun.
It is great to hit a home run
If it is a long hit then
run as fast as you can and get a double.
Billy Stricker, Grade 4
Liberty Elementary School, IN

Rain

I never understood,
the meaning of umbrellas
why cover the rain,
when all it's trying to do is,
kiss your skin
with his silvery liquid drops
Grace Orndorff, Grade 5
Steeple Run Elementary School, IL

The Flowers

Sweet in the spring
Singing in the sunshine
The flowers fill the air with joy
The spring
Chelsie Beckner, Grade 4
Robein Elementary School, IL

The Person I Love

The person I love is very sweet
The person I love is very neat

The person I love is kind to me
The person I love sticks up for me

The person I love is older than me
The person I love is the same size as me

The person I love is a friend to me
The person I love is "CORTNEY"
Cassandra S. Roberts, Grade 4
Hoagland Elementary School, IN

The Forest

As the elk go ambling by
The eagles patrol the sky
The wolf down upon the ground
Waiting, not making a sound
While the fish in the brook
Avoiding the fisher's hook
Upon the sky look
As the trees are swaying
Matthew Meyer, Grade 5
Countryside School, IL

Hogan's Heroes

I very do think,
that you know Colonel Klink,
but do you know Shultz,
he does not play with the Colts.
Noah Pierce, Grade 4
Goodfield Elementary School, IL

Ode to Deodorant

Deodorant, oh deodorant,
Your scent makes me smell great.
You even help me get a mate.
My armpits aren't sweaty anymore.
My armpits are dry galore.
When I smell like an ape,
You make me smell great.
Whether you're mango or pear,
I will never care.
When I get out of the shower,
You make me smell good once again.
Kenedy House, Grade 5
Morgan Elementary School, IN

Dolphin

D iving dolphins
O ver the waves
L eaping into the sun
P layful animals
H uge
I ncredible and
N ice!
Brandon Lawless, Grade 5
Floyds Knobs Elementary School, IN

Papitas

BIG chocolate brown eyes,
Stare at you sweet fully.
Begging for a home,
To be loved and cherished.
Her brown and white,
Inside she is saying,
"Take me home, take me home"
Until she can't wait anymore.

Throw, run, and catch!
The little Shih Tzu bounced,
And skipped and jumped!
The dog for me must be hyper,
And she's rambunctious enough for me!

The pup was filled with glee!
Only one thing left to do, NAME!!!!!
Lina? Skippy? NO!
Papitas! Third time's a charm!
Leaping out of the car door,
Into her new home.
Just awaiting her beginning
Of a new life, and love.
Sydney Kaplan, Grade 5
Ranch View Elementary School, IL

Blue

What color is Blue?
Blue is the color of the sky.
Blue is the color of the lake.
Blue is the color of the night.
Blue is also the color of my heart.
Diane Hardy, Grade 4
Lavizzo Elementary School, IL

Four Wheeler

Four wheeler
Loud, monstrous
Zooming, screeching, mudding
Fun riding with friends
Riding, gliding, pedaling
Smooth, colorful
Bicycle
Seth Head, Grade 5
Staunton Elementary School, IN

Basketball

Basketball is heaven
Like taking a free throw
Basketball is winning
Like taking your friend one-on-one
Basketball is thrilling
Like leaving the locker room ready to play
Basketball is being prepared
Like knowing you'll be taking the winning shot
Basketball is responsibility
Like taking a picture with your team
Basketball is happiness
Like throwing the ball in the air with joy
You just won the championship!

Nick Sagastume, Grade 5
St John of the Cross Parish School, IL

Ode to Christmas

Stockings hung by the chimney
Christmas trees so glittery
Ornaments held with care
Smells of cinnamon in the air
Snowflakes nip your nose
And maybe even your toes
Warm fuzzy sweaters around your neck
Everything has to be spotless not even a speck
Sounds of jingles on the rooftop
When you go outside you have to wear a cap
Crinkly wrapping paper tied up in bows
I love Christmas I think you know

Jaclyn Swanson, Grade 5
Morgan Elementary School, IN

My Country

My family and friends went back to Bosnia.
We saw lots of lakes.
The food was great.
That is what I saw.
It made me the happiest I ever was.

Emin Jakupovic, Grade 4
Haugan Elementary School, IL

Monkey Business

I have a monkey he's really cute
But you have to be careful he just might toot
It's really funny he wears one boot
And he likes to play the flute
But what's weird is he likes to hoot
And sometimes I wish he had a mute
Other times I want to throw him down a laundry shoot
And he loves all kinds of fruit
But you have to be careful he likes to bite
And he loves to fight
And he never does anything right
You may call him weird but I call him Jakite

Reno Casanova, Grade 5
Center Street Elementary School, IL

Man of Snow

I am an ordinary man
Many kids made me out of snow
They made me as tall as a tree
Then they added a carrot nose and a red bow

After that they left me standing in the snow.
As I stare into the street.
Busy people honk and beep.
Many people stopped from the heavy sleet.

I stand for about a month,
On the white gleaming snow, that is freezing
I hope I don't catch a cold
Especially when I start coughing and sneezing

The kids are sad because spring is coming soon.
I know this is when I melt away,
Drop went the kids' tears.
Hopefully they will remake me another day.

Scott Mitchell, Grade 6
Our Lady of Peace School, IL

Dragons

There are stories of dragons from long ago,
Are they real, nobody knows.
Some are great, some are small,
There are some that rule them all.
Some live in cold, some live in hot,
Some breathed fire, others did not.
They live in the mountains; they live in the sea,
And some live on land, like you and me.
Dragons are the coolest things,
The best ones are in Beijing.
They might have lived anywhere,
But mainly in our own nightmares.

Steven McReynolds, Grade 6
McHenry Middle School, IL

A Strange Foreign Exchange Student

I live in a classroom.
I wear a uniform every day.
It gets boring some of the time.
But when it's science, hooray! Hooray!

I love fifth grade.
But I don't in some way
I like it, because for me there's no homework.
I don't like it, because when everyone leaves
I'm stuck there until the next day.

It's fun and cheerful.
Every day I smile with glee.
I learn a lot.
From my teacher Mrs. Gianotti.

Bella Antoniolli, Grade 6
Our Lady of Peace School, IL

Track

running fast and strong,
people are cheering me on,
give it all I got.
Andrew J. Coontz, Grade 6
Rochester Middle School, IL

Cats and Dogs

Cat
cute, soft
sleeping, eating, drinking
hissing loudly — playing fetch
barking, jumping, digging
obnoxious, loud
Dog
Alexis Gleason, Grade 5
Hiawatha Elementary School, IL

Fun Summer Baseball

Hot summer practices
The taste of cold water
Tickles my tongue
Coaches yelling out signals…
Fundamentals…
Need to be improved
Batting…fielding…pitching
And base running
Practices are hard…but exciting
All preparing,
For the critical first game
It's fun…
It's summer…
It's baseball
Clayton French, Grade 6
Linton-Stockton Elementary School, IN

Goodbye My Dead Friend

I wish you were here
I miss you so much my dear.

Why did you go
I miss you so.
After the day you left
I felt like I never meet you.

Oh why do I think
And why do I dream
So much about you.

Every day I think about you
My heart tells me
You will always be with me.

I wish you were still here
And you were right next to me.
Armando Rodriguez, Grade 6
Peck Elementary School, IL

Mrs. Whitacre

Mrs. Whitacre is
cleaning her new
house in Kentucky.
Mrs. Whitacre.
Jessica Hein, Grade 4
Bright Elementary School, IN

Martin, a Great Man

Martin
Strong, brave
Helping, protesting, caring,
Will be remembered forever
Martin.
Daniel Villa, Grade 6
San Miguel School, IL

Snow

Snow
White, cold
Freezing, sliding, running
Shiny, icy
I love snow!
Adrianna Patterson, Grade 5
Cloverdale Middle School, IN

Hope

If hope could be a color
it would be as white as snow.

If hope could be a taste
it would taste just like ice cream.

If hope could be a smell
it would be a summer day near a lake.

If hope could be a sound
it would be the sound of chirping birds.

If hope could be a feeling
it would be a perfect summer day.

If hope could be an animal
it would be a dove gracefully flying.
Patrick Smith, Grade 4
St Agnes School, IL

Lighthouses

Lighthouses are so bright
They light the sea up for ships;
They are a good help.

Light houses are so bright;
Jesus is the bright lighthouse
To show us the way.
Brett Simpson, Grade 6
First Baptist Christian Academy, IL

Spring

Spring
Cloudy, rainy
Planting, eating, playing
Flying kites in the air
Fun
Mohayad Alzein, Grade 4
Universal School, IL

Snow Day

A day for snow play
Sliding, sledding, snow fight fun
Forts with wars from me
Wars all day 'til we're all cold
Snow, snow everywhere and more
Zane Seal, Grade 4
Goodfield Elementary School, IL

In Space

I am a poet in space,
looking for galaxies and Milky Ways,
To touch the moon at noon.
Pierre Matienzo, Grade 4
Haugan Elementary School, IL

Best Friends

Helping with problems
Trusting, someone with secrets
Having a best friend
Andria Welty, Grade 6
Rochester Middle School, IL

Softball

Besides the uniforms,
Across the field,
Against the pressure,
Despite the fear,
Down the line,
Until you win,
From batter to pitcher,
Along the line,
As the ball flies fast,
Toward the batter,
As I swing and hit,
Along the bat my fingers with pain.
Briana Sauls, Grade 6
Michael Grimmer Middle School, IN

A Girl Named Abby

There was a girl named Abby.
Who was feeling a little crabby.
Because her flute went splat!
Which made it end up flat.
So she had to play Bobbi Jean's.
Who was very mean!
Abigail Trotter, Grade 5
Center Street Elementary School, IL

Mama's in the Kitchen

Mama's in the kitchen making fried chicken
Daddy's in the hall, resting on the wall
Sister's in the room, riding with a broom
Brother's in the attic, fixing on the static

Armand Nutall, Grade 4
Martin L King Elementary School, IL

The Shoe

I am a shoe,
I like to walk too.
My owner's feet really stink,
Did his huge feet really shrink?
I just went for a ten-mile jog,
It was a race beside a bog.
I'm getting torn up and old now,
I will never get thrown away I vow.
Although the end is near,
I will just sit here.
My laces are permanently soggy,
My soles are all chewed up by the doggy.
Putting me on the market was smart,
But I still wish I was back in K-mart.
In this closet it is very dark,
I think I heard that dog just bark.
Please look down at your feet now,
Try and treat my relatives the same somehow.

Austin Scott, Grade 5
Dee Mack Intermediate School, IL

Disney World

Cinderella's castle pointing to the sky
Pastries from Main Street Bakery
Screams of children on rides
Sun beaming on my face
Hot buttery popcorn
It's going to be an exciting day

Morgan Kaptur, Grade 5
Frank H Hammond Elementary School, IN

Nothing

Nothing's ever what you think
Everything happens in one little blink!

Nothing's ever what you are
Only because you're always a shooting star!

Nothing ever goes your way
Only because you had a bad day!

Nothing's ever what it seems
Only if you make ice cream!

Nothing's ever what you think
Everything happens in one little blink!

Grace August, Grade 6
St Anastasia School, IL

Solar System

Pluto so cold
Sun so bright
Saturn is a spectacular sight
Jupiter is big
Mercury is small
Venus is not far from our star at all
Mars is Earth's sister
Uranus and Neptune both bright blue
I enjoy observing the solar system with you

Matthew Rappe, Grade 4
Pritzker Elementary School, IL

Night Time Sky

When I look out my bedroom window I see
stars in the night time sky
Sometimes I wish I could fly through the night clouds
I want to jump out my window and see all the tiny roof tops
When I am soaring through the sky I see little tiny cops
chasing a criminal in my eyes
Finally ending my adventure I gracefully
float into my bedroom and gently fall asleep

Luke Robinson, Grade 6
Central Jr High School, IL

Snow Globe Sadness

A snow globe's life is a sad life.
I wake up from my sleep to realize I'm being shaken.
I wake and smell bacon.
I'm allergic to bacon.
I just lie down and cry.
I wish I could die.
A snow globe's life is a sad life.

Connor Braeger, Grade 6
St Pius X Catholic School, IN

Frozen

cold as ice frozen like a pond *beware* for it is frozen!
freeze stop forget! read laugh learn.
cold jacket yell echo
echo
echo
froze frozen freeze like ice cold as snow!
Frozen

Megan Smaltz, Grade 4
James R Watson Elementary School, IN

Snowman

S o many people made of Snow.
N ever melt in the winter.
O n top of the snow.
W ould like to stay warm.
M aybe put a carrot, scarf, and a hat on it.
A re hard to make.
N ever move a muscle.

Christian Lewis, Grade 5
St Michael School, IN

Give Me

Give me neatness.
Give me knowledge
And I will use it to get A's.
Give me honesty.
Give me kindness
And I will help everyone that trusts me.
Jonathan Figueroa, Grade 6
Norman Bridge Elementary School, IL

The Red Dot

He ran across the floor
He sprang up on a chair
His tongue was hanging out
But he didn't really care

The dot dashed left
As did he
The dot jumped on his paw
He heard laughs of glee

The dot just ran in circles
Finally he got bored
The laser sight had grown old
The one he so adored

The cat gave up
And walked away
The people stood there, open mouthed
In a state of dismay
Kyle Jackson, Grade 5
Twin Branch Model School, IN

Seasons

Today is the day
We go outside to play.
But did you know
We played in the snow?
I also found a leaf,
I called it, "The Chief."
I sat at the beach
and ate a tasty ripe peach.
My mom said to take a shower,
then I went outside to pick a flower.
The last thing I did was pick a clover.
Then the seasons had to start all over.
In bright beautiful spring,
I got my mom a diamond ring.
In freezing cold winter,
I oddly got a tiny splinter.
Hot, warm, nice summer,
this year was a total bummer.
The nice leaves falling fall,
actually wasn't bad at all.
That is the end, my friend.
Courtney Groh, Grade 4
Study Elementary School, IN

Friendship

My friendship is like a merry-go-round,
Sometimes I have fun,
Sometimes I don't!
It is like a light bulb,
It goes on and off,
And sometimes it just doesn't work!
Alexis Gillum, Grade 6
Laketon Elementary School, IN

The Nightmare

I went to bed last night.
And woke up to a fright.
I had a terrible nightmare.
I would tell you but I don't dare.
I can't believe what happened last night.
It hurts just to think of the sight.
Zach Wright, Grade 5
Perry Central Elementary School, IN

Basketball

Basketball
Orange, round
Bouncing, dribbling, moving
Like a big orange.
Dwayne Wade.
Christopher Simmons, Grade 4
Cynthia Heights Elementary School, IN

If I Could Be...

A baseball player.
I would hit
Home runs,
Get outs,
Make great plays,
Help my team win games.
I love baseball!
Trevor Fetscher, Grade 4
Cynthia Heights Elementary School, IN

The Funeral

I miss you so much
Though you're still here

I still think of you
Even though you're with me

I wish you were here
To watch me grow up

I know you're watching
Though I can't see you

I miss you so much
But I know you're near.
Ashley Egan, Grade 5
Norman Bridge Elementary School, IL

By Myself

When I'm by myself
and I close my eyes,
I'm as tall as a tree,
I'm light as a bee.
I'm as powerful as a bear,
I'm as invisible as the air.
I'm as aggressive as a lion,
I'm immense as a canyon.
And when I open my eyes,
all I want to be is me.
Bartosz Kozminski, Grade 6
Norman Bridge Elementary School, IL

My Dearest Thing

All my pets are so great
My dogs will bark
When a stranger is outside
Are fun to play with
My family is also great
Make good cookies
They look out for me
My friends are cool
Have been friends for a long time
We look out for each other
Even like the same things
Brian Murphy, Grade 5
Churubusco Elementary School, IN

Grasshoppers

Grasshoppers like to
Sing at night to put us all
Asleep every night.
Matthew Gough, Grade 4
Robein Elementary School, IL

Jungle of Life

One day as I was walking...
Exploring...

As I proceeded farther
Searching...

For a way out
The crooked vines snapped,
I ran away quickly

But everywhere
I turned I was caught
Panicked and scared

I hurried...
But the bushes prickly and piercing
Stopped me
Help! I'm tangled in this jungle.
Amy Horn, Grade 6
Linton-Stockton Elementary School, IN

Star

Star oh star
Show me your secrets,
You float far away,
Yet you glow so brightly
As if taunting me to see.

Sam Griffin, Grade 4
Country Meadow Elementary School, IN

Tracker

I had a dog I loved so much,
He never played double-dutch.
We would hide then he would seek,
But he would cheat cause, he would peek.

A few years after we got him,
He go shot right in the limb
He was suffering a lot.
Now we put flowers on his plot.

Kelsey Prichard, Grade 4
Adams Central Elementary School, IN

School's Out

It's the last day of school yippee hurray
No more school as of today
I run out the door inhale the breeze
I see the sunshine and the green trees
Going off on adventures in the wild blue yonder
Was summer made for kids, I wonder
This is what my parents say
"School will start again someday"

Brett Geever, Grade 6
Rochester Middle School, IL

I Am

I am a cheerleader
I wonder about life
I hear whispers
I see the stars in the sky
I want to go out

I am a cheerleader
I pretend I am a bird
I feel tickles on my face
I touch the clouds
I worry about things that may never come true
I cry when I get hurt

I am a cheerleader
I understand that things won't come easy
I say cheers for my team
I dream of being a professional cheerleader
I try to do my best
I hope I will make the best of my life
I am a cheerleader

Alexis Gutierrez, Grade 6
Cassell Elementary School, IL

School's Out

A vacation is being free
It's as cool as a brand new toy
It's as hot as hot chocolate on a cold winter's day
Like the color of a blue-green sea
And sounds like a rushing of waves on a beach.
It tastes like warm, fresh chocolate chip cookies
It smells like apples in the fall
It looks like a plane ready to take off
It feels smooth as the water surface.
It moves like a boat through the water.
I love vacation
School's out!

Maggie Vallone, Grade 5
St John of the Cross Parish School, IL

Red

Red is the color of cherries and strawberries.
Red is our school colors and our mascot's feathers.
Red is my favorite color, except for blue that's my other.
Red is the color of cupid's darts, and some people's hearts.
Red is an awesome color!

Kelly Tokarz, Grade 4
Oak Hill Elementary School, IN

Seasons

The seasons of the year are spring, summer, winter, and fall.
In the fall, the leaves change colors and fall off.
In summer, it's hot and you can go swimming.
In spring, it rains and starts to warm up.
In winter, it's freezing cold and snowy.
Can you guess which season is my favorite?

Samantha Roldan, Grade 6
St Joseph School, IL

Sounds

The softest sound
The loudest sound
The sound that makes us go around

Every sound has a beat
They can make you tap your feet
Some sounds may be sweet

Sounds can turn into a song
Some sounds can turn into a rap
Some can make you take a nap

Some sounds are long
They can sound like, "ping-pong"
Or they are just very long

Some sounds make you run
This poem was fun
My poem is now done

Dan Gunckel, Grade 6
Emmanuel-St Michael Lutheran School, IN

Benched

Got to keep my butt down
Or I'll get benched.
Got to move my feet
Or I'll get benched.
Got to box out
Or I'll get benched.
Got to play with passion
Or I'll get benched.
Got to play with intensity
Or I'll get benched.

I forgot to do everything
So now I'm benched.
Grant Schuler, Grade 6
Laketon Elementary School, IN

Scared

Way back when
One dark night
I was scared
and full of fright.

I had been out
all day that day
I was sweaty
from my play.

I heard hissing
and saw eyes
Eyes of yellow
Oh my, my.

It was just
a cat that night
A cat that filled me
full of fright.
Dalton Troy Moody, Grade 6
Haubstadt Community School, IN

Wagging Wonders

To show their love they lick you.
Happily they wag their tails.
Their paws are big and padded,
but watch their long, sharp nails.

They like to roll and wrestle.
When they play — they bite.
If you hear a growl or snarl,
be prepared for a fight.

They say they're man's best friend,
but also women's too.
I think dogs are wonderful!
How about you?
Matthew Kelly, Grade 6
Rochester Middle School, IL

My Brother Ate My Homework

My brother ate my homework, it was quite a nasty sight.
He put it in his mouth, and gave my Mom a fright.
I screamed at him, "Spit it out!" But he wouldn't even budge.
I shook him hard, he gulped it up. "Wow," he said, "it tastes like fudge!"
I screamed, "Oh no! Look at what you did!"
Turning in fright, he ran and hid.
I chased him around, he darted left and right.
Until he saw my math book…and took a big old bite!
I let out a scream of terror and sunk slowly to the floor.
He ate all my homework, then he ate more and more!
He gobbled up all the pages, words and problems, too.
And this is why I'm sitting here…with lots of homework due!
Marissa Roper, Grade 5
Bell-Graham School, IL

Sitting in a Cemetery

Here I am sitting in the cemetery
watching the grave stones wear away like glass in the ocean.
All of them still showing importance of the people who were.
Well, at least trying.
As they fade away, those people are fading away from our memory.
But we must remember that they were special.
They lead their own lives like we do but then life slipped away from them.
So here I am sitting in the cemetery
watching the grave stones wear away like glass in the ocean…
And still trying to figure out what they say.
Jessica Campbell, Grade 6
Rochester Middle School, IL

Ode to My Cat Misty

My cat Misty is gray. She has tan designs on her too.
She is two years old and I love her so and she will always love me too.

She loves to prowl and hop and play.
She rolls her ball back and forth all day.

She is really special to me and really special to you.
She will be in my arms and my heart and your arms and heart too.

She loves to dash and run
And have fun all day in the sun.

When she dies we will all cry and miss her too.

Sierra Lori, Grade 5
Morgan Elementary School, IN

Unicorn

Galloping on the magic trail
wings made of red roses full of sparkle
fairies ride on the white unicorn
as it gallops on passing lilies and butterflies and other dimensions
the unicorn finally enters a dimension
trotting on a shooting star's trail leading her back home
above space and through the stars

Mallory Burke, Grade 5
Noonan Academy, IL

Ode to My Grandpa!

My grandpa was funny but he is gone. I miss him a lot. He made my heart warm and cozy. But now I'm sad. I loved him so. When I was little I was afraid of him. He needed me now me and my grandma need him. He died. Years ago I never knew he's go so soon. Now I feel so sad because I loved him so. He has always been there for me. Life is not fair because they took him away. Grandpa loved me so but now I know you're never coming home. You dressed up like an elf for Christmas. You always made me feel like I was on my best behavior. I cry every night hoping you'll come home. When my cousins were mean to me you made them say sorry. You made me feel so important. Now I am lost. Bye Bye Grandpa.

Amber M. Manship, Grade 4
Morgan Elementary School, IN

Team Work

Passing the puck can be fun because when you pass it and they score your team could have the lead.
When you shoot the puck it's like passing but you shoot you can score.
Then when the other team has the puck you can hit them (known as a check).
Then you can steal the puck and have a chance to score.
Then if the other team blocks the puck and then you can just steal the puck and have a chance to score.
Then after the time goes out at the end of the game the team with the most goals win.

James Timmerman, Grade 6
St John Evangelist School, IN

Bio

Shelby
Athletic, funny, shy
Sister of Lesley and Emily
Lover of basketball, summer break, and bicycle rides with my family in the spring
Who feels happy when we win the championship, nervous before a piano recital, and anxious for summer break
Who needs love, joy, and happiness
Who gives a helping hand, time to others, and listens to people's stories
Who fears spiders, heights, and failure
Who would like war to end, seeing people smile, and joy all around
Who lives in the country in a brick house on Winter Road
Toennies

Shelby Toennies, Grade 6
Damiansville Elementary School, IL

Ode to Thanksgiving

The food is delicious. The turkey is the best part. The pilgrims called it a feast. Thanksgiving is fun. It is a time for your family to come to see you and the dinner. That's what Thanksgiving is about. But Thanksgiving is in the fall. That's when the leaves go to the ground. That's the best part of Thanksgiving. It's a good day to eat turkey. You can see your family and friends. They just don't come for the food; they also come to see you. The guys just don't come for the game; they come for the food too!

Tristen Goodwin, Grade 4
Morgan Elementary School, IN

Drums

I have drums that are really loud and my mom usually gets really wowed
I love drums because they're cool I think drums rule
Bass drum, snare drum — lots of fun; drum a cool song — then I'm done
Hitting cymbals — clang, clang, clang, when you drum, it goes bang, bang, bang
Drumming a song is just my thing; when people hear me, heck they'll even sing
If you have a drum, you need a band; some people say no, but I say, "Oh, yes you can!"
On my bass drum I have a skull; when I play, it sounds like rock n' roll
Hitting the snare drum, it goes bam, bam, bam; when my mom hears me, she's my #1 fan
With a microphone, I can sing with my voice; I can sing anything of my choice
As a player, I'm average, but with lessons I'll have leverage
Drumming sometimes tires me, but someday, someone will hire me

Max Steinkuhl, Grade 6
St Theresa School, IN

Ladybug
They have black spots
They are the best insect,
Because of its spots
It will tickle your nose
It is my Love Bug
The ladybug!
Megan Nika, Grade 6
Rochester Middle School, IL

Class
Into the class go,
About to start,
Before I sit I go,
Toward the air vent,
Into the basket I get my book.
In front of me the teacher stands.
According to the teacher we have to learn.
Along with reading and English,
Aside from homework I love this class.
Out of this class I go,
Since the bell rings.
Like any other kid I got to seventh hour.
Kristi Merta, Grade 6
Michael Grimmer Middle School, IN

Friends
Friends are cool.
My friends and I love to get wet.
Yesterday we went to the pool.
Something was floating in there
So the lifeguard got a net.
Anthony Walter, Grade 4
Central Elementary School, IL

Chihuahuas
Mean, grouchy
eating, biting, sleeping,
cute, adorable, lovable, brown,
loving, munching, crabs,
black, noisy,
dogs.
Sara Rebus, Grade 4
Liberty Elementary School, IN

My Fat Cat
My cat is fat
My cat is lazy
She sits on my lap
And her name is Daisy.

She doesn't like to play
She doesn't like to leap
That is how lazy she is
She gets it from me.
Luke Short, Grade 6
Rochester Middle School, IL

Library
Librarians and books
Tables and computers
Books so good
Kids and their tutors
Reading and writing
Some books are scary
Let's read! Let's read!
This makes the library.
Kelly Kiolbasa, Grade 5
Our Lady of Peace School, IL

Dark Ages
Back in the time of knights and kings,
back in the time of magical things.
Witches and wizards,
magic and stuff.
Dragons with fire,
and smoke that they puff.
Castles with draw bridges over a moat;
farmers in fields herding their goats.
Horses for jousting,
to get their troops ousting.
Amour for battles,
their chains they would rattle.
Honor and glory,
was their entire story.
These were the Dark Ages,
when medieval man rages.
Though times were primitive,
and their soundings limited;
the allure for me was eminent.
That's why it fascinates me,
because of all its mystery!
Ryan Minton, Grade 6
Central Jr High School, IL

A Rat Story
I once knew an ugly rat,
That was really really fat.
He lives by a mill.
He is very still,
And his best friend is a black bat.
James Swanson, Grade 6
ROWVA East Elementary School, IL

Spring
When all the flowers bloom
You might just assume
A bird will flap its wing
And lots of them will sing.
The grass is turning green
It's time to plant the beans.
So now it's time to bring
The first signs of Spring.
Abby McNutt, Grade 5
GCMS Elementary School, IL

What Is Nature?
Nature is beauty.
Nature is mysterious.
Nature is loving.
Ally Czerwonka, Grade 5
St Jacob Elementary School, IL

A Reflection
I am here,
Sparkling every night,

I sit and watch every sight,
Above the world,

During the day,
I am gone,

But, at night,
I see a reflection of me.
Logan Wisniewski, Grade 6
Linton-Stockton Elementary School, IN

Friends
F riends forever
R espectful to each other
I mportant people in your life
E ncourage each other
N ever lies
D on't leave you for another
S hare with you
Kirsten Burris, Grade 5
Staunton Elementary School, IN

Sports
Soccer
Run and pass
Passing dribbling shooting
Turnover, the other team has it
Passing faking shooting
Shoot swish
Basketball
Kyle Kostell, Grade 6
St Matthew School, IL

The Silly Zoo
Guess what's at my zoo,
Lions you betcha,
How about snakes,
Or giraffes' tall necks,
Birds glide through the treetops,
Monkeys throw birthday parties,
While rhinos have horn battles,
And little penguins do a dance,
It's such a silly zoo,
So come and be you!
Jessica Pletsch, Grade 6
Rochester Middle School, IL

Fishing

Cast the line out far.
Catch the little or big fish.
Go eat the fishy.

Zacarias L. Garcia, Grade 4
McKenney-Harrison Elementary School, IN

Give Me

Give me power.
Give me peace
And I will bring peace to the world.
Give me confidence.
Give me hope.
Give me strength
And I will save the world from any danger.

Furqan Muneeruddin, Grade 6
Norman Bridge Elementary School, IL

Respectable

R espect everyone and each other
E veryone should be treated equally
S aying yes to your teacher Ms. Nolen
P eople should treat others as they would like to be treated
E very time the teacher asks you to do something, do it
C are for everyone and everything
T ake care of your classroom
A ll people should then you should be kind
B e kind to others and animals
L etting everyone be your friend
E very teacher deserves respect

Brandon Johnson, Grade 6
Edgebrook Elementary School, IL

Hurricanes

Destroying our homes, Why?
People are homeless
Some are injured and lost their lives
People are crying and screaming for help
Still the question is, Why?

Kyle Stuetelberg, Grade 4
Bell-Graham School, IL

Friends

Friends are like family
Staying with you forever
Someone to talk to
Someone to share with
Someone to laugh with and have fun
Friends are like crayons
They are many different colors, shapes, and sizes
Someone to play with and someone to have over
Someone to cheer you up when you're down
And not to make you frown
Someone to make your world turn upside-down
Friendship is like a good book you can never put down.

Tyler Zampa, Grade 5
St John of the Cross Parish School, IL

Sugar Cookies

Sugar cookies are fun to eat when
dipped in milk, it's so unique when taking
a bite it's so moist and round it'll melt
in your mouth so tasty it sounds. So
grab a glass and say 'got milk' to
the freshness of cookies piled up in
your mouth. Yummy, yum, yum, I can't
wait till they're done, of the freshness
of cookies piled up in the oven.

Dilma Samayoa, Grade 5
Levan Scott Academy, IN

In Indonesia

In Indonesia
A little girl is jumping for joy
'Cause someone has decided to sponsor her.

Her community gets wells and medical help.
The whole community is happy.
Their lives have changed forever.

I know this,
'Cause I have decided to sponsor her.
We communicate through letters
And will meet each other some day.

World Vision has made a difference in the world.
I have made a difference in the world.
Now you can make a difference in the world.

Erica McKinley, Grade 6
Laketon Elementary School, IN

Ludington, Michigan

I love to see,
The radiant sunset at the end of a Ludington day,
Water bolting upon shore,
The sun glistening on the settled water,
I love to hear,
The roaring of the water,
The loud call of the seagulls,
Water slowly drifting down the river,
I love to feel,
The warm sand on my feet,
The warmth of the sun streaming down on my face,
I love to smell,
The soothing smell of the beach,
The smell of Ludington nothing can compare.

Rachel Jones, Grade 5
Churubusco Elementary School, IN

Spiders

Spiders all around,
Hanging, hanging upside down.
On their very silky web.

James Riley, Grade 4
McKenney-Harrison Elementary School, IN

I Am

When I am by myself
and I close my eyes…
I am as tall as the Sears Tower
I am full of power
I am a butterfly
I am flying in the sky
I am as small as a mouse
I am wearing a blouse
And when I open my eyes
all I want to be is me.

Remah Aby-bashish, Grade 4
Norman Bridge Elementary School, IL

There Once Was an Elephant

There once was an elephant
who dreamed he could fly with his ears
he jumped off a cliff
and now he can't fly anymore

Paul Crowe, Grade 5
Gard Elementary School, IL

Moving

I hate moving
so hard, painful,
you lose your friends,
you have to make new ones,
the truck comes,
the truck leaves,
so hard to move,
feel the pain.

Jack Johnston, Grade 6
Sacred Heart School, IL

Playing Baseball

When I play baseball,
I hit some home runs
and when I hit them,
I have fun!
When I hit a fly ball
high up in the air,
when it comes down,
it never lands fair.
When I get out,
I never pout.
I just go up to the plate
and swing again!

Dalton Johnson, Grade 4
Marine Elementary School, IL

Squirrels

One day I went into the park.
I watched a flying squirrel.
I watched it jump from tree to tree.
It landed on a girl.

Zachary Shappell, Grade 4
Adams Central Elementary School, IN

What Is Yu-Gi-Oh

What is Yu-Gi-Oh?
Yu-Gi-Oh is a game.
It is not lame.
It is a television series.
Joey is so furious.
Ugimoto is a duelist.
Dark Magician is my favorite monster.
My other is Turtle Catapult.
That is what Yu-Gi-Oh is!

Jonathan Southern, Grade 4
Morgan Elementary School, IN

Lawyer

L ucky people
A lways working
W hy do I live with one?
Y ou are lucky
E vil people in town
R eally nice suits are good for court

Blythe Borton, Grade 4
GCMS Elementary School, IL

Golden Wing Warbler

Golden Wing Warbler
Unmistakable, dazzling,
Migrating, trilling, foraging
Nesting in broad road ranges
Hovering, breeding, soaring
Colorful, appealing
"Vermivora Chrysptera"

Kush Patel, Grade 4
Dixie Bee Elementary School, IN

Love

Love is a feeling inside
All over in your mind
You can't stop thinking about it
He can't stop thinking about her
And she can't stop thinking about him
Love is something to explore
Love is something we all should adore
Love

Corrie Fay, Grade 6
Central Jr High School, IL

Goodbye Winter

Winter is gone.
It left one day at dawn.
I will miss the hot cocoas,
and how the wind blows.
It will not be snowing.
All the big winter coats will be going,
but spring his here!
It brings me so much cheer.

Cassie Crawford, Grade 6
Rochester Middle School, IL

Storms

Bad, cold, wet, ice, snow
Ice storms make trouble each year
Cold, snow, mittens, ice

Trevor Heavilin, Grade 4
GCMS Elementary School, IL

Spring

S o wonderful we won't go inside
P icnic in the park
R iding on my bike
I nches and inches of rain
N othing but playtime
G reen green grass

Maggie Popken, Grade 4
Robein Elementary School, IL

Give Me

Give me luck.
Give me knowledge
And I will use it to help people.
Give me peace.
Give me friendship.
Give me light
And I will lighten the world.

John Samek, Grade 6
Norman Bridge Elementary School, IL

Flowers

Flowers
Beautiful, colorful
Budding blossoming, blooming
Always making me feel bright
Shines

Sarah Hassan, Grade 4
Universal School, IL

Spring

Spring
Happy, cool
Playing, singing, riding
Many, many blooming flowers
Awesome

Abaan Merchant, Grade 4
Universal School, IL

Baking

Mixing bowls and wooden spoons
Milk and butter
Oven so hot
Served to each other
Frosting and chocolate
Poured in a pan
Getting bigger and bigger
Cake made by my Gram.

Kylie Broadway, Grade 4
St Robert Bellarmine School, IL

Basketball

Basketball is my favorite sport
I love when I dribble the ball up and down the court
When I shoot at the ball into the big round hoop
I get such a thrill
That my whole body just might get a chill

To hear all the crowd cheering when you make it
Or sighing and maybe even crying if you miss it
So it doesn't matter at the end of the game
If you win or lose
How many baskets you made or missed
Or even what the score is
All that matters is if you played your heart out
So go ahead play with all you got
Get with it
Get your head in the game

Natalie Hynek, Grade 6
St John Evangelist School, IN

Cars Are My Life

Cars are my life.
Cars are so cool.
Like Lambo, Saleen and GT
I love these cars, they love me.
Their engines purr like little kittens.
Their tires serve as mighty mittens.
Traction control keeps from rolling over
Big SUVs are kings of red rover.
With big beasty engines
And total bling rims
The muscle car era will never be again.
I love all the cars even the uglys,
The muscle cars of yesterday and Fords Model A.
I think about cars every day
R8, Exige and DB9.
One day they'll all be mine.

Cars are my life.

Chris Schmitt, Grade 6
Haubstadt Community School, IN

My Family Is a Racetrack

My family is a racetrack.
My dad is the road and barricade,
all tough and leading me to my future.
My mom is the crowd, cheering me on and helping me.
My younger brother Ryan is the repairman and station,
telling me cool new things and helping me through tough times.
My even younger brother Sean is the race car,
driving me crazy!
My youngest sister Molly is the grassland in the middle,
looking oh so soft, cute and kind.
I am, well, the race car driver, driving my way to
victory and having a purpose in the stadium.

John McCabe, Grade 6
Cassell Elementary School, IL

Fun

What is fun?
Fun is laughing
Fun is smiling
Fun is spending time with family and friends
We take time
Out of our day
To do what we love
Spend time with our best buds

Lauren Johnson, Grade 6
St Mary School, IL

Apple Pie

The aroma is unforgettable,
Like newly bloomed roses.
The taste so magnificent,
Like the frosting on a cake.
When you eat it your insides will hum with joy.
It is a treat sent down to Earth from the gods.
Sometimes it comes in a box,
Like babies come in a basket.
Some people like pop as a treat,
Or cake and ice cream.
But that's definitely not for me,
I LOVE apple pie!
Some people have best friends,
And I also do, but my friend isn't human,
It's APPLE PIE!!

Riley Lindholm, Grade 6
McHenry Middle School, IL

Skulls

I love skulls
They are so cool
They are usually bad to the bone
They also have cross bones
You can see them everywhere
They are on shoes, shirts, if only people cared
They are even in the head of people at the pool
May I say skulls are cool.

Shelby Kimmel, Grade 5
North Intermediate Center of Education, IL

Friends 'Til the End

You are the best,
There is no contest
You put your mind to the test
For those reasons, you are my friend
You always have a hand to lend
You laugh at all my jokes
(That aren't funny)
And you are kind to my folks
You are always there for me
As I can see
I hope you are my friend until the very end

Marissa Maeder, Grade 6
St Mary School, IL

Martin Luther King Jr.

Martin Luther King was good
he fought for people's rights
he never gave up
Alejandro Luna, Grade 6
San Miguel School, IL

Hope Is

If hope could be a color
it would be red as a ruby.

If hope could be a taste
it would taste just like chocolate.

If hope could be a smell
it would be the smell of flowers.

If hope could be a sound
it would be the sound of birds.

If hope could be a feeling
it would be a happy feeling.

If hope could be an animal
it would be an eagle soaring in the sky.
Noé Márez, Grade 4
St Agnes School, IL

Family

They always love you,
Even if it doesn't seem they do.
They've always got your back,
And are there to cut you some slack.
Family is a pure love,
Sent from above.
Kacee Hall, Grade 6
Rochester Middle School, IL

Awake and Asleep

Awake
Loud, rowdy
Playing, jumping, swimming
Skip, laugh, lie down, cover up
Snoring, tossing, turning
Quiet, peaceful
Asleep
Lauren Nagle, Grade 5
GCMS Elementary School, IL

Piglets

Piglets
Squeals are painful
Snorting, running, eating
Running joyfully around pen
Noisy
Zack Meyer, Grade 6
Milan Middle School, IN

Grandpa

He was at the nursing home every day.
We visited him every week.
When we saw him at his weakest point, we always cried.
The day I heard what happened to him.
Thinking about the past, knowing there were no more fun times with him.
We did everything together, from fishing, to farming.
We still hold our hearts close to each other.
Even though he's gone, we still are best friends forever.
Heather Hubert, Grade 5
Perry Central Elementary School, IN

Wrong

Sitting here thinking of all the wrong I've done. Just way more than one.
Having no fun at all. Feeling like I'm going to fall.
Thinking about you makes me cry. Why won't you just let me lie?
Waiting for you to fail. So they set no bail.
Freaking out too much. About such and such.
Waiting for the world to end. Trying to find a friend.
Bleeding hearts dripping all over. Never finding a four leaf clover.
Watching your eyes fade. Even the bluish shade.
Waiting for the passing day. Walking beyond the bay.
Missing your loving smile. Making that extra mile.
Walking away from me so fast. Missing everything from the past.
The plain white sheets now are red. They are even taken off the bed.
Please remember me for no wrong. But sitting with you all along.
Christina Isaac, Grade 6
Bon Air Middle School, IN

Fall

"Come" The trees seem to whisper
I walk into the forest where
The jumping jackrabbits joke around
And the birds twitter in the sunlight
A branch falls from the highest tree bringing golden leaves with it
I am mesmerized with the colors of fall
Yellow
Purple
Brown
Gold
Orange
Red
The leaves are the colors of the rainbow as they fall
Fall is the greatest time of the year
Luke Landiak, Grade 5
Beebe Elementary School, IL

If I Could I Would*

If I could I would bring you back.
If I could I would go to New Years and stay awake to see you again.
If I could I would have made sure you never went to where you were.
If I could I would have made sure you didn't do all the things you did.
If I could I would bring you back.
R.I.P. Marcus Adams
Brianna Kinzer, Grade 6
Three Rivers School, IL
*Dedicated to Marcus Adams

Love

Love can be confusing
It can be what you make it
It can be frustrating and fun at times
But it can make you sad in a matter of minutes
You can be happy at first
Then slowly turn to sad
I have experienced it, it was fun at first
but the fun was slowly diminished

Aaron Porter, Grade 5
East Elementary School, IN

Snow

Wishing for snow before I go to bed, I watch the
news for the weather forecast

While I am asleep of
snow I am dreaming

Dreaming of making a snow man
maybe the whole snow family

Making snow angels with my brother, dreaming
just dreaming of how much fun it will be

Then, when I wake up, quickly
I go downstairs to take a shower

Go back up the stairs to put on some jeans
with a turtle neck sweater

Then my coat and mittens
and everything

Go outside just to see nothing
nothing at all but grass and bare trees

Joi Gillespie, Grade 5
Benjamin Franklin Elementary School, IN

Math

Why should we learn math?
Shouldn't we just learn to follow Jesus' path?
Addition, subtraction, multiplication too,
It's so confusing I don't know what to do.
My teacher is really nice,
But she has friends that are mice.
My grades were not good,
But then they got better.
Until I found out I had to give Dad a letter.
I gave him the letter, went straight to my room,
And waiting and waited to hear a big boom.
I heard no boom so I came out of my room,
To find my dad singing zoom zoom zoom.
he said that I had won a shiny little star,
All because of that teacher who told me I could go very far.

Jaylene Thompson, Grade 6
St Mary School, IL

Captive

Captive
Scared, lonely
Thinking, stressing, hoping
The eyeglasses slip on his face, he sees in a new way
Freeing, exploring, loving
Memory, happiness
Free man

Ciara Kerckhove, Grade 6
Stanley Clark School, IN

Education

E very child goes to school
D evelopment in your grades
U sing good vocabulary
C hicago Public Schools
A sking questions
T eachers teach the class
I ndependent reading
O beying the teachers
N ever break the rule

Kenneth Yan, Grade 5
Mark Sheridan Elementary Math & Science Magnet School, IL

In a Forest Lush and Green

In a forest lush and green
There walked a girl whose name was Maureen.
Lovely flowers of pink and blue
Were in the forest lush and green.

Maureen met a lovely green bird.
It asked her nicely, "Have you seen my friend Jean?"
"No, I have not seen Jean,
And I can't be seen with a bird so green!"

Before long the time came
That Maureen saw a lovely unicorn.
After a bit she heart it mourn,
"Have you seen some nice fresh corn?"

"No, I have not seen some corn,
And I can't be seen with a unicorn!
With you creatures I cannot be seen
In this forest so lush and green!"

Nafisa Syed, Grade 4
Countryside School, IL

Parents and Kids

Parents
responsible, cautious
laboring, caring, supporting
worrisome, dependable, energetic, playful
clowning, daring, sharing
crazy, irresponsible
Kids

Marcus Braun, Grade 6
Perry Central Elementary School, IN

Monkeys

Long, stretchy tail swing
Monkeys move like acrobats
Screeches heard around
JJ Lee, Grade 5
Stanley Clark School, IN

Orange Soda

Orange soda,
YUM! YUM!
I love soda.
I really do!
It tastes like
ORANGES.
It really does.
Orange soda is refreshing.
It is good!!
Blake Cavins, Grade 4
Marine Elementary School, IL

Gecko

The scaly gecko
Crouching, tiger-like, stalking
Smoothly, silkily.
John DeBuysser, Grade 5
Stanley Clark School, IN

The Puppet
(A Poem for Two Voices)

Puppet
Dancing in the moonlight
Dancing
Twirling all alone
All alone
No one by its side
By itself
Scared and sad
Sad
Crying all alone
Puppet
Dancing in the moonlight
Zachery Hubbard, Grade 5
Tremont Elementary School, IL

Clouds

Watch the clouds roll by
Look for animals in them
Swiftly through the air
Paige Melissa Cowell, Grade 5
GCMS Elementary School, IL

Tree

Tree waving in the breeze,
Leaves blowing around the yard,
Tree so beautiful at fall.
Zachary L. Fuller, Grade 5
Hendry Park Elementary School, IN

Victory

It's a hot day today,
It is green, and it is Spring.
Who's going to win this tennis game?
We don't know — it's going to be hard.

My partner and I serve.
The ball soars through the air.
The other team hits it back.
The ball goes back and forth.

My team scores!
The other team does the serve.
The ball goes back and forth
Like two bulls are hitting it.

The crowd is going to scream
Because the score is all tied up!
Who will win? Nobody knows.
My partner does the serve.

Bounce! Bounce! We win!
Ryan Mondak, Grade 4
Countryside School, IL

4-Leaf Clovers

Look down at the grass,
Those green little strips.
Do you see any different?
With 4 rounded tips.
Have you ever seen one?
Sleeping in the dirt.
He's so tired,
From a long day at work.
What does he do for a living?
You don't know?
Must I say?
He hides down deep,
Because you've scared him away!
Caroline Patz, Grade 4
Oak Hill Elementary School, IN

The Farm

Farms are a great place
Much to see while you are there
Pigs, sheep, and horses
Ryan Morgan, Grade 6
Elwood C C School, IL

Cats

Cats
Fluffy, playful
Hiss, climb, scratch
Loving, nice, exciting, cute
Calico
Samantha Hill, Grade 4
Coal City Intermediate School, IL

3 Things to Hear

God died
for my sins
mom had me
as a baby
called me her baby boy
my dad loved me
people said I look just like him
Logan Hart, Grade 5
Churubusco Elementary School, IN

Black

The color of despair
The color of a broken heart
The color of depression
The color of betrayal
Black, a mysterious friend
The color of mourning
The color of disappointment
The color of a midnight storm
The color of death
Black, a mysterious friend
Miranda Hasler, Grade 6
Linton-Stockton Elementary School, IN

John's Long Legs

There once was a boy named John
He had legs so skinny and long
But one day he fell
Right down the well
And now his tallness is gone
Hannah Huxhold, Grade 6
St Pius X Catholic School, IN

Blue

Blue is a color
When you are down.
Blue is a song
When you have a frown.
Blue is the color of the sky.
You think of blue
When you want to cry.
Blue is the color of a shirt
Or a blue ink pen.
Blue is also the color of my eyes.
Theresa Johnson, Grade 5
Staunton Elementary School, IN

August

A lways running around
U nexpected hot weather
G rilling delicious foods
U kulele to make some music
S wimming in every pool
T aking long quiet naps
Allison Skolds, Grade 6
Elwood C C School, IL

Friday Afternoon

It is Friday 2:00 p.m., again;
We are in Science class working on our science projects;
The room is silent;
You can hear the rain hitting the window panes;
Splish, spash, plop;
Each drop sounds like it is raining cats and dogs!

Bang, bam;
Test tubes fall and crash;
Sizzle, boom, pop, ssss, shhh;
Chemical reaction!

Ring, ring;
Noise forms;
Laughter, screaming, shouting, buzzing;
That's all you hear;
Everyone leaves;
The room is silent again;
You could almost hear a pin drop!

Night falls;
Darkness engulfs;
Everyone is gone;
All of this will happen again, next Friday.

Simone Siew, Grade 4
Timothy Ball Elementary School, IN

Spring

Spring can be warm like the glowing sun
It sounds like firecrackers in the air
Moves like a light beam traveling through space
Feels like a fresh meadow breeze
It tastes like fresh berries
Smells like fresh spring flowers
Like soft, green grass
Blue like cold stream water
Red like the fire hydrant passing by
To me spring is peace on Earth!

Michael Yu, Grade 5
St John of the Cross Parish School, IL

Memories*

I hear the sound of the waterfall, tinkling
The dogs barking uncontrollably
I smell the damp odor of the animals, as I walk in the door
In the glare of the aged, dusty fans' lights
I hear my cousins running through her tiny house

I see her unique, childlike body making us lunch
I observe her arguing with Grandpa
Always sticking up for us when we get in trouble
As I hug her goodbye, I never come to think
That it could be the last time I ever see her again

Joie Gadberry, Grade 6
Linton-Stockton Elementary School, IN
*In loving memory of Wanda E. Pitcher

Heart Attack

The screaming sound of the cutting chain saw
Slicing and dicing the thick wood
The sudden halt, the loud thud on the cold ground
The close sound of the hovering chopper
Flying above the colorful sky
Thinking and hoping, is he alive?

The sudden call of the doctors
The waiting room filled with joy
The relief, but hoping we don't have to go through this anymore
Now my grandpa is home
Living the retired life
He still has to watch his heart because of that night

Koye Kaiser, Grade 6
Linton-Stockton Elementary School, IN

Praise

Praise the Lord Almighty!
Look what he has done!
He's given us the flowers
He's given us His son

Praise the Lord Almighty!
His promises are true
He sent His son to die for us
To save both me and you

Praise the Lord Almighty!
In good times and in bad
He gives us life eternal
For that I'm very glad

Jacob Reinking, Grade 6
Emmanuel-St Michael Lutheran School, IN

The Simpsons

The Simpsons are my favorite show
Homer always says DOH!
There is Bart
And the Kwik-E-Mart
If the nuclear power plant blows up, oh no!

CJ Baker, Grade 6
Rochester Middle School, IL

Who I Am

I am the fall wind, reaching out
I am a soccer goal, waiting
I am a branch on a tree, calling
I am a whispering mouse crawling inside my hole
I am a nail polish, colorful
I am a shopping bag, ready to be full
I am a cat, very lazy
I am a turtle in the morning
I am a bird ready to fly
I am a book ready to be read.

Alissa Rex, Grade 5
Churubusco Elementary School, IN

Jess

There once was a girl named Jess
She loved to wear a dress
She fell off the stool
And into the pool
And that was the end of Jess
Beau Carter, Grade 4
Robein Elementary School, IL

Assignment

Teacher wants me to write a poem.
My patience is wearing thin.
I really don't like English class.
How do I begin?

I see a poem taking shape.
It's right in front of me.
Verses, refrain, stanzas of course.
I get it! Don't you see?

I turned it into teacher
I'm feeling better now.
She's handing them back to
everyone…
A D+ but how?!
Jack A. Riedy, Grade 6
Gray M Sanborn Elementary School, IL

I Can

I can't wait till the sun comes
It is a breath of fresh air
Until the clouds, oh how beautiful
The sunset is like a princess's dress
So pretty and pink
Then the moonlight gives a chill
To every country there is.
Oh, how it looks like an eyeball
Sitting there watching you
Until the dawn brings fresh air
Like an early morning fall day
Amber Schuyler, Grade 5
Tri Elementary School, IN

Skateboarding

Aboard the skateboard,
Despite the danger,
Above the trucks come the wheels,
Throughout the town you ride,
Below you is the pavement,
Without the thought of danger,
Up and down you go on the half pipe,
Like a little kid on a swing,
Near the end of the day,
Out you go,
Toward your house you go.
Anas Suleiman, Grade 6
Michael Grimmer Middle School, IN

Running

The sun is big and bright
orange and yellow
Outside in a chair
staring up
I want to skate
it's too hot
I want to ride
is it still to hot
I say
I want to run
Run
Run
Run
Faster
Faster
Faster
Then I stop
I say
I will run another day
Dawnn Chapman, Grade 6
Central Jr High School, IL

Music

A rhythmic sound
That has a beat
It makes you want to move your feet.

The sounds will come
The sounds will go
And usually
The sounds will flow.
Thomas Naragon, Grade 6
Laketon Elementary School, IN

Football/Baseball

Football
Tough, exciting
Training, diving, catching
Pads, helmets, jerseys, gloves
Hitting, jumping, throwing
Fantastic, upset
Baseball
Joseph Trowbridge, Grade 6
St Mary Elementary School, IN

Inside My Desk

I looked inside my desk,
It was a real big mess.
I found loads maybe tons of paper,
Then I found my old stapler.
The stapler hurt my finger.
Then I found a picture of a singer.
Next I found a pile of junk,
And then I found a smelly skunk!
Nicole Lakomski, Grade 5
Fredrick Nerge Elementary School, IL

Hangin' Loose

On the floor I was wandering,
Now I'm sitting just pondering,
Would life be different if I did not fall?
I might be up there standing tall.

Being home would be great,
Because I'd have a different fate
I would see my old friends again
On the shirt favored by men

So small and young on the cuff
I am a rock that has grown tough
Being out in a jungle-like state
Has helped me see my one true fate.
Ryan Somerfield, Grade 6
Our Lady of Peace School, IL

Water

Sparkling, wet blue waves
splashing on the lush, hot bays
surging toward the sun.
Tymothy Pomykala, Grade 5
Our Lady of Peace School, IL

Bird of Prey

The hunting hawk is gigantic.
Circling the sky,
searching for their prey.
A loud screech can be heard
from all around the world.

The great majestic vulture
Scavenges for their prey.
Vultures hunt in the Amazon.
His red face shows his hunger
as he eats his dead prey.

The Harpy eagle is the biggest
eagle in the world.
They live in rain forests
in South America.
Huge feet and sharp talons
help him chase his prey
through the trees.
Snake and lizard devourer.
Raymond Kopkowski, Grade 6
Thayer J Hill Middle School, IL

Christmas

Christmas
Gleeful, lovely
Giving, caring, sharing
Cheerful, merry
That's why I love Christmas.
Kyle Manion, Grade 5
Cloverdale Middle School, IN

Mrs. Hawkins

M y teacher is
R eally naggy and
S he actually likes Purdue for that she's

H orrible but
A wesome I suppose but
W orse than spinach also
K ing of reading but
I mpossible to not do work when she's around and
N ot nice but
S weet!

Logan Albright, Grade 4
Shoals Elementary School, IN

Ode to Soldiers

They are fighting for our lives, even when we sleep at night.
Protecting lives for you and for me,
Their hearts aren't always filled with glee.
When they come to see their families they always plead,
Please stay and comfort me.
But he says, Sorry but I have no choice.
He says good-bye. I love you.
His family says their good-byes as his mom starts to cry.
He said, "I'll be back after the war so wipe your eyes."
She said, "I love you son, I'll see you then."
One year later a note was received. His family cries.
At the funeral his mom begins to cry.
She went over to her son's casket she said,
"I let him go even though he's at his true home in Heaven."
She thought, "He was brave and now he is in his grave."
I wish he didn't have to go.
Right then they started to play "American Soldier."
She thought again, why was it him?
Why wasn't it me? She prayed before she went to sleep.
She lay down and smiled, take care of my child,
My brave little soldier.

Breanna Wilson, Grade 5
Morgan Elementary School, IN

Ode to Sneaky

You're black and white and very sneaky
You cuddle up in my arms so neatly
When you're outside and the doors unlocked
You jump on the handle then the alarm goes off
Your owner is Allyson, you're her favorite pet
When you're bored you come up for a snack
When you eat a snack you feel so glee
Then you go away to climb a tree
In that tree you find a flea
You chase that flea right up that tree
Then Allyson Lockhart comes for a hug
You run down to her even though you're a little scared
Then you jump on her without your claws in the air
Then you guys fall asleep in a big warm chair

Lindsey Bowe, Grade 5
Morgan Elementary School, IN

School

All the pencils are sharpened and ready to go,
as I try not to write way too slow.

The lined paper is in a stack
as I try to fit it in my backpack.

I thought I heard an angel sing,
when I heard the bell ring.

That meant it was time to leave,
I hope on my test I will achieve.

Whitney Misfeldt, Grade 4
Erie Elementary School, IL

Blue

Blue is the color of my old skateboard shoes.
Blue is the color of my bright blue eyes.
Blue is the color of an October sky.
Blue is the color of my front door.
Blue is the color of my bedroom floor.
Blue is the color of a big blue rug.
Blue is the color of a big bad bug.
Blue is the best color of all time.

Cody Minor, Grade 5
Staunton Elementary School, IN

The Song of Life

Look into the forest, the colors of the wind
Listen to the living rain, to the bare earth sing
Listen to the silent beat, of the forest, alive
Look at small birds' beating wings, to the sky they strive
Listen to the song of life, to the source itself
Listen to all creatures sing, with boldness or with stealth
Look into the heart of trees, in the souls of vines
You will be a part of them with life you'll be entwined
Watch with awe at jumping fire, love the pulsing waves
Be enraptured, captivated, by the morning haze
See the freedom of the bound, of the white-tailed deer
The fire in every creature's heart, will forever sear
Hear the wail of the dove, the piercing shriek of hawks
Listen, you'll hear harmony, of roars, hoots, and squawks
Look for signs of true freedom, it flies just like the lark
In every creature's glowing eyes, it sings in every heart
All this is the song of life, wrapped around each other
Listen closely, you will know, we all need each other

Lizzy Oi, Grade 5
Gray M Sanborn Elementary School, IL

Harry McScary

There was an old lady quite scary
She met a man very hairy
They soon got married
Lived near people buried
And that is why my name is Harry McScary

Ghrae Dolan, Grade 6
Christian Life Schools, IL

What Is Music?

What is music?
   Music is emotional
   Powerful vocals
   Inspiring people
   Endless sound
   Magical solos
   Peaceful violins
   Amazing noise
   Having fun
   Hanging with friends
   Headbanging headaches
Now that's music!

Brandon Haluta, Grade 5
Hiawatha Elementary School, IL

Rogers Farm

Lying in the hay
Soft, warm, the sun on my face
Quiet and peaceful.

Matthew Schoen, Grade 5
Stanley Clark School, IN

A Young Girl

A young girl
Smart, stubborn
Loving, caring, daring
Saving someone takes a lot of courage
Jumping, running, hugging
Champion, impatient
Teenager

Makaela Douglas, Grade 6
Stanley Clark School, IN

My Dad*

I feel sad about my dad.
I get sad when my dad is gone.
I think about my dad when he's gone.
I feel bad when my dad is gone.
I get bored a lot when my dad is gone.

Nick Bryant, Grade 6
Rochester Middle School, IL
*Inspired by Nick's dad who is going blind
and is away a lot learning how to function.

Friend

Friend
Nice, kind
Talking, smiling, giggling
Honest, loyal, mean, hateful
Stealing, cheating, lying
Unfriendly, rude
Enemy

Erica Bluhm, Grade 5
Adams Central Elementary School, IN

Fried Ice Cream

Cling, cling, cling as the bowl came down
Because I was acting like a clown.
Then it gave me an idea,
I'm going to make fried ice cream but first I have to cook the tortilla.
I can't wait to use the honey,
because it dribbles really funny.
What a lovely smell,
except for my brother's stinky gel.

Raven Hensley, Grade 5
Levan Scott Academy, IN

If I Were a Flower

If I were a flower… I would hear everyone's conversations outside.
I would be so beautiful.
I would be different colors like pink and purple.
Or even yellow daisies.
I would be a perfect gift for a girlfriend from her boyfriend.
I would look so pretty mixed in with baby's breath and a pretty red
bow tied around my lovely green stem.

Kelsi Dempster, Grade 5
Floyds Knobs Elementary School, IN

The Clay Pot

Big and round, colorful on the sandy ground.
I collect broken pieces and put them together.
Hey, look there's another!
It started out as a beautiful pot,
but now it is not.
I bet it would have looked better
if it hadn't been in such horrible weather!
There are so many things from the past that I would like to learn!

Jenna Wisneski, Grade 5
Freeburg Elementary School, IL

The Leprechaun

Once there was a leprechaun, who had a pot of gold.
Said he'll never let go of it, even if he gets old.
But soon he lost, all his gold and his pot.
For the thieves who stole them, escaped on a yacht.

The leprechaun was mad, so he went to a place (to find his gold) called L.A.
When he asked about his gold, they didn't know what to say.
Then we went, to a place called Peru.
He asked about his pot, they laughed until they turned blue.

The leprechaun went to every place in the world.
But when he didn't find his gold, he went back home with his back curled.
When he went home, he found his pot.
It came with a note, and also all his lot.

The note said, 'I'm sorry all your gold I stole.'
'It's in front of your house, under the pole.'
The leprechaun rejoiced, for all his gold was back.
And just to be safe, he hid it in a big brown sack.

Sohum Chokshi, Grade 5
Fredrick Nerge Elementary School, IL

Unhappy

My family had been unhappy
My family had two people
Me and my mom
Not having much wealth
Living in an apartment in Newburgh
Home alone while Mom works 12 hour days

Going to daycare at dawn
Sitting alone shooting baskets
Wearing old hand me downs from my cousins
Going to bed early, not seeing much twilight
Then my mom married Matt
March 15, 2003

Electricity doesn't get shut off
More wealth, not home alone
Mom doesn't work
Totally seeing twilight
More importantly, I have a dad

Aspen Taylor, Grade 6
Linton-Stockton Elementary School, IN

Summer Vacation

Summer vacation is the best time of year,
because you are out of school and all you can do is cheer.

I like to go to the city pool,
hanging with friends is really cool.

I visit my relatives from out of state,
my aunts, uncles, and cousins are great.

On summer vacation I bike ride around,
on summer vacation you can't keep me down,

We go to Holiday World every summer,
if we don't go it is a big bummer.

The Zinga slide in the water park,
is my favorite I wish it was open after dark.

Summer vacation it never lasts,
with all the good times it goes by too fast.

Kane Garcia, Grade 5
North Intermediate Center of Education, IL

Friends

F antastic people you can
R emember, share laughs and smiles.
I t's fun to go places and
E njoy passing
N otes and secrets to one another.
D on't know what I would do without them,
S helby S., Shelby P., and Hayley.

Shelby Snyder, Grade 4
Liberty Elementary School, IN

Zoom

HONK! HONK!
That's the noise I hear
As I zip quickly
Up and down the street.
With my new gold rims and nitrous purge.

I'm a car that can't be beat.
I'm registered at 120
Ha! I'm running 173.

My brand new supercharger making an uproar,
Like a thunder cloud in the sky.
Ha! You can't see me.

HONK! HONK!
The sound fades slowly in the dust,
As I zip
Up and down the rough, old street.
There's just one problem,
I can't stop.
I'm gaining speed but…
OUCH!!!
There's a dangerously sturdy tree.

Brent Dunn, Grade 6
Linton-Stockton Elementary School, IN

Sports

S o many different activities
P lay with friends and compete with friends
O nly some junior high schools have cuts
R ace to get first
T o many people want to play sports so there might be cuts
S o much fun and so little time

Erin Kennedy, Grade 6
Elwood C C School, IL

The Sun and the Moon

The sun, the sun shining bright
Glowing from the day till the moon shines at night
Now the moon is showing up over the bay
Shining bright till the day.

Matthew Rueger, Grade 4
Creekside Elementary School, IL

Bay

One day,
Looking over the bay,
Hearing the seagulls screech,
Mingling with the sound of laughter and merriment,
I come to wonder,
How did it get here?
Did it come with clouds of thunder?
Then I say,
This is a thought for another day.

Connor Gleason, Grade 6
Rochester Middle School, IL

Theseus and the Minotaur

In a maze of fog and fear, upon the floor lie men with spears.
In the maze, day seems like night, within its wall there is no light.
In the maze lies the blood of men, in the place known as a Haunted Den.
A man with a plan, a man with a spear, through the maze with only one fear.
Hunting the exit from the maze, the thing he feared fell upon his gaze.
The creatures sat crouched in the den, the beast feasting upon the fallen men.
The creature took one glance at him, then the creature's eyes grew dim.
The creature's name was Minotaur, thick blood dripping from its jaw.
Two fearsome horns grew from his head, 'He could not be killed,' was often said.
The man held his spear ready to fight, Minotaur's eyes glowed with devilish light.
It leapt from the ground towards the man, who stood still just like his plan.
The creature leaped right onto the spear, roaring in pain, his own death he did now fear.
Minotaur struggled back onto the floor, an exit beyond the thing, the man now saw.
Leaping from the floor, it charged towards him, stopping as the spear cut into its limb.
The beast did roar and cry in pain, the man wouldn't stop until the Beast was slain.
A man with a plan, a man with a spear, now in the battle he had no fear.
The spear he threw at the Minotaur, and escaped the maze to return no more.
The spear had flew right through its head, finally, the cruel minotaur was dead.
In a maze once filled with fear, upon the floor lies bones and spears.
This maze once made day seem night, through its evil, shone no light.
In the maze lies the story of men, in the place once known as Haunted Den.

Daniel Rosenberg, Grade 5
British School of Chicago, IL

Sara's Poems

I am a dancing poet
Dancing on streets, at home, and any where I can
My poems are dancing to their own rhythm as they're sliding across the floor

I am a spring poet
Sitting in the park watching the Earth come to life
My poems are doing the same and they're more beautiful when they are growing, reaching towards the sky

I am a basketball poet
On the court while people are cheering us on
M poems are aiming up high taking a shot and making the point — helping us win

I am a fantasy poet
Riding on a mystical creature soaring through a world of wonder
My poems are exploring the dangerous and new world

Sara Beck, Grade 6
St Barbara School, IL

The Joker

I have a brother like no other who is silly and annoying.
I tell him to stop but he says not and simply keeps on going.
He jokes all day and calls it play and tumbles all about.
He stubs his toe and lets us know with a never ending shout.
He makes more noise than all the boys and we tell him he's being a pest.
We send him to his room but he comes out too soon because he thinks he's better than the rest.
He pouts and shouts whenever we go out and makes my dad uptight.
He always eats only his treats and leaves his dinner with only one bite.
He takes a shower for half an hour and drives my mother insane.
But in the end he's still my friend even though he's such a pain.

Joshua Rivera, Grade 6
St John Evangelist School, IN

Looking for Love

Looking and searching for my one true love.
I think about it everywhere I go.
It's like I am a very desperate dove.
A dove, looking for a someone to know.

The search for love is a marvelous thing.
Loving someone brings happiness each day.
Love is deep and thoughtful, not just a fling.
When love appears, splendor is there to stay.

When you are in love, your heart always glows.
The moments you share are gleeful and sweet.
The excitement of your heart always shows.
Hand in hand you walk, down a sunlit street.

Looking and searching for my true soul mate.
Onward I'm walking, awaiting my fate.

Lisa Holm, Grade 6
McHenry Middle School, IL

Presidents

P eople vote for the president.
R unning for president is hard.
E lecting is also real fun.
S ometimes I kind of want to be president.
I might even try being it.
D o presidents go around the world?
E very time I see the president on TV I keep watching.
N ot every time a president was voted for he or she wins.
T V is a place where you might see the president.
S o I guess presidents are important.

Brett Salyards, Grade 4
GCMS Elementary School, IL

Exercise/In Shape

Exercise
Running, jumping, jogging
Walk mill, dumbbells, jump rope, and roller blading
Walking, climbing, surfing
Sweaty, hardworking
In shape

Julia Rowley, Grade 5
St Joseph School, IL

My Favorite Thing

Rocks and fossils are my thing
  They can be found in anything.
Different shapes, sizes, and colors galore
  Look I found a dinosaur!

Let your imagination soar
  And never be afraid to explore.
Look in caves, creeks, and even on the floor
  And maybe you'll find a dinosaur.

Alec Soer, Grade 5
Gard Elementary School, IL

Myrtle Beach

My favorite place is Myrtle Beach
At Myrtle Beach I hear the peaceful sound
Of the waves washing on the shore
At Myrtle Beach I smell the aroma
Of the salty sea water
At Myrtle Beach I see the lovely dolphins
Leaping out of the water
At Myrtle Beach I feel so excited because
I am in my favorite place
I am very happy when I am at Myrtle Beach
At Myrtle Beach I see the seagulls
Myrtle Beach my favorite place

Morgan Turner, Grade 6
Linton-Stockton Elementary School, IN

Super Hero

I know a super hero
Who isn't very tall
Whose muscles really aren't that big
And I've seen this person fall
Whose name isn't Superman, Spiderman, or Flash
The person is my mother
Who I have loved all my past

Mark Heaton, Grade 6
Rochester Middle School, IL

My Grandma's Purse

My grandma's purse is a great big mess!
She won't throw anything away, she'll confess.
A tube of red lipstick, to make her look pretty,
And a small book of jokes, because she is witty.
A few packs of tissues, just in case;
An old pair of jogging shoes, just right for a race.
A case of ticket stubs from her favorite shows —
Why she needs them, nobody knows!
A small sandwich in case she is hungry;
A little wallet filled with money.
Some old melted lollipops, gooey and sticky;
A lot of dirty wipes, all yucky and icky.
A pair of pink sunglasses, just right for the beach;
A box of chalk, because she likes to teach.
An old checkered tablecloth just waiting for a picnic;
A lot of medicine, in case she gets sick.
If my grandpa sees inside it, he'll have a cow.
That's why she'd better clean up her purse out right now!

Claire Michael, Grade 4
St. Matthew School, IL

The 70s Disco

My name is Billy Joe and I have an afro.
I like to do the 70s disco and eat a yummy Oreo.
They call me Billy because I am a hillbilly,
like Billy Bob Thornton.
Ridin' cowboy yall!

Kyle Sullivan, Grade 4
W E Wilson Elementary School, IN

Candle Light

Orange…
Like the flickering flame
Of a burning candle
Orange…
Like an enormous jack-o'-lantern
On Halloween
Orange…
Tastes like a fruity tangerine
Orange…
Thumps
Like a basketball
When you drop it
Orange…
Like the fluttering leaves
Of a spring day
Orange.

Tanner Hall, Grade 6
Linton-Stockton Elementary School, IN

Abe in the Elevator

I saw him! I saw him!
In the elevator the other day
Abraham Lincoln, in the flesh
Just believe me, ok?

What could I do? Talk to him?
But only a few seconds till the next floor
Just then, it hit me
He was going to the
Abe-Look-Alike convention next door.

Shannon Drage, Grade 5
Bell-Graham School, IL

Mayday

Something flies over my head,
At the speed of sound,
But then I hear a loud pop,
And it crashes to the ground.
I walk over to the site
And rush to the crumpled jet.
I see the cockpit glass is cracked,
And I begin to fret.
Is he alive?
Is he dead?
Did he get hit very hard,
Smack dab in the head?
I see his eyes blink,
And I smile and wave,
And I worry no more
About digging his grave.
Then I wake up,
Filled without any dread.
It was all just a dream,
It was all in my head!

Mario Cannamela, Grade 6
Rochester Middle School, IL

Dingoes on the Hunt

Dingoes run over grassy plains,
Then catch a meal of meat.
They sink their teeth into their prey,
And take a bite to eat.

Chelsea Emenhiser, Grade 4
Adams Central Elementary School, IN

Friends

Roses are red
pigs are pink
flowers are sometimes yellow
what color are you
it doesn't really matter
it only matters if you are
a true friend

Codie Jo Brown, Grade 4
Tallula Elementary School, IL

Birds

Fly high in the sky
Wish I could try
Beautiful to see
Better to be
To be free
A bird I see

Marc Dubrick, Grade 6
St Mary School, IL

Purpose

Purpose…
Once I wondered
Why I was put on
This Earth…

Was it for helping others
Or for destruction…

I don't really know,
For me life is like a
Question waiting to
Be answered…

I am always trying
To find my meaning in life,
But I have all this time
To decide…

Alejandro Castaneda, Grade 4
Peck Elementary School, IL

School Bell

I like the school bell
But sometimes it smells
I like it when school is out
It makes me want to shout.

Katie Cooper, Grade 4
Goodfield Elementary School, IL

How Long Is Your Chain?

How long is your chain?
Chains are like colorful, shiny, jewelry
that can webble to the floor.
Maybe your chain is a spinning rim
in the necklace that spins on your neck.
Is it made with diamonds that
are as shiny as stars twinkling
in the midnight sky?
Anyway that you make a chain
it will always be colorful jewelry
of any kind.
How long is your chain?

Christian Crook, Grade 6
Haubstadt Community School, IN

Graduation Day

Graduation Day.
That's fun to say!

I'm finally going to 1st grade.
I hope what I learned will not fade.

But that's okay.
I'll have new friends anyway.

Jasmin Magdaleno, Grade 4
St Robert Bellarmine School, IL

The Coming of Spring

Spring is arriving.
The robins are coming alive.
The water is summoning,
"Come and take a dive!"

Spring is finally here.
Flowers are blooming.
Summer is now near.
Over you, green trees are looming.

Spring is far gone.
Summer is here.
the sun rises at late dawn.
Amid school children's cheers!

Rachel Koch, Grade 5
Tremont Elementary School, IL

Ode to Presidents

How you keep me safe
You make a lot of rules to obey
I do not like it when you trade
There are many of you
Never come to say
I hate it when you go away
But when it comes to President Bush
He can come but not stay

Dairian Lewis, Grade 4
Morgan Elementary School, IN

Night

Through the dark night sky,
where crickets chirp and fireflies fly,
I see moms tuck their children in their beds,
they close their eyes and rest their heads,
the stars beyond the trees the cool night summer breeze,
the moon so bright it's a wonderful sight,
the children are now asleep as they dream of Little Bo Peep.

Allison E. Huston, Grade 6
Rochester Middle School, IL

Got Cold Milk?

The smell, smell, smell,
Fills me with anticipation
Can't wait, wait, wait,
My emotions are restless
The room is as warm as a summer day
Tick, tock, tick, tock,
The timer is teasing me
Buzz, buzz, buzz
Finally they are done.
I take them out, the
jumbo chocolate chip cookies
call my name,
"Staisy, Staisy, Staisy, come and eat us!"
I put them on a big plate.
Thinking, thinking, thinking,
What am I forgetting?
Aha! I'm forgetting something very important.
"Got Milk?" a cookie asks me.
I think, I don't.
Uh oh! What about you,
do you GOT COLD MILK?!

Staisy Cardenas, Grade 5
Levan Scott Academy, IN

Black

Black-thing
Frightens, unclear
Creeping, overpowering, hating
A void of darkness unlighted by goodness
Fearing, breathtaking, stifling
Undefined, nightmare
Dark-midnight

Andy Bartels, Grade 6
Stanley Clark School, IN

Summer and Winter

Summer
Balmy, worn out,
Swimming, smelling, playing
Scorching, sweaty, snow pants, hot chocolate
Snowing, fighting, sledding
Snowflakes, arctic
Winter

Courtney Bryers, Grade 5
Neil Armstrong Elementary School, IL

I Am

I am a floating cloud, always on top of everything.
I am a calendar, filled with so much I can't do it all.
I am a pen, writing a story of my life,
I am a quilt, with so many patches,
    Who or what am I?
I am a bookshelf holding too much.
I am an old toy, that's never used,
I am a new car, with no scratches at all.

Brooke Foote, Grade 5
Churubusco Elementary School, IN

Family

Mom's in the kitchen making chicken.
Dad's in bed halfway dead.
Brother's in school acting like a fool.
Sister's in the hall coloring on the wall.
Family — can't live with them, can't live without them.

Kayleen Grable, Grade 4
Forest Park Elementary School, IN

Man

Man
Devil-eyed, convincing
Aiding, providing, wondering
Watch out — his red eyes can hypnotize you!
Aggravating, upsetting, provoking
Dull, ordered
Master

Madelyn Lee, Grade 6
Stanley Clark School, IN

Undead

To the graveyard I went, deep in the night
Not obeying my mom's words, I went in spite
I slept there facing my fright,
I awoke at day and soon it was night
There I saw, what I tried to escape from
Then I sat there, teary eyed and glum.

There they were, on the twilight grounds,
Hundred of them, heads dented in, making no sounds,
A phantasm of a man, the undead
I was scared, heart beating with that said,
Their eerie shadow filled the graves,
Looking quite a bit like slaves

I stood there, mad with fright,
I didn't want to put up a big fight,
With these mean creeps of the night,
Still paralyzed with fear, I was no knight
I wanted to go home
Home for tea, but

They stood there, walking towards me.

Jason Krause, Grade 4
British School of Chicago, IL

You Captured My Love

There's this
special someone
you really like
who captured you
by sight
and your head
is gone,
your heart pounds.
You give him
a special kiss
and make your dream
come true.

Dusti Guthrie, Grade 6
Laketon Elementary School, IN

Happiness Is…

Happiness is like our yellow sun
It smells like fresh cut flowers
It tastes like creamy, milky chocolate
It sounds like silly laughter from a clown
It feels like joy exploded inside of you

Austin Ellingwood, Grade 5
East Elementary School, IN

Cat

Cat
Furry, cute
Meowing, purring, scratching
They are very cuddly.
Kitten

Austin Lofton, Grade 5
Staunton Elementary School, IN

Football

Here are some ways to describe
Football:
Catching a pass
Throwing a pass
Running to the end zone
Passing the football
Tackling the runner
Rough sport
Tough sport
Intense
Tossing a football
Fumbling a football
Tumbling to the ground
Blitzing the quarterback
Intercepting the football
Celebrating a touchdown
Kicking a field goal
Winning the game
There are a lot of ways to describe
Football, but overall football is fun!

Isaac Pauli, Grade 6
St Theresa School, IN

Hope

If hope could be a color
it would be green like a stem on a rose.

If hope could be a taste
it would be the sweetness of chocolate.

If hope could be a smell
it would be a sweet vanilla candle.

If hope could be a sound
it would be a beautiful orchestra.

If hope could be a feeling
it would be a kiss form a loved one.

If hope could be an animal
it would be a cute little puppy.

Jessica Sellers, Grade 4
St Agnes School, IL

Elysa, Mellisa, and Marysa

My best friend ever is Elysa.
Who then met chunky Mellisa.
They became preachers,
Then horrible teachers,
So, then decided to work for Marysa.

Miranda Shryack, Grade 6
ROWVA East Elementary School, IL

Rabbit

Rabbit
Cuddle with you
Their bounces are like springs
They can bite you if they are mad
Love them

Kristin Bergdall, Grade 5
Adams Central Elementary School, IN

The Race

A horse goes swoosh around the track
Up and down its mane flopping
You know he's coming down the track.

Allison Kern, Grade 4
Goodfield Elementary School, IL

The Big Rock

Hikers and tourists
Sturdy and tall
Rock so big
Makes people look small
Hard to climb and easy to see
Gaze for an hour
'Wyoming!' 'Wyoming!'
It's the Devil's Tower

Anna Baio, Grade 5
Our Lady of Peace School, IL

Hero

Hero
Loving, caring
Strong, dependable, cool
Fearless, awesome, fearful, weird
Mad, mean, kooky
Evil, crazy
Villain

Jenny Schultz, Grade 5
Adams Central Elementary School, IN

The Crook

There once was a crook
With a hook
Who stole a book, a library book
He gave a dirty look
At the guard, who said, "Gobbledygook!"
It's a crook with a hook!

What'll I do?
Boo-hoo boo-hoo!
That book was brand new
And I don't know Kung Fu!

That crook could be in Timbuktu
Since I don't know ju-jitsu
What'll I do?
This is such a hullabaloo

Wait a moment —
That book will soon be overdue!
Whoop-dee-doo!

Robby Welch, Grade 5
Countryside School, IL

Busy Bees

Buzz Buzz go the bees
I see them in the flowers
They take the nectar

Hannah Petty, Grade 5
Seton Catholic School, IL

Blake, Blake

Blake, Blake, barking wild
In the weather oh, so mild.
Go get the ball
And bring it back again.
Then we'll lie down
And rest 'til ten AM.
When we stand up
My sister will be here
She'll get your back
And ride you like a horse
I'll be outside
Making an obstacle course.

Rachael Hopp, Grade 4
Creekside Elementary School, IL

I Want a Phone!

I once asked my dad for a phone,
"When you're older," he threw me a bone.
But that wasn't nice.
And I was precise,
And that's why I'm writing this poem.

Elisa D'Amico, Grade 5
Tri-State Christian School, IL

Excuses

Excuses build nothing but trouble, exhaustion, and pain
Who ever invented excuses should be ashamed
And if you used an excuse,
then man you will be in pain
Because pretty soon they will find out
and you might want to cry or runaway
You will cry to me and I will say
excuses will build nothing but trouble,
exhaustion, and pain.

Grace Qualkinbush, Grade 4
John Simatovich Elementary School, IN

Summer

Summer can't come too soon for me
For I can't wait to be free
Free from the daily grind
Studying will be off my mind
No more early to bed, early to rise
Summer is the time when no one cares if you're wise
So come summer, come, I don't even care if you bring flies

Stan Richard Rinehart, Grade 5
GCMS Elementary School, IL

My Horrendous Birthday Party

The day of my horrendous birthday party,
I though my party would be fantastic,
It took a turn and went drastic,
All of a sudden the fun disappears,
You could hear the noise right at the Sears,
The popcorn plummets to the floor,
Right now the party is not such a bore,
Someone splats the cake on the wall,
The vibration causes presents to fall,
Children put beans in their straws as if loading,
Right after that the balloons start exploding,
The day of my horrendous birthday party,
The party is still as chaotic as could be,
Right now all I want to do is flee,
You have no idea what they will do,
The wall has turned a deep, deep blue,
It was from the icing and from the cake,
Another is what I might have to make,
I wish I was in my bed fast asleep,
Instead of being here in this big heap.
The day of my horrendous birthday party.

Hannah Day, Grade 4
British School of Chicago, IL

If Hope Could Be…

If hope could be a color
it would be blue as the color of the sky.

If hope could be a taste
it would taste just like a chocolate chip cookie.

If hope could be a smell
it would be a cherry candle.

If hope could be a sound
it would be an electric guitar.

If hope could be a feeling
it would be a hug from my family.

If hope could be an animal
it would be a dog with lots of love.

Michael Cristelli, Grade 4
St Agnes School, IL

Thunderstorms

They sound very loud
They produce more than a cloud
Might even produce a funnel cloud

I'm pretty sure lightning comes from the ground
I don't know what makes
The sound of thunder
I think it's the rumble
From down under

Is a squall rare in the fall?
Do they produce hail or high winds?
They can pick up cows and hurl them around

They might be strong enough
To destroy people's grounds
If rain is good for farms
If it will help the farmers
It won't do any harm

When the storm moves on
It all will be gone
When the storm will cease
I will be relieved

Matthew Ours, Grade 6
St Theresa School, IN

I Am

I am a cat, waiting to be petted
I'm an inspector, waiting for a case
I'm a chalk board, waiting for life
I'm a pen writing a poem
I'm a clam, hiding something beautiful within

Chelsea Bennett, Grade 5
Churubusco Elementary School, IN

Clay Pots

Hidden in the sand,
Secrets of the desert land.
Almost discovered,
Covered with a brown color.
Now held in my hand.
Sara Hilpert, Grade 5
Freeburg Elementary School, IL

Imagination

Creativity
daydreaming and getting lost
just dare to daydream

lose focus, cut loose
go into la la land
let your mind wander

sweet, peaceful calmness
think about whatever you want to
let your thoughts run free.
Taylor Maharrey, Grade 5
Floyds Knobs Elementary School, IN

So Much to Do

So much to see, so much to do
Go to places like a zoo
Play a sport like volleyball
Make a painting for the wall
Jump into an ice-cold pool
Buy our Dad a brand-new tool
Suck on a banana pop
All the fun is o'er the top
Take me to a baseball game
Camping is my claim to fame
Eat a hot dog off the grill
Listen to the whippoorwill
Think of all the things I'll bake
I can't wait 'til summer break!
J.P. McDermott, Grade 4
Winston Campus Elementary, IL

Pine Trees

Never loses leaves
Birds go in and out of you
Snow on top of tree
Faith Duke, Grade 4
GCMS Elementary School, IL

Ode to Paige

Paige is my best friend.
She likes to stay the night at my house.
She's never as quiet as a mouse.
I'll never let her go
Rain or snow I'll always be her friend.
Kayla Deneen, Grade 4
Morgan Elementary School, IN

Friends

Friends are the greatest things to have, always there when needed,
And most stick up for you in any situation, without being pleaded.
Friends are someone to talk to, and are always there to listen,
But the ones that stay by you for life are the ones that truly glisten.
Victoria Joy Gaesser, Grade 5
GCMS Elementary School, IL

Bobby Wayne Jones

Strong, helping, caring, thoughtful
Felt like I was his own dear child
Who cared deeply about my mom and I
Who felt it his duty to fight for his country and everyone in it
Who needed us when we were not with him then
Who gave his life when he graduated from the U.S. Marine Corps
Who fears only dying, losing his family, and not getting married and having kids
Who would like to have his own house with a wife and two kids
Who would like to see my sister and I grow up, get married and have kids
Resident of the small town of Folsomville, Indiana
Bobby Wayne Jones
Strong, helping, caring, thoughtful
Bobby Wayne Jones
My personal hero
Cheyenne Brinksneader, Grade 6
South Spencer Middle School, IN

The Balloon

I was asked to hold a large, pink piece of string, had no idea what for,
But had felt my fingers reaching out, as I walked right out the door.

Gripped the string with all of my might, my fingers tight and neat,
My feet were lifting off the ground, slowly rising from my seat.

I looked at what was on the long string, a shiny purple pink balloon,
I was lifting higher and higher, for right above me was the moon.

Jumped off my floating ride to space, ran across the bumpy moon,
I had lost my way while in paradise, couldn't find the balloon till noon.

Once again, I gripped my floating ride tight, with all my extra strength,
Popped the balloon with my ten fingers, falling, trembling, for quite a length.

Tumbling down my neighborhood hill, I found my house real fast.
Walked into my house silently, afraid the silence wouldn't last.

But yes, indeed I found my room, just like it had been before.
And I quickly jumped into my bed, right when my mom was about to open the door.
Melanie Betbadal, Grade 6
Thayer J Hill Middle School, IL

Grandpa

Watching his spirit whisking away like the wind
knowing he's in a better place.
The beautiful summer day slowly turning into a dark stormy night
never being able to see him again.
Holly Haupricht, Grade 4
Churubusco Elementary School, IN

Interesting Boy

I am an interesting boy who dreams.
I wonder why there is terrorism.
I hear the guns of war.
I see the people running from bombs.
I want to help but I don't know how.
I am an interesting boy who dreams.

I pretend I can fly forever.
I feel the warm moist air against my face.
I touch the moon and the stars.
I worry how long this will last.
I cry when it is over.
I am in interesting boy who dreams.

I understand what makes the wind blow.
I say I can't do everything.
I dreamt that I could, and did.
I try to picture things in an understanding way.
I hope I can be very helpful one day.
I am an interesting boy who dreams.

Alexander T. Davis, Grade 6
Rochester Middle School, IL

Loud as an Elephant

I'm as loud as an elephant.
Running up and down the steps
Screaming at the top of my lungs.
Loud as an elephant. Opening and slamming my closet door.
Loud as an elephant. Stomping on the floor.
Loud as an elephant. Knocking down the door.
Loud as an elephant. Getting kicked out of the store.
Loud as an elephant. Shooting fireworks at 12:00.
Loud as an elephant. Waking the town.
Loud as an elephant. Here me roar!

Austin Jones, Grade 6
Haubstadt Community School, IN

Happy?

Do you need some happiness
I don't know do you
Do you want to smile
Or scream or frown or cry boo hoo
Are you shy or are you hyper
Do you fight or do you run
Are you in the inner group
Or are you just an alone one
Do you get A's and B's
Or are you flunking out of school
Are you just uncomfortable
With everything you do
Are you all for fun
Or do you just enjoy sitting home and watching tv
You might not want to be happy
But will you do it just for me?

Amanda Mankovich, Grade 6
Battle Ground Middle School, IN

Kid

Kid
Tall, red-headed
Loving, looking, enlightening
Always looking for adventures; loving to others
Persuading, sensing, helping
Blue-eyed, skinny
Boy

David Madden, Grade 6
Stanley Clark School, IN

My Favorite Place

My favorite place is at home
In my home I smell green apple candles
In my home I see dazzling quilts everywhere
In my home I see my family

In my home I feel the sleep carpet
In my home I taste delicious chocolate chip cookies
In my home I hear the oven talking (beep)
In my home is the perfect place for me

Cody Crichfield, Grade 6
Linton-Stockton Elementary School, IN

Bird Hunting

Bird hunting is sometimes fun,
But don't forget to take your gun.
You'll have to lie down on the ground,
Right beside your trusty hound.
Then you'll have to sit and wait,
Unless you have a good bird bait.
Then make sure you are ready,
And you might need a lucky teddy.
Sometimes nothing is what you get,
And then don't throw a fit.
But maybe just maybe a bird you'll see,
You might want to say yippee.
If you say it you'll scare the birds,
Your friends will then think you're a nerd.
Then you'll get really mad,
As a bird hunter you're bad.
You might want to send back in the mail,
The license you got to hunt quail.
But you won't think that's a good choice,
If you did, you'll yell and lose your voice.
The next year you'll be better.

Cody Simpson, Grade 5
Center Street Elementary School, IL

The Sea

Deep down in the sea where it's dark.
I turn around and I see a shark.
When I look up, I'm in a tree.
When I look down, I'm in the sea.
I try to run but I can't get away because it's dark!

Quonellis Williams, Grade 4
Lavizzo Elementary School, IL

Beautiful

Not everyone thinks they're
beautiful not even a waterfall.
A celebrity has a lot of money,
they don't care at all a seed
is not beautiful when it's
small, it just needs a little more
love that's all. When you're small
sometimes you're not beautiful at all
but later on in life you'll
be standing tall.

Kimberly Alvarez, Grade 6
San Miguel School, IL

Truck

T ruck
R oads take them places
U nbelievable powerful engine
C autious not to get in an accident
K eys will start the engine

Jonathan Chapman, Grade 5
Staunton Elementary School, IN

Jesus Is Born

Hay and old wood
Shepherds and sheep
Wise men so old
Jesus is falling asleep
Mary and Joseph
Angels singing through infinity
"Rejoice. Rejoice"
This makes the Nativity

Alexis Topel, Grade 5
Our Lady of Peace School, IL

Hawk

Soaring through the sky,
Strong winged bird flying so high,
Wind beneath his wings.

Travis Hendrickson, Grade 4
Dixie Bee Elementary School, IN

Why

Why did he go
Why did he leave
Why did God take him
Why did he get cancer
Why was it him
Why did he die
Why didn't he stay longer
Why did he leave me
Why did we cry
Why was it him
Why did I love him so much
Why?

Elizabeth Erhardt, Grade 6
GCMS Middle School, IL

My Bed

My bed, my bed
I love my bed
On my pillows
I rest my head.

My bed, my bed
It is pink and red
As I lay there
I feel dead.

My bed, my bed
I watch Ned, Fred, and Ed
As they're sliding
On their sled.

Dawn Failla, Grade 5
Hiawatha Elementary School, IL

Nascar

N avigating the track
A mazing noise
S liding into the wall
C olorful race cars
A mazingly fast cars
R acing is fun

Jake Burns, Grade 5
Seton Catholic School, IL

Basketball

Shooting the jumper
Hear the swish.
As a fan cheered
His cola took a splish.

The championship is almost yours,
Just a few seconds left.
4,3,2,One!
Your dreams have only just begun.

You were the underdogs,
That didn't stop you.
Now the trophy
Is such a marvelous view.

Ethan Maurer, Grade 6
St John Evangelist School, IN

Gone

Standing there, wet eyes,
Tears ready to drop,
Gazing at a stiff dog,
Not just any dog,
My dog, a dying dog,
Suffering, and breathing hard,
Nothing we can do,
Except, wait.

Brittney Shambaugh, Grade 4
Churubusco Elementary School, IN

Football

Hard hitting
Cracking helmets
Coaches screaming
Fans yelling
Smell concessions
Green grass
Boiling sun
Crunching cleats
Sweaty jersey

Tony Giannini, Grade 5
Bell-Graham School, IL

Christmas/Halloween

Christmas
Santa, presents
Giving, caring, listing
Snow, cold, candy, bats
Buying, scaring, fooling
Fun, costumes
Halloween

Jessie Zepeda, Grade 5
Village Elementary School, IL

Sue

There was a lion named Sue;
Her best friend's name was Drew.
But when she said, "Hi,"
Drew started to cry
For they were trapped in a zoo.

Allie Dussliere, Grade 5
Seton Catholic School, IL

My Book Is Missing

My book is missing.
Where'd it go?
I don't know where it is,
And why it's missing.
I've been looking for it for a while now.
Why?

I laid it by my front door,
And now it's not there.
I wonder why.
Maybe someone stole it,
Maybe someone hid it or
Maybe my dog ate it.
My book is missing.

Dane Schuler, Grade 6
Laketon Elementary School, IN

River

Water glistening
Water flowing all day long
Sparkling clearly

Matt Mersinger, Grade 5
St Jacob Elementary School, IL

Personality
Dad
Tall, smart
Blue eyes, black hair
Family, fishing, hunting, swimming, friends
Friendly

Marybeth Rohrig, Grade 6
Milan Middle School, IN

Under My Bed!
Under my bed is tragic.
When I look under I scream:
Stinky socks, dust, books and everything.
My mother says just a second, she takes the vacuum cleaner
and it's clean I should "Hurray!"
I am glad and proud, not much for my mother to say.

Marcelina Puc, Grade 4
Norman Bridge Elementary School, IL

My Poems
I am a chocolate poet
Sitting on a chocolate chip cookie
In a chocolate river, my poems fall
Into the river and turn into chocolate
And flow with the river.

I am a flower poet
Sitting in the middle of a daisy watching
The bee's buzz all around,
My poems fall to the ground
And turn to beautiful flowers.

I am an Earth poet
Sitting on top of the Earth writing my poems,
My poems soar around the world
To learn different cultures
And meet new people.

I am a day poet
Writing my poems under
The night time moon and day light sun,
My poems go to the past and future
To write more for the days to come.

Antigony Mendez, Grade 6
St Barbara School, IL

Daydream
As I lay in the snow looking up in the sky
Soft bits of God's dandruff fall on my face
Melting away
Slowly making my face wet.
All of a sudden
My face is dry
And I catch myself
Looking out the window.

Chloe Leifer, Grade 6
Laketon Elementary School, IN

Giving
To receive is nothing but to give is something
that will make you and everyone else happy.
Give, give to those who are sick or dying,
Give, give to those are helpless,
Give, give to the homeless,
Give, give, give.
To Receive is nothing but to give is something
that will make everyone else happy.

Blake Gross, Grade 4
Churubusco Elementary School, IN

Every Year
Every year leaves start to change and fall
The weather gets a little colder
And windshields start to blur
We know fall is here,
'Cause it happens every year

After autumn comes the cold and snowy time of year
When holidays are 'round the corner
Bright lights on houses and on trees
White flakes slowly drift to the ground
That's when we know that winter's here
'Cause it happens every year

After winter snow melts into slush
Rain falls and flowers begin to grow
It warms up, and birds sing their songs
School lets out until next year
'Cause it happens every year

When it gets hot
We play outside a lot
People take vacations to places far away
Then we know that summer's here
'Cause it happens every year

Anna Kanfer, Grade 5
Countryside School, IL

School's Out
School's out I can smell the fresh summer air.
Twisting and turning and jumping about.
School's out, no more cranky librarian.
Playing sports no homework, hooray school is out.

Kyle Sisk, Grade 4
Oak Hill Elementary School, IN

My Sister
My sister is nice and funny,
She can be as sweet as honey.
You don't want to get on her dark side,
Or the next day you'll come with a purple eye.
She's encouraging and cool,
In fact she's my sister.

Krystal Cobos, Grade 6
San Miguel School, IL

Buried for Years

B uried when I was lost,
U sed to hold flowers.
R uined after many rains.
I n sand for many years,
E ventually found.
D ug up to be studied.

F inally taken out of sand,
O ut of the sand I go,
R iding in a soft container.

Y ears have gone by now.
E veryone looks at me.
A day feels like a minute.
R ight by me a pot like me.
S ee he's broken just like me.

Auggie Ward, Grade 5
Freeburg Elementary School, IL

My Mixed Family

We may not be at our real homes
But we accept the fact that it's true
My dad's a beaver
My mom's a cat
My brother is a pig
My sister is a monkey
And I'm a snake
We make a happy family
We all love each other

Jesse Torres, Grade 4
Haugan Elementary School, IL

Squirrels

Small little critters.
Chubby cheeks, cuddly fun.
Fuzzy, nutty guys.

Alexander Wilkinson, Grade 5
Stanley Clark School, IN

Hermit Crab

In a cage,
The hermit crab sleeps,
I pick him up
And he awakens deep,
Pulls out his pinchers
And tries to pinch me,
Comes out of his shell
And looks at you,
Put your finger toward
Him and he goes back
In his shell,
I put him back in his
Cage and say hope
You sleep well

Lowell Lynde IV, Grade 4
Creekside Elementary School, IL

Cardinals

C hampions
A ggressive
R eally good
D etermined
I nvincible
N umber one
A wesome
L egendary
S ignificant

Nick Murphy, Grade 6
Rochester Middle School, IL

What I'm Thankful For

T o loving
H appy families
A dog
N ice friends
K ind people
S anta's presents
G rilled chicken
I ce cream
V ictory dinners
I ce water
N ew things
G atherings

Madeline Schwartz, Grade 4
Adams Central Elementary School, IN

Cranky Corbin

Cranky Corbin creeps around
The corner of the condo
Cautiously keeping an eye out
For his curious cousin Calvin

Corbin Froderman, Grade 5
Staunton Elementary School, IN

Bubble Gum

Bubble gum, bubble gum
Pink and blue
I like bubble gum how 'bout you?
Bubble gum, bubble gum
Cherry and blueberry
I like bubble gum how 'bout you?
Bubble gum, bubble gum
Blow a BIG bubble
Pop! The bubble gum is all over!
Bubble gum!

Schyler Tully, Grade 4
Oak Hill Elementary School, IN

Autumn Flowers

They are very bright
flowers will reflect the light
in the Autumn sun.

Hannah Hanford, Grade 5
St Jacob Elementary School, IL

Homework

Homework is not fun.
I can't wait till it's done.
Sometimes I don't do it.
At home I have a fit.
My mom never watches me.
Sometimes I get up and flee.
I never want to study.
But I always do it with a buddy.

Max Gantman, Grade 5
Fredrick Nerge Elementary School, IL

Oh I Love Her Dearly

I have a cute
little puppy
Oh I love her dearly
She can be
a pest
But oh I love her dearly
she can get
on my last nerve
But oh I love her dearly
I may tell her
bad girl bad girl!!!!
But oh I love her dearly

Coty Huebschman, Grade 5
Perry Central Elementary School, IN

Trapped in Outer Space

I am trapped in deep dark space
No one around
Floating…floating
alone
I am scared
Suddenly…
I hear a clanging sound
What should I do?
I reach for the massive ship
Safe…at last
I fly away…home

Bradley White, Grade 6
Linton-Stockton Elementary School, IN

Poems

poems, poems,
hear the beat,
which words can you defeat,
it will take some time,
to make the rhyme,
when you start,
all you can do,
is let it flow and your pencil dart,
but if you get poem block,
go down the letter line,
and you'll do fine.

Madeline Koldos, Grade 4
Creekside Elementary School, IL

Boys

Boys Boys Boys,
They make way too much noise.
They don't say thank you or please,
They don't even wipe their nose when they sneeze!

Boys Boys Boys,
They steal everyone's toys.
They don't care for any of us,
And they make such a fuss.

Boys Boys Boys!

Bailey Pierson, Grade 5
Lincoln Trail Elementary School, IN

My Rabbit

My bunny rabbit, so sweet and cute,
Munching on her bits of fruit;
Over there, she sits in her hutch,
jumping around very much.
My rabbit you must understand
is much like one from a fantasy land.
In some ways she may appear strange,
but much more interesting than the one I exchanged
You see…She has the horns of a goat, a lions throat
and ears of a great blood hound:
She's the size of an otter, quite a good trotter
yet only weighs half a pound;
She may be moody, but sure is a beauty,
with the eyes of a teddy bear;
With the wings of a fairy, and color of a cherry;
You see, THIS is my hare.

Lauren Brooks, Grade 5
Gray M Sanborn Elementary School, IL

Teacher's Tools

I can be as black as the night.
I can be anything but white.
I produce ink
On something that dissolves in the sink.

I help the teacher write with glee,
Knowing what I write could help shape the students' destiny.
Across the paper I fly,
Like a graceful humming bird flying through the sky.

Once I was lent to Ben
It was on the day he turned ten.
I can be put in an art bag,
I can also have a name tag.

You can buy pens in herds.
We are twigs next to the trees that make us form words.
My point can be as sharp as a knife.
But then again this is my life.

Joseph Amari, Grade 6
Our Lady of Peace School, IL

Volleyball

You run out the door
You look at the floor
You feel like to cry
When she looks you in the eye
You fall to the ground
Staring all around
You get back up with embarrassment
And go to your huddle
You feel the pressure pounding
You see the opponent
And you release your anger
You feel that one drop of sweat, tears, and blood
Fall to the ground
You think for a second…
The opponent stares
You give a glare and BAM you spike it
Your feet are about one foot in the air
All of a sudden you hear the buzzer
You fall to the ground with pity
Thinking of what just happened
You look around and say, this is the real game of volleyball

Rachel Skinner, Grade 6
St John Evangelist School, IN

Go Anywhere You Want to Go

A fun place to go every once in a while
With swimming and adventures
Formed every day
A new place to visit
To learn something new
To have a little fun
With me and you
You'll see the Arch
Or a statue or two
As long as I'm with you during this time,
There is always something fun that we can do.

Annie Gustafson, Grade 5
St John of the Cross Parish School, IL

Sweet Goodnights

Has there ever been someone or something that they say,
That means so much in each and every way?
Well I have that feeling too,
With my mom and dad and their sweet goodnights too,
They're sincere to say it every night,
Especially when I have a fright,
Wether I'm sad,
Or whether I'm mad,
They're sure to make me glad,
I'm sure to never go to bed without hearing them say,
Goodnight and I love you in each and every way,
We say this each and every day,
Because we love each other in a special way.

Kenzie Glassburn, Grade 6
Bon Air Middle School, IN

My Love Bug

I remember the evening
I wanted
To see my grandma,
I had a bad feeling,
When we got to the hospital
I felt better
But…when we left
I felt miserable,
I went to bed,
And when I woke up
We got a call,
They said, they tried
To resuscitate her,
But nothing happened
I dug my head into my pillow
I remember what she called me,
Her little love bug,
I guess
It was her time to move on
I love you, Grandma
From your Love Bug
Cody Wilson, Grade 6
Linton-Stockton Elementary School, IN

Sunset

A river flowing,
A kingdom of life and love…
Rushing to the sun.
Baani Singh, Grade 6
St Scholastica School, IL

My Friend

My friend
I like her
Ask me why
Because she is always there for me
Because she makes me feel better
Because she is there to play with me
Because she is my dog
Because, because, because
I like Daisy
Shaylynn Stratton, Grade 5
Staunton Elementary School, IN

Happy Time

Happy time is spring time,
It's wonderful to me
All the birds are coming out
And flowers so nice to see

The bumble bees are buzzing
They're flying all around
Everyone is singing
Such a beautiful sound.
Sara Whiteley, Grade 4
Oak Hill Elementary School, IN

Hope

If hope could be a color
it would be pink as pretty as the sunset

If hope could be a taste
it would be sugar

If hope could be a smell
it would be flowers

If hope could be a sound
it would be the sound of birds singing

If hope could be a feeling
it would be like winning the lottery

If hope could be an animal
it would be a cat
Samantha Powell, Grade 4
St Agnes School, IL

Spencer

He looked so cute,
So small,
So helpless.
As we walked in
I touched him.
He was as soft
As a pillow.
He was like
A mini furball,
All black with
Some white
On his chest.
Wagging, wagging
His tail.
He was as fast as
A bolt of lightning,
Or somewhere close.
Spencer,
He shall be.
Brandon Hoeg, Grade 4
Creekside Elementary School, IL

People

Tall, short
Fat, skinny
Brown, peach
Poor, rich
Different people
Different lifestyles
But everyone is treated equally
And everyone together makes
Up our big big
World
Rachel Bank, Grade 4
Winston Campus Elementary, IL

Spring Fever

The snow is melting
Birds are chirping
March is ending
Nature is coming back to life

People play in parks
Baseball begins
Spring cleaning sweeps the nation
We are out of hibernation!

Showers are quenching the Earth's thirst
Flowers bloom and petals burst
Daffodils, roses, daisies, and sun
Gardeners are having fun

School is out in June
A heat wave on its way
Temperatures are rising
Spring is swept away
David Dworkin, Grade 6
Charles J Caruso Middle School, IL

Chocolate Fudge Sundae

Cold and delicious,
Whipped cream on top,
Coated with chocolate fudge
Sprinkles,
Topped with a cherry,
Flavors of any ice cream,
Topped with pineapple,
Or anything you want.
With a long banana,
Blueberries,
Yes, you may.
The taste will make your day.
It all tastes so yummy,
Hits the spot in your tummy!
Tori Fahse, Grade 4
Cynthia Heights Elementary School, IN

The Invisible Me

I am unknown as
the element in the sky as
the wind in disguise or
Snow white and blue as
a clear blue sky that's
invisible to the human eye
Richard Mares, Grade 4
Haugan Elementary School, IL

Sunsets

Sunsets on the coast
Water shines from the sunset
Quickly it gets dark
Michael Gregory, Grade 5
Bell-Graham School, IL

Puppies

Puppies are cute and adorable.
They are fun and affordable.

Puppies like to play and bark.
Unlike people they don't make bad remarks.

I like puppies that are brown and black.
And maybe ones that enjoy a scratch on the back.

Now my poem is coming to an end.
Be nice and adopt a furry little friend!

Kiresten Gibson, Grade 5
Staunton Elementary School, IN

The Earthworm and the Elephant

An elephant went walking up a hill;
At the top he saw an earthworm strong and still.
He said, "Get off my hill, or I'll eat every bit of you!"
Said the worm, "Sir, don't say that, or I'll eat you, too!"
And so a quarrel came upon those two,
The earthworm and the elephant.
The elephant got impatient and bit the earthworm,
And the earthworm bit the elephant back.

The elephant angrily said, "Move, or this will be over!"
The earthworm said, "Dear elephant, just go the other way!"
And so the quarrel continued on
Between the earthworm and the elephant.

Finally, the elephant became too impatient
And yanked the earthworm out of the way.
The earthworm did the same to the elephant,
And they both became even more angry.
At last they became too angry to control themselves.
They both threw each other off the hill.
They slid down very, very fast
And got hurt very, very bad
With only themselves to blame!

Akshay Bhardwaj, Grade 4
Countryside School, IL

God

As a Catholic I believe that God is up above,
I go to church every Sunday and pray,
I pray to God that someday in the future,
I will join Him in His kingdom up above,
Everyone joins me and prays to God on Sunday,
I hope that each one of us prays to God each day,
I love God and I hope to join Him at His side.
Dear Lord I love you,
And I know You love me too,
Oh God I praise You,
You are the king of all.

Conor Adler, Grade 6
Sacred Heart School, IL

Day at the Beach

Undulating ocean
Pungent sea air
Gulls crying above
Waves flowing
Brackish water
Floating away

Akash Shah, Grade 5
Frank H Hammond Elementary School, IN

Summer

I hear the sun whisper words of warmth
I feel an early summer breeze fill the sweet-smelling air
I see the sun saying good bye,
Slowly fading away into the evening sky
I smell the aroma of freshly cut grass
I taste the red delicious apples straight from the orchard
Sweet summer

Kwynsee Kaiser, Grade 6
Dakota Elementary School, IL

Your Eyes

Your eyes are as bright as the stars in the sky
But I think it is time to say good-bye.
Your smile, it sparkles, it dazzles, it shines
My sadness rings out like the quietest of chimes
You know I would save you, if I could.
If I could, surely I would.
But though your eyes are as bright as the stars in the sky,
Now I know it is time to say my final good-bye.

Mckenna Moseley, Grade 4
Bell-Graham School, IL

Why Can't I See?

I love like a puppy and hate like any other human
But mostly I love
You visualize all I can't, but I do hear
And what I hear each night, cuts me deep
Why? Why? Why? Can't I see?

The yells of a woman in pain,
The cries of a child who is ashamed,
And the yelp of a man who is to blame.
I look but I can't see
Why? Why? Why? Can't I see?

But then I stop…and I know
That the cuts in my society resemble me
And the place that I want to see,
and the people that I want to be
Why? Why? Why? Can't I see?

My cuts,
My skin,
My eyes…I can see!

Alyssa Boatright, Grade 6
Linton-Stockton Elementary School, IN

Christmas/Halloween

Christmas
Beautiful, cold
Relaxing, calming, glistening
Snow, ice, candy, costumes
Tricking, treating, trading,
Freaky, scary
Halloween
Jordyn Budreau, Grade 6
St Mary Elementary School, IN

Grandparents

Grandparents
Nice, lovely
Caring, laughing, revolting
Happy, loyal
I love my grandparents.
Adrianna Freeland, Grade 5
Cloverdale Middle School, IN

Spring

Spring has flowers.
And April showers.
With some wind,
Flowers should bend.
Spring brings back the fish,
So I can have a seafood dish.
Alex Nettleton, Grade 5
GCMS Elementary School, IL

My Seasons

Spring
Hot fun
Splashing, boiling, hiking
Dad, pool, pumpkin, aunt
Freezing, trick-or-treating, spooking
Cool, spooky
Fall
Dakota Koontz, Grade 4
Liberty Elementary School, IN

I Played with a Ball

One day I played with a ball,
Then I ran into a wall.
First I got sad,
Then I got bad,
So I threw the ball hard at the wall.
Alyssa Bean, Grade 6
ROWVA East Elementary School, IL

Moon

The moon shines so bright
It guides you through the night.
As the stars guide you through the night
As it is so bright.
Joey Bell, Grade 5
GCMS Elementary School, IL

A Bird's Point of View

The wind flies freely above my wings.
I would love to join along as the autumn mist sings.
Soon there will be colorless snow,
It will be fun, as on the ground it will glow
We birds have to go, so bye bye cold, where we go, the sun is gold.
Back we will return, in the sunny days,
To migrate in winter, we have many ways.
This is a worriless life of a bird, if you listen, you'll remain stirred.
With no worries about restrictions, we live many happy years,
A life of a bird, is without any fears.
This is a wonderful blessing we possess, what can be better than a life without stress?
Janki Brahmbhatt, Grade 5
Neil Armstrong Elementary School, IL

Ode to My Friend Haley

She's in my classroom every day
We would jump and play
She came to my house around the hay
But one thing she doesn't know is that she's my friend in every way.
A friend always sticks together
And friendship is the golden thread that ties our hearts together.
Kayla Cash, Grade 4
Morgan Elementary School, IN

The Fourth of July

The Fourth of July is a fun experience.
There are red, white and blue fireworks that light up the sky.
Glow sticks that lead the way, flags blowing in the wind,
funny hats and glasses on me.

We all feel like kids again,
no one dresses fancy but just like kids.
We all have fun and laughter. I smell smoke and hot dogs on the grill.
Ellen Prange, Grade 4
British School of Chicago, IL

Winter to Spring

I'm walking in the woods with just a slight "wisp" of wind.
The squirrels scurrying all around hoping that the winter would end.

The butterflies are flying up, up in the sky.
They're all traveling to the south and I ask myself…Why?

I walk past the pond and there I see nothing,
No birds, no geese, no ducks not even a bird to sing.

I keep on walking even though I feel like a fish out of water,
With nothing to keep me company except the coming of winter.

The trees are totally covered in a white blanket of snow.
The snow is covering everything that's all I really know.

I made it through the winter, and all I have to know,
Is that winter is almost over and that spring is coming to melt the snow.
Christina Rees, Grade 6
Belzer Middle School, IN

Stars and Stripes on Iwo Jima

I am the book Flags or our Fathers. I am being carefully, contently, calmly read.
About all our country has to be thankful for. Our country has freedom because of all the brave lives shed.

I am new, soft covered, and small. Looking at my cover can fill anyone with mystery.
The statue on my cover is standing as tall as a proud American flag. I am about the greatest picture in United Sates history.

My word font is smaller than an ant. The story in me is more than a metaphor, simile, or rhyme.
I am about six of the greatest soldiers, frozen, in the film of time.

I am about these six flag raisers' lives, their bravery, their love for their country. I tell about their brave, unique stories,
In a place far from home, about the United States war glories.

Everyone will celebrate freedom in America, because of the soldiers like the ones you read in me.
In the long-lost footprints on Iwo Jima, about the heroes they came to be.

My cover is the statue in Arlington, Virginia. It may look to some serene,
With six ordinary boys raising the U.S. flag on the battered mountain on Iwo Jima, but I am all about a United States marine.

Allegra Wozniak, Grade 6
Our Lady of Peace School, IL

School

S ome time schools fun like going outside or doing since also talking with your friends.
C an go home at 3:00 it's really fun when it comes to the end of the day.
H aving fun on the bus talking to your friends and making plans after the bus ride home.
O n Wednesdays we go home at 2:30 it's a fun day.
O n some days we go and have open gym it's really fun!
L earning is fun because you can learn things that you haven't heard of.

Briana Zagonek, Grade 5
Fredrick Nerge Elementary School, IL

Likes

Things I love to see:
    I love to see my dog when she looks like a puppy dog,
    she loves to see the garage, and I love to see the catalog on the table next to my dog.
Things I love to hear:
    I love to hear music because it is artistic,
    the sound of snoring puts me in comfort, also the TV quiet at night.
Things I love to feel:
    I love to feel the warmness of my coat on a cold winter day,
    also the cushion in my Grandpa's boat, fuzzy stuff feels good when you come in from the cold.
Things I love to taste:
    The pumpkin pie is as good as the sky, pizza is also a thing I love because it is as warm as a glove,
    and also ice cream lets have a dream.
Things I love to smell:
    I love to smell apple pie, and the sky,
    also fresh air so let's go out there.

Brandon Goepfrich, Grade 5
Churubusco Elementary School, IN

Starry Night

I see a castle with a dark and unpleasant past. I hear merciful screams in the castle halls. I see a black castle towering over a helpless village. A crescent-shaped moon shining in the night sky. A crashing waterfall that soon calms into a glossy moonlit lake. A peaceful wildflower meadow sits undisturbed. The rolling wind blows the flexible grass to the damp cold ground. The warm sun to come, the cotton candy pink skies are about to awaken.

Alexis Marie Bridgwater, Grade 6
Central Jr High School, IL

The Slave

You're a slave.
Aren't you afraid
To get whipped
And treated like dust
To work all day
And never get paid
Never play and
Never have a good day?
Keep holding on.
You will be set free
For this is what you really need.

Patrick Anderson, Grade 6
Countryside Montessori School, IL

What Is a Female Lion?

Does all the work.
Fights with the male when she sees him
Sitting around the den.
Lives in a pride
eats zebra, bears, and antelope.
Is a carnivore.
Brings down large pray.
Takes care of the cubs.
Finds a mate.
Has four cubs.
Is happy and a big cat in the wild.
That is a female lion!

Haeven Davis, Grade 4
Morgan Elementary School, IN

Ballet and Tap

Ballet
Point, stretch
Gliding, leaping, turning
Friends, teachers, studio, shoes
Tapping, competing, bending
Flap, shuffle
Tap

Jenna Rolowicz, Grade 5
Our Lady of Peace School, IL

The Clock

A clock can
ring with his
big ding
he is large
and will
barge outside
on noon
there is a full
moon
He will stop
and get to
the top.

Jasmine Carrillo, Grade 5
Gard Elementary School, IL

Softball World Champion

This is what we've been waiting for
To see who is number one.

We all meet in Illinois
To show how it is done.

We pound the ball with all our might
And run like the wind.

The team that crosses the plate the most
Goes home the champion.

Kalene Freshour, Grade 6
Laketon Elementary School, IN

King

I am a king,
a ruler.
I am in control.
I take over my thoughts,
my emotions.
I grasp the power in my mind,
in the palm of my hands.
I don't let go.
I am a king.

Zoe Spruston, Grade 6
Haven Middle School, IL

Hammy the Hamster

Hammy is small
and so are you.
But don't worry
he's just an inch or two.

Ryan Lamb, Grade 4
GCMS Elementary School, IL

Streams

Hear the streams flowing.
Trickling down crisp mountains.
Quiet and peaceful.

Danielle Pasalich, Grade 5
Stanley Clark School, IN

Storm

Boom! Thunder in my ear.
This I do not like to hear.
Lightning crashes on the ground,
But it does not make a sound.

Kinzey Stoll, Grade 6
Rochester Middle School, IL

Chicks

Cute little chickens.
About to hatch from their egg.
Beautiful chicks, cute!

Addi McAteer, Grade 4
Marine Elementary School, IL

Cardinal

Cardinal
Beautiful, dazzling,
Flying, soaring, diving
Charming people all around
Landing, nesting, hatching
Awesome, amazing
Cardinals

Mark Drake, Grade 4
Dixie Bee Elementary School, IN

The Big Run!

I ran from the cops.
I had on big flip flops.
I ran so fast,
They ran out of gas.
So, I went to go get some cute tops!

Sydnee Redlich, Grade 6
ROWVA East Elementary School, IL

Jail Monkey

There once was a monkey
Who was very funky.
He played all day
In the farmer's hay.
He did the locomotion
And caused such commotion.
He was put in jail
Without any bail.

Blake Peppers, Grade 5
Seton Catholic School, IL

Dead Rat

School is like a dead rat,
Sometimes it can be fascinating,
Other times it stinks,
And the stink is long lasting,
But so is the fascination,
And you remember it all of your life.

Vladimir Kistler, Grade 6
Laketon Elementary School, IN

My Pet Dog

My pet dog
Is not so bright,
She has a fear
Of rain and night.

If you've
Had a dog like this,
You've been prepared for
A big sloppy kiss!

Border Collies aren't just pets,
They're Family.

Matthew Henkels, Grade 4
Creekside Elementary School, IL

River of the School

I'm shiny and silver attached to the wall.
People line up to use me, sometimes they stall.
I pour my clear blood, and quench their thirst.
My switch is never clean that bothers me the worst.

I'm not the kind with pennies in me,
Nor one in the park next to a tree.
I'm just going to be a pile of rusted junk,
Only worthy of that smelly local dump.

I'm scared when my switch goes screech,
Children chug my cool liquid as their teachers teach.
I am like a train station, people come and go,
I'm always busy, but I never move to and fro.

Lauren Janek, Grade 6
Our Lady of Peace School, IL

Dogs

I have two dogs at my house
Neither is afraid of a mouse
They're playful inside and out
They both love their Frisbees
One stays in, and one stays out

They will keep you warm when you sleep
They even may like to herd sheep
They make great guardians
When you are scared,
They will comfort you
They can be your best friend
If you're bored, play with them
You can teach them tricks
They wag their tails when they're happy
So keep them happy, and the tail will be wagging

You can have a ball with them
They will forever chase a ball
Sometimes they chase squirrels
They hate taking baths
They sometimes go swimming
Dogs are my best friends.

Thomas Mooney, Grade 6
St Theresa School, IN

Poochy

Doggy
I like her
Ask me why
Because she's so cute when she smiles
Because she talks into the phone
Because she protects me when I'm scared
Because I'm her Little Bub and she's my Poochy.
Because, because, because
I like Poochy!

Cody Van Horn, Grade 5
Staunton Elementary School, IN

A Piece of Paper Feels Hurt

A piece of paper feels hurt.
People stabbing and sticking pens and pencils into it.
No one ever thinks to be more gentle.
It's always press harder.
But papers are sad.
People stabbing and sticking pens and pencils into them.

Sean Horwitz, Grade 6
Norman Bridge Elementary School, IL

Yellow

Yellow is the bright sun in the morning.
Yellow is leaves in the fall.
Yellow is a buzzing bee.
Yellow is the stars and the moon at night.
Yellow is sweet laffy taffy in my mouth.
Yellow is the color that I like the most.

Megan Byrer, Grade 5
Staunton Elementary School, IN

Championship Game

In the bottom of the 1st inning,
5-0, my team was winning.
My team was having fun,
Until Sean hit a 3-run home run.

We went to the 5th,
Thinking it was a myth.
5-3 with Sean up to bat.
He went deep, and that was that.

Going to the last inning,
5-4, we were winning.
Sean was trying to come in the clutch,
But I made a pitch that he couldn't touch.

Adam Nauracy, Grade 6
St John Evangelist School, IN

Trying to Be a Calm and Happy Person

I am a calm and happy person.
I wonder if I will ever be sad.
I hear people talking about me.
I see some of my friends leaving my life.
I want to keep my closest friends.
I am still a a calm and happy person.
I pretend to be a calm and happy person.
I feel alone at home.
I touch the pictures of the past.
I worry I might be depressed.
I cry in the cold and lonely darkness.
I am still trying to be a calm and happy person.
I understand that things change.
I say I will move on.
I dream of my life in the past as a calm and happy person.

Matthew Jalac, Grade 6
St Matthias/Transfiguration School, IL

Guitar

G uitarist
U are so good
I play great songs
T uner
A wesome
R ock and roll

Austin Davis, Grade 4
Morgan Elementary School, IN

Spring

S o much warmer than winter
P retty flowers are in bloom
R ainy days are very common
I nch by inch the temperature rises
N esting birds are in the trees
G reat summer days are soon to come

Dana VanDuren, Grade 5
Beebe Elementary School, IL

School

S cience can be fun.
C omposition can be tricky.
H omework during the day.
O n time for class.
O n the ball when doing homework.
L earning can be difficult.

Jacob Bernhard, Grade 6
Elwood C C School, IL

Fairies

They dance and they play
in a jolly good way,
and they do it all day
no matter what the others say.

They frolic and run
under the big, shining sun,
and they all have fun
making up silly puns.

By the end of the day
they have nothing to say,
and no fun games to play
that's the fairies' way.

Leah Holsclaw, Grade 5
Floyds Knobs Elementary School, IN

Hummingbird

Hummingbird
Small, sweet,
Humming, sipping, squeaking
Winging, flying, zooming
Dazzling, colorful
Swift

Sheraya Greene, Grade 4
Dixie Bee Elementary School, IN

Liquid Crystals

Rain
Cool, wet
Pouring, drizzling, falling
From the sky to the ground
Glorious

Adam Aldabe, Grade 4
Universal School, IL

Clouds

The clouds in the sky
Shaping, floating in the air
Lovely, fluffy clouds

Ali Noe, Grade 5
Seton Catholic School, IL

Dear Mom

Be my valentine
I want you to be mine

I want you to sign
My valentine
I did not ask nine

I think you are fine
With you I would like to dine
I will whine
Until you are my valentine
I will sit under a pine

I know I write more than a line
Mom I love you

Brittany Watson, Grade 4
St Colette School, IL

Summer

Summer
Raining, sunny
Swimming, sweating, playing
Playing outside so I have fun
School break

Artana Sherifi, Grade 4
Norman Bridge Elementary School, IL

Chinchilla

C alling all animal lovers
H aving nice fluffy fur
I love them so much
N ew or old it doesn't matter
C ome on buy one
H olding them in your hands
I need one or my life would be over
L oving little animals
L iving with them every day
A lways coming your way

Katie Johnston, Grade 6
Elwood C C School, IL

My Pets

Daisy is my cat
She is SUPER NICE
And very gentle
Isabella is calm and quiet
NICE AND SWEET
And never bites
Pepper is my chubby cat
Her meow is super loud
But she is a very sweet cat

Audrey Person, Grade 5
Churubusco Elementary School, IN

Christmas

Christmas
Presents, family
Eating, playing, exciting
Fun, marvelous
Santa Claus comes.

Heaven Taylor, Grade 5
Cloverdale Middle School, IN

Parrots

Parrot
Colorful, smart
Flying, mimicking, chirping
Perching on someone's hand
Bird

Brandon Zhou, Grade 5
Seton Catholic School, IL

My Grandparents

My grandma is nice.
Her house has no mice.
My grandpa is cool.
He has a nice pool.
My grandma is sweet.
And she is really neat.

Andrew Young, Grade 5
GCMS Elementary School, IL

My Mom Love

Whenever I felt sad
you were there or
whenever I felt lonely
you were there to care.

You always there when I need you
and so the word to say is "Thank You."
You mean to me through my heart
and take all my pain to the apart.

So nobody can destroy
the love of the mothers
because it can't replace it to another.

Khin Si, Grade 6
Liberty Elementary School, IL

Memories of the Past

Memories of the past
   I used to have a cast
   Which wasn't such a blast
   I never was harassed
   Me and my brother used to wear masks
That is all from memories of the past

Mattie Swan, Grade 5
Gard Elementary School, IL

I Am

I am a girl who loves to sing.
I wonder if I will ever sing on a stage.
I hear the crowd roaring when I come out to sing.
I see myself singing on a stage.
I have wanted to be a singer ever since I was 4 years old.
I am a girl who loves to sing.

I pretend my room is a studio to record the songs I sing.
I feel the emotions of the song when I sing.
I touch the microphone and feel as if I'm dreaming.
I worry my dream for singing will be shattered.
I cry when I'm told I'll never make it in the music business.
I am a girl who loves to sing.

I understand that I might not make it.
I say I'll make my dream come true.
I dream of singing forever.
I try to sing songs all the time.
I hope singing will be not just a dream but real.
I am a girl who loves to sing.

Jamoni Reynolds, Grade 4
Levan Scott Academy, IN

What If…?

What if the world was a rainbow?
Would we reach the pot of gold?
What if the world was age?
Would we reach the age of old?

What if the world was a television channel?
Would we be channel 55 or channel 2?
What if the world was me?
Would there even be a him or a you?

What if the world did not exist?
What if there were no rainbow?
There were no age or emotion?
There were no behavior or tv?
There were no you?
There were no me?

What if the world did not exist?
What if…?

Arrielle Terry, Grade 6
Chicago International Charter School - Longwood, IL

The Forest

Such beautiful trees.
Birds whistle while they make their nests.
I love the outdoors.

Brad Lehman, Grade 4
Goodfield Elementary School, IL

Grandparents

Grandparents are as nice as saints!
Loving and caring
Having a bad day?
Grandparents will make you feel a lot better!
Grandparents make the world
A better place!

Katie McAuliffe, Grade 5
St John of the Cross Parish School, IL

My Dog Maggie

My dog Maggie is the best,
She doesn't have to prove it on a test
She is a great listener,
I always love to be with her
Running around, she loves to play,
When she looks at me I know she's here to stay
Her big brown eyes stare up at me,
Wagging her tail happily
I know she'll always be my friend,
All the way to the very end

Molly McNamara, Grade 5
Bell-Graham School, IL

My Love

I once had a love named Diana.
My love for her burns with the
hot intensity of 1000 suns.
But I didn't know if she loved me back.
She always made me smile when she could.
She knew that I was in love with her at first sight.
But I don't think she loved me back.
If I had one wish…
I would wish to be together forever.
I hope she loves me back.

Nick Rizzotti, Grade 6
Thayer J Hill Middle School, IL

Book

If I were a book,
when I am opened I would say,
"Readers beware! You are in for a scare!"
I'd mold the shelves with my scariness,
and I'd pledge to be a best seller.
I'd be a paperback with worn pages.
I would also make my readers
read me over and over again.
Life would be a nonstop scary nightmare.

Corey Welch, Grade 6
Lombard Middle School, IL

A Candle

Flickering softly,
So much like hope —
A faint glow that warms the heart,
Too easily extinguished.

Sally Ploch, Grade 6
Gray M Sanborn Elementary School, IL

Hunt/Fish

Hunt
Deer hunt, bird hunt
Shooting, hiding, scouting
Track, pursuit, explore, search
Casting, angling, hooking
Fish

Jake Briggs, Grade 5
Tri-State Christian School, IL

Cougars

One day as I walked in the dark,
I spotted something sly.
How I wanted to run away,
But I would surely die!

Coleton Wilkins, Grade 4
Adams Central Elementary School, IN

Mrs. Harmon

M iracle
R are
S pecial

H umble
A ngel
R eal
M akes me laugh
O ptimistic
N ice

Zachary Dale Jenkins, Grade 5
Morgan Elementary School, IN

Mom

Roses are red; violets are blue
I would be very sad without you
Will you be my awesome valentine
And I will be your valentine too

You look so very fine
In the pretty sunshine
On you I can depend
To me you are divine

This letter that I will send
Will ask you to be my friend
And be my very best bud
Our friendship will never end

Sara Fecko, Grade 6
St Colette School, IL

Inside a Black Hole

Inside a black hole I see nothing but a light
A light like no other light
A light so bright brighter than the sun itself
This light is as bright as the yellow on a new yellow marker
This light inside a dark hole is the light of heaven coming closer to me
The darkness is the underworld

Greg Chastang, Grade 6
St Pius X Catholic School, IN

The Loveless Skyscraper

It is nightfall and the lonely skyscrapers are sitting in rows trying to sleep.
The skyscrapers are like a box of treasure waiting to be opened.
They are little cats dreaming of the love they feel
From all the people who stop to admire them.
There is one ugly skyscraper that never gets noticed.
He is the ugly duckling that will never get to experience love.
He hears people all day saying that he should be torn down.
He is sad all day and weeps through the night when the others are sleeping.
All he ever asked for is someone to love him.

Tori Singleton, Grade 6
St Pius X Catholic School, IN

Mom and Dad

M other, you are always here for me.
O ver there, always there, if I need help and love, you are there.
M other, you cheer me up when I'm gloomy, Mommy I love you.

A lovable family we shall stay.
N ever will we part.
D ependable family

D addy, I wouldn't forget you
A lways caring and helpful too!
D addy, I love you.

Patricia Kania, Grade 4
Norman Bridge Elementary School, IL

Under the Big Top

Round and round goes the circus clown.
So many faces a smile a frown.
But when the performers took the stage
The attention was given to the strong man Gage.
He'd perform a stunt so stupefying,
When the people would tell their friends they'd think they were lying.
But the biggest stunt was still to come,
The one that would guarantee you'd have fun.
The act that would follow belonged to the clowns.
The act made you laugh, and you'd never see a frown.
It was the biggest food fight you ever have seen.
The food was flying all over and in between.
As the stadium squealed loud with delight,
Goofy threw a pie that hit Jimbo and blocked most of his sight.
There was only one thought in everyone's head,
I want to come back again before I am dead.

Kevin Wenzel, Grade 5
Hadley Middle School, IL

What Is My Hand?

My hand is useful in many ways.
My hand does many hard jobs.
My hand has five fingers.
My hand has five finger prints, finger nails.
My hand has one thumb, one pinky, one index finger,
one middle finger, one finger that's bigger than the middle.
My hands help me do things like homework.
My hand has five fingers that look alike.
My hand is an inspiration to my body.

Josh Chinn, Grade 5
Morgan Elementary School, IN

You Know It You Want It

You know it,
You want it,
You need it, you love it,
You just gotta have it,
Hopefully you don't know it, because I do,
So don't get you're hopes up I'm not telling you.

Mitchell McDonald, Grade 5
Country Meadow Elementary School, IN

Victor

Victor
Deliberate, scared,
Blinking, thinking, loving,
I can't love wickedness, but I *can* love wickedness' hostage,
Gaining, crying, hugging,
Ecstatic, joyful,
Girl

Stacie Skwarcan, Grade 6
Stanley Clark School, IN

What Is Yrteop (yer-tee-op)?

The FBI can't figure it out.
The world doesn't know what it's about.
Something from out of this world in space.
It comes from another galaxy's race.
It's in my dictionary which is insane!
It can be a very colorful…thing.
It's a symbol of uniting.
Can be a very neat sighting.
It's absolutely full of words.
It's "poetry" spelled backwards!
That is yrteop!

Brianna Jacobi, Grade 5
Morgan Elementary School, IN

What Happened to Jan When She Tanned

Hi, my name is Jan.
I have to go tan.
I burnt myself now.
So, I look like a cow,
And now I am a tan man.

Shelby Simmons, Grade 6
ROWVA East Elementary School, IL

End

Tears will overcome you,
Crystal drops will fall

You may fall too,
But that isn't all

Happiness is far away,
Now you are speechless, without a word to say

Will you love again?
Are you ever going to win?

Will you ever be sane?
Can you get over the pain?

Yes, you will be fine,
Just give it some time

Dyllanne Deischer, Grade 6
Linton-Stockton Elementary School, IN

Katie

Katie
Funny, gullible, sweet
Sister of Lance, Britt, and Ryan. Daughter of Judy and Bryan
Who loves to run, be with friends, and go shopping
Who feels happiness, pride, and when St. Louis Cardinals win
Who fears bugs, losing loved one, and failure
Who need help getting through hard times in life
Who gives time with other, love and support
Who would like to graduate school, move to North Carolina
Haubstadt
Allen

Katie Allen, Grade 6
Haubstadt Community School, IN

If Hope Could Be…

If hope could be a color
it would be blue as bright as the sky

If hope could be a taste
it would taste just like chocolate ice cream

If hope could be a smell
it would be lots of lit candles

If hope could be a sound
it would be a beautiful soft piano song

If hope could be a feeling
it would be a joyful hug in the heart

If hope could be an animal
it would be a puppy cuddling with me

Bianca Delgado, Grade 4
St Agnes School, IL

Dearest to Me
My dogs are loving and soft
My mom helps me and loves me
Even when she gets mad at me
She still loves me
Tristan Selby, Grade 5
Churubusco Elementary School, IN

Memories
The times we spent together
The moments that we shared.
I'll cherish in my heart forever
Knowing that you cared.
I'll try to be strong and move on
Because you would want it that way.
It will be hard without you by my side
but I will remember you every day.
Taysia Fulkerson, Grade 5
Perry Central Elementary School, IN

Friends
Friends never bail out
They know what you are about
They let you borrow their shoes
They never let you catch the blues.

Friends never make you sad
They help you through the good and bad
They talk to you on the phone
And never make you groan.
Nicole Tabatabai, Grade 6
Rochester Middle School, IL

Spring Break
It is a wonderful time
Grass — the color of a lime
Flowers blooming in a row
Butterflies dancing
Some the colors of a rainbow
The sun is shining
All bright and fun
I see families dining
Outside in the sun
The clouds in the sky
Make me wish I could fly
They are pure and white
On a background of light blue
All the beautiful colors
All the delicious smells
As I walk through the town
A week away from school
Lets us do things that are quite cool
Fun walks in the park
The sound of a dog's bark
Spring…I hope it's not dark
Elisha Hoffman, Grade 6
St Theresa School, IN

Florida
F antastic
L ounging in the sun
O pulent
R unning in the sand
I s the best place ever
D ynamic
A wesome
Whitney Baller, Grade 5
Adams Central Elementary School, IN

Christmas
Christmas
Cold, fun
Freezing, giving, getting
Icy, big
This is God's son's birthday.
Kyle Everhart, Grade 5
Cloverdale Middle School, IN

The Skateboard
B est skateboard I think.
L ooks cool on the bottom.
I t has a skeleton on the bottom.
N ever confused with others.
D o you have a BLIND board?
Cameron Brach, Grade 6
Elwood C C School, IL

Spring
I love spring
It makes me sing
The birds and the bees
The grass and the trees
The flowers sprout
Squirrels come out
Spring! Spring! Spring!
Jenna Jurewicz, Grade 5
Norman Bridge Elementary School, IL

Rollerblading
Focused.
Going forward,
Heel down,
Incredibly slow.
What a ride!
Katelyn Benningfield, Grade 5
GCMS Elementary School, IL

Johnny Cash
Johnny Cash
Music-maker, talented
Playing, writing, crying
Dresses like he's at a funeral
Band leader
Daniel Kimball, Grade 5
Staunton Elementary School, IN

I Am
I am kind and intelligent.
I wonder where God will lead me.
I hear Christians singing.
I see me in the future.
I want to live a God-fearing life.
I am kind and intelligent.

I pretend I am older.
I feel angels guiding me.
I touch the gates of Heaven.
I worry I might not make it to Heaven.
I cry for the people I've lost.
I am kind and intelligent.

I understand God's love.
I say God's word is true.
I dream I will go to Heaven.
I try to be nice to my siblings.
I hope my friends and family
Will all come to Christ and go to Heaven.
I am kind and intelligent.
Angie Koch, Grade 5
Tremont Elementary School, IL

Something Special*
I have something
Something special
It's there when I need it
And it's there when I feed it
It has an eternal place in my heart
And its favorite words are bark, bark
I'll love it forever
Its name is Peluche Hernandez
My baby dog
Lisbeth Hernandez, Grade 6
Hannah Beardsley Middle School, IL
*Dedicated to my family
and my "special" dog.

Tree's Characteristics
Help us breathe and live
Trees have a lot of branches
You can climb all trees
Geoff Mathis, Grade 5
St Jacob Elementary School, IL

Brain
Brain
Terrible, smart
Pulsing, quivering, nauseating
Ruler of the whole Planet X
Seizing, controlling, commanding
Powerful, rhythmical
Mastermind
Andrew Hildreth, Grade 6
Stanley Clark School, IN

The Little Fairy

The Little Fairy
There once was a fairy
that couldn't decide
whether she should fly.
So she climbed to the top of a mountain you see
and then shouted with glee,
and that was the end of the little fairy.

Natalie Henrikson, Grade 5
Cumberland Elementary School, IL

Shy

Shy is a dark shadow it follows you through your life
The bigger the group
The more your shadow goes away with slight

Shy can be overcome
But you have to try hard
It may take forever
Just wait till you draw the right life card

Then you will scream
Jump up and yell "I WIN"
You then will say "Wow I'm not shy!"
And on your face will be a big grin!

Crystal Coble, Grade 6
East Elementary School, IN

Blue

Blue is like bruises, painful and serious.
Blue is like the summer sky.
Blue is like midnight, light and dark at the same time.
Blue is like a kite in the sky.
Blue can be books.
Blue can be anything.

Cody Market, Grade 5
Staunton Elementary School, IN

Music to My Ears

Music is like gentle waves washing ashore.
Music sparkles in your ear,
Making you want to dance,
When dancing,
Music is singing in your ears,
The music is telling you to dance,
Like the waves,
Swoosh, Swoosh,
You dance to the right,
Then to the left,
The music keeps you up all night,
Telling you not to go to bed,
Music to me is like being on the beach,
Watching the sun going down,
Swoosh, Swoosh.

Kylee McDermott, Grade 5
St John of the Cross Parish School, IL

Window

A blanket of cotton balls
Horses neighing, cows mooing
The smell of dust blowing making me sneeze
Feeling of breezes blowing in my face
Seeing lambs grazing in the fields
Hearing dogs bark and birds chirp

Savannah Mettler, Grade 4
Erie Elementary School, IL

Karson Klyber

K ind to people a lot
A wesome in football and other sports
R ocks on the drums
S occer is fun to watch
O nly four people in my family
N ot mean to people

K ind to animals like rabbits, dogs, and cats
L oser I am not
Y ellow is my 4th favorite color
B lue is my 1st favorite color
E verybody is my friend in my class
R ude to people not me

Karson Klyber, Grade 4
Robein Elementary School, IL

Raining Paintballs

Paintballs were falling from the sky rapidly,
as if they were rain.
They were falling from the sky,
hundreds, thousands, millions at a time.
The sound of them soaring through the air was quite,
like a mouse.
They stung like a bee.
Falling freely through the sky,
hitting every person and object,
in sight.
Everything covered in paint, looked like a rainbow.
What a beautiful sight.

Tannor Bittner, Grade 6
Haubstadt Community School, IN

The Fish

There in the tank, there is a fish,
Watch it flip and do its tricks.

But in the fish, there is a yearning,
To go to sea and start its learning.

So, to a school of fish he'll go,
To learn the things all fish must know.

Here comes the bus with all his friends
It's off to school for Fish and his friends.

Briana Dearing, Grade 5
North Intermediate Center of Education, IL

Conner

Conner
Has curly hair
Plays lots of basketball
Is a very athletic boy
Awesome
Nick Baumer, Grade 5
Adams Central Elementary School, IN

Waiting

Standing in the outfield
Waiting for the ball
The hot sun stings my face
I feel like I could fall.

Everything is boring
I have nothing to do
Everything is boring
'Cause I have to wait for you.

Smack! The ball flies
Way up in the air
It rolls on the ground
I run without a care.

I pick the ball up
I throw it with all my might
My eyes are still blinded
'Cause the sun that's oh so bright.

They catch the ball
They touch the base
A smile comes
Upon my face.
Bekah Brunn, Grade 6
Laketon Elementary School, IN

Tall Trees

Trees are very tall
Stretching so high to the sky
Trees start their life small
Jacob Cygan, Grade 5
St Jacob Elementary School, IL

Flying

My only wish is to fly
Soaring through the sky
I'll take dips into clouds
I'll feel moisture all around
I'll fly with the robins, hawks, and eagles
Maybe even with the seagulls
It will be the best time ever
I know it will because the plan is clever
This time I will never forget
Never, never, never
Abrar Najjar, Grade 5
Universal School, IL

Eagle

Eagle, Eagle of browns and whites,
Reaching up to wondrous heights.
Tell me please, what do you do
When the hunters catch sight of you?
Amanda Jones, Grade 4
Cynthia Heights Elementary School, IN

Spring

Spring has come
Spring has come.
Spring is a good
Time for fun.
I like spring
Yes I do!
I like spring
I hope you do too.
Jared Davis, Grade 5
GCMS Elementary School, IL

Bald Eagle

Bald Eagle
Huge, beautiful,
Soaring, diving, catching
Proud American National Symbol
Hunting, feeding, swooping
Amazing, glorious
Bird
Zachary Reisinger, Grade 4
Dixie Bee Elementary School, IN

Freak the Mighty

F ighting
R owdy runt
E ager to get a new body
A dventures
K evin

T eamwork
H onesty
E nergized

M axwell
I s Killer Kane's son
G iant
H auls Kenin around
T ough
Y ou have to read *Freak the Mighty*!
Taylor Elmer, Grade 6
Perry Central Elementary School, IN

Spring

Flowers smell fragrant
Wind is blowing the new buds
Birds sing all day long
Katelyn Worley, Grade 5
Hiawatha Elementary School, IL

Trapped in a Jungle

I am dashing through the foggy jungle
Not knowing where I am going
Just running…
I hear heavy footsteps
I feel rough hands grasping my body
I call out for help
Nobody hears me
I scream louder
Is this real?
Is this a dream?
I do not know, but…
I am trapped
Cole Riggleman, Grade 6
Linton-Stockton Elementary School, IN

Zuzu

Zuzu is my Shih Tzu dog,
She rolls around just like a log,
Her favorite toy is a stuffed bone,
And she gets sad when she's left alone.

On stormy nights she has some fear,
But not as much when I am near,
She sticks her face deep in her bed,
So I can't see her tiny head.

She loves to fill me up with joy,
Even when I'm so annoyed,
Even when I want to cry,
I know she will be by my side.
Taylor Ortiz, Grade 6
St Matthias Elementary School, IL

Witnessing a Murder

A flurry of movement
Catches my eye.
As I look at it,
I break down and cry.
I see a horse
Get shot in the head.
I want to save it,
But I run away instead.
I felt everything,
Even her sorrow.
That she would not live
To see tomorrow.
I felt her sway,
As she took her last breath.
And the gentle thud
To her death
I write this poem
Not to scare you,
But to think twice
Before everything you do.
Elizabeth Krilich, Grade 6
St John Evangelist School, IN

Love from Pa

There has been a hole in my heart since Pa died.
No one to call Pa anymore.
Playing pick up sticks or doing puzzles was fun!
When I ate ice, Pa told me I would turn into an ice cube!
But now when I do that stuff, my hole is filled.

Alyssa Muscato, Grade 5
St Anthony's School, IL

Spring

I can't wait the day is almost here
And it is very near,
To hear new things, to see,
And smell the spring cool wind will blow
My hair with the air

Birds will sing time to time
As a flock of other birds in the air
Will fill the sky with their beautiful wings.
It is like they color the sky

I will run to the field of flowers.
When I look around,
The flowers are like the colors of the rainbow

When kids laugh it makes me laugh with joy,
As kids play rope, ball, and other stuff

So, I say goodbye cold days
And hello cool, fun, and nice spring
But still I can't wait for spring

Alexandra Sosa, Grade 4
Peck Elementary School, IL

Wet Paint

Boy am I tired, I need to sit down,
So with one small gesture he stepped into town.
There is a seat not occupied at all,
And I do want to sit or I'm likely to fall.
He walked 'cross the street and sat down on the chair,
'Til the scream of a voice put him into the air.
"What's the matter with you, can't you read the sign?"
He looked at the board with it's scribbles and lines.
He didn't know what it meant he thought with a grumble,
But a look at the man's face and he knew he was in trouble.
He ran and ran as fast as he would,
Not to stop 'til he knew that he could.
Without even knowing it he sat down near Big Ben,
'Til he heard a shout and repeated the cycle again,
Now rather lonesome he looked down at his shirt,
Blue and red polka-dots don't go well with dirt.
He went to his house and was rushed to a shower,
"I didn't expect you home for another half an hour."
And then for a while he thought of his day,
Then he remembered "wasn't my shirt colored gray?"

Austin Hatch, Grade 6
Rochester Middle School, IL

Obstacles

It could happen again today.
How can we protect the future every day?
Take the next step
Abandon wannabes
Help
Do it now
Because putting it off 'til tomorrow isn't an option
Just be the one to
Make it happen
Be that one.

Ashlyn Twibell, Grade 5
Twin Branch Model School, IN

Cafeteria Noise

The talking and chatting of the kids.
The zip, zip, zipping of the lunchboxes.
Crumbling bags, and sliding of chairs.
The cafeteria noise it just blares.
The talk of kids trading their lunch.
The burps of boys there are a bunch.
Stacking of chairs as lunch draws to an end.

Abby Eichholtz, Grade 6
St Pius X Catholic School, IN

Winter

Winter, very frigid
Makes you sick
Snow is very cold.
The cold air will eventually freeze the cold water,
Which will turn into ice.
Ooh pumpkin pie, can I have a slice?
Yummmmmmmmmmm!!!!!

Peyton Randolph Janney, Grade 4
Liberty Elementary School, IN

The Owl

I am the owl
My home is being destroyed
Some giants are running over me
Some have noticed me
And those are on my side

Some are helping me
Protesting the Mother Paula's Pancake House
And messing up the site
So the builders won't move on

They care about me
Those nice giants
They're not going to let anyone win
But them

The owl

Elise Gray-Gaillard, Grade 6
British School of Chicago, IL

My First Day as Aspirin

I sit in the cupboard
Alone in the dark.
Nervous and impatiently
I wait to be opened.

With my safety seal on
I sit.
Waiting, waiting
Hours have passed.

I hear several 'thumps'
Coming towards me.
Coming closer, closer,
The cabinet opens…

The strange thing emerges,
Like a giant smashes me open.
"Oh no!" It's too late.
This is nothing like I had in mind.
Stephen Knecht, Grade 6
Our Lady of Peace School, IL

Why Must She Die

when my grandma had a stroke
a little girl asked me why
when they took grandma to her car
the little girl asked if she was ok
I didn't think I told her a lie
two days later grandma was in ICU
I asked myself if she was going to die
I think I told myself a lie
one month later at the funeral home
I realized, I told myself a lie
why must she die!
Allison Parker, Grade 5
Perry Central Elementary School, IN

My Beautiful Shell

I can hear the crashing ocean,
The music of the glistening dolphins,
The waves splashing,
Children yelling,
Having fun,
I taste the bitter water,
Warm and wet,
I see the dazzling ocean,
In my beautiful shell.
Monica Burks, Grade 6
Linton-Stockton Elementary School, IN

Raining

It started to rain
The lightning was beautiful
The rain turned to snow
Charlie Garrett, Grade 5
Seton Catholic School, IL

Address

Elizabeth Street,
So quiet,
So peaceful,
Until
Someone zooms by,
Swish!
Slow down! I then yell,
But do they listen
I can never tell.
In the morning,
I hear the birds,
Chirp! Chirp! Chirp!
At night
I hear the train
At the end
Of our street
Then it wakes me up
With its loud horn.
Elizabeth Street,
So wonderful
To live in.
Rachel Ziemba, Grade 4
Creekside Elementary School, IL

Basketball

Michael Jordan got the ball
Charles Barkley came to stall
Michael shoots
Then he makes the coup
Michael Jordan and Dominique Wilkins
were in the dunk contest
The Dominique scored less
That's all I have to say,
Have a nice day
Victor Johnson, Grade 4
Martin L King Elementary School, IL

Dog

I have a dog her name is Maggie
Her fur is extremely shaggy
She runs and runs and plays all day
And doesn't listen to a word I say
At night she comes in my bed
And steals the pillow from my head
Lexi Sigler, Grade 5
Lincoln Trail Elementary School, IN

Baby/Adult

Baby
Playful, young
Observing, napping, giggling
Infant, toddler, grownup, mature
Busy, older
Adult
Bethany Galle, Grade 5
Tri-State Christian School, IL

Spring

S plashing in the water
P laying in the sun
R ain, rain, rain
I ce cream melting
N oises outside
G etting ready for break
Holly Tompkins, Grade 5
GCMS Elementary School, IL

Bugs

Bugs
Smelly, Slimy
Crawling, Wiggling, Hopping
Slow as a snail
Furry
Lucy Cathcart, Grade 5
Floyds Knobs Elementary School, IN

Birds

They fly high,
High in the sky.
My, oh my,
Their spirits never die.
They have wings,
Unlike some things.
Wings help them fly,
High in the sky.
They look so graceful,
High in the trees.
They are so beautiful,
As they fly with the bees.
Birds are magical,
The chirping that I hear.
I listen to it sometimes,
It soothes my ears.
Phillip Williams, Grade 6
Rochester Middle School, IL

Ocean

I am the ocean.
I wonder if I can be something else.
I hear my waves.
I see my waves reaching to shore.
I want people to be safe.
I am the ocean.
I pretend to be something else.
I feel happy.
I touch people's hearts.
I worry about people.
I cry for people who die in me.
I am the ocean.
I understand why people die.
I say there must be more lifeguards.
I dream for people to be safe.
Israel Padilla, Grade 6
St Matthias/Transfiguration School, IL

You

For what you do, is up to you
Though sometimes you may have to face the new
Not everything is under your control
But everything can be like a bull
Fearless and tearless you must be
Like this bull in life
For you might find much strife
It is the extra thing that you do
That will make up most of you
The thing will seem unnecessary at the time
Undone the time will come when you will whine
Everything is possible though you may think that it's not
For that will be true if it is your thought
Think about what you want carefully
Because that is who you'll be
Don't leave goals untouched
Because you will be such
Only you can save your date
I am just a common mate

Dylan Pulver, Grade 6
Hawthorne Scholastic Academy, IL

Family

My family yells and sometimes pushes,
My brother pushes me hard and sometimes in the bushes.
But when we fight I think how lucky I am
To have a family and to know that we can,
We can fight together and push through our hardships,
And love and help each other with our friendships.
My brother loves me, that's all I have to know.
And so does my family, I love them so!

Haley Kontol, Grade 4
Oak Hill Elementary School, IN

The War of Narnia

T'was the war of Narnia,
Though many men were catching malaria.
When the battle seemed one thousand to one,
Our work was never done.
After the reinforcements arrived,
It appeared our army had revived.
The reinforcements helped a bunch,
I wonder when they have lunch.
It wasn't long before we demolished half of the group,
They fell to the ground like gloop.
When the queen was the last one standing,
She looked far too demanding.
Although the battle with the queen took forever,
It was a great endeavor.
When she fell face-flat on the ground,
We made sure she was defeated with a pound.
So the land of Narnia was at war,
But they are no longer anymore.

Logan Garner, Grade 5
North Intermediate Center of Education, IL

Snowboarding

S uper fun!
N o better way to spend a weekend
O utstanding!
W aves of snow
B etter bring friends, just in case you get lost
O ut of this world adventures
A great way to meet people
R eally relaxing
D id I mention jumping and tricks?
I f in Colorado, there are amazingly cool mountains
N ice runs…and no injuries = a great time
G ood way to get in shape

Matt Karlins, Grade 6
Thayer J Hill Middle School, IL

Abedallah, My Dear Brother

Abedallah, my dear brother loved me.
He loved my parents, my sister and baby.
Now that he's gone we have nothing to do.
Before his life was through,
He made duaa and did other good things too.
He read Qur'an and prayed slowly like he knew.
Once his soul was not on Earth anymore,
All of us knew, us four.
I saw a tear roll down my mothers face.
I ran to her like I was in a race.
"What happened," I asked in fear.
My mother replied, "His death is very near"
Then I shed a tear.

Saja Hamayel, Grade 5
Universal School, IL

What Is a Friend?

A friend is a person
A person who is kind
A person who helps you out
When you are sad they make you feel happy
A friend will never lie to you
A friend will never let you down
A friend is always there to make you laugh when you are sad
A friend is always nice to you and friendly
A friend will tell you the truth
Friends will never talk behind your back

That's what a friend is!

Jill Book, Grade 4
Morgan Elementary School, IN

Excitement Feels Great

Excitement is multicolored
It smells like chocolate cake,
And tastes like it too!
It sounds like cheers, claps, and people shouting great things.
And it feels great.

Riana Richey, Grade 6
East Elementary School, IN

I Am

I am a happy girl who loves to write
I wonder if there is a 50,000 page book
I hear the flipping of pages
I see a golden book and silver print
I want the best handwriting
I am a happy girl who loves to write

I pretend I can write forever
I feel a leather journal and a metal key
I touch a smooth pen
I worry I will write something stupid
I cry when I can't think right
I am a happy girl who loves to write

I understand I can't write all the time
I say all people should write
I dream I will be the best writer ever
I try to write about all things
I hope to be an effective writer
I am a happy girl who loves to write

Mikayla LaRocco, Grade 5
Hiawatha Elementary School, IL

School

Grateful class
Lovable teachers
Mad workers
Learning experiments
Exciting field trips
Wild after-school activities
Stunning sports
Exploding fun
Cheering kids
Best principal.

Logan Hanni, Grade 4
Adams Central Elementary School, IN

Me

A ngelic
R eads a lot
D uck lover
E verybody's friend
N ever gives up

T houghtful
H appy
O beys my parents
R espect
N ice
B right
E nergetic
R eliable
R ickety
Y oung

Arden Thornberry, Grade 4
W E Wilson Elementary School, IN

My Poems

I am a crying poet sitting on my tear
I watch my poems drop like rain as they seek a puddle of water under my feet.

I am a star poet riding a shooting star as I write my poems
They fly off and I hope one day they will be as bright as a star one night.

I am a nature poet sitting on a branch as I write my poems
They fly off into the sunset.

I am a wind poet sitting on a gust of wind whispering to people as I write my poem
They blow away twisting and twirling to be read.

I am an ocean poet sitting in a reef as I write my poems
They are taken away by bubbles and brought to the top.

Erin King, Grade 6
St Barbara School, IL

Cute Little Squirrel, Sitting in a Tree

I am brown and plump with cute little whiskers.
I am almost like a fat mouse.
I just love to eat nuts of any kind.
In her backyard I have a big, wooden tree house.

During the winter I look for good food.
I find food that has a good crush, crackle, and crack.
When I find a really good nut to eat,
I put it in my mouth and carry it up to save in my little tree shack.

As time goes by I get fatter and fatter.
As time goes by I look for food and run.
As time goes by I get cuter and cuter.
In her backyard though, it is always just a bowl of fun.

Josephine Baio, Grade 6
Our Lady of Peace School, IL

My Dear Mother

The first thing I heard was your heart beat way before I was born.
The first thing I saw was your smile when I was born.
The first steps I walked were toward you.
You heard my first words.
You helped me, cared for me.
All I want to say is:
I thank you very much,
My dear mother.

Adriana Garcia, Grade 4
Haugan Elementary School, IL

The Day My Dog Got Fired

I have a dog named Sirius who's crazy for his job
He's not the average slob
When I got home the house was shining
But my dog was whining
He told me what happened so now he's fired
He wrote my mom a letter and it said your phone is now rewired.

Nikki Harper, Grade 5
Center Street Elementary School, IL

Hawaii

H awaii has lots of luaus and it has lots of beaches
A lways bring shorts, short-sleeve shirts, and a bathing suit
W indy sometimes it gets very windy up there
A nimals love Hawaii and people love Hawaii
I n Hawaii it is always very hot
I t is never cold in Hawaii, even during the winter it is hot there

Amanda Wells, Grade 6
Elwood C C School, IL

School

School is a place fun and cool,
Some hate it so they drool.
Some kids are good in math,
But it's not always an easy path.
Reading is a fun sensation,
Because you use your imagination.
So as you can see,
School is the place to be.

Logan Kennard, Grade 5
North Intermediate Center of Education, IL

Rainbow

"Red" is the color of blood,
that leaks when I cut my hand,

"Blue" is the color of the sky,
I look at when I lay in the grass,

"Violet" is the color of the sweet juicy plum,
I picked from the tree,

"Orange" is the color of the ball,
you gave me and I continue to play with,

"Yellow" is the color of the sun,
so bright in my face,

"Green" is the color of the grass,
which you and I play in,

This is my rainbow,
for you and I.

Kimisha Glasper, Grade 6
Emmett Louis Till Math & Science School, IL

Sky Shimmer

Unreal wisps floating by,
Forming shapes in the sky,
When people spot it, it might look fluffy,
But in the midst of it, it's a far cry from stuffy.
The shape can be a placating, whitish-blue,
Or suddenly take on a much more threatening hue.
All this, I'll say, describes a cloud;
A beautiful, shimmering, nature-made shroud.

Laura Lee, Grade 5
Canterbury School, IN

Stormy Night

It was late on a stormy night,
And I was still awake
My dog tried to be brave for me,
But I could feel him shake
A crash of thunder shook the room
And took me by surprise
And in the dim light I saw
That fear was mirrored in his eyes

The world outside was blurry;
Rain spattered on the windowpane
And sudden crashes of thunder
Were driving me insane
I closed my eyes and told myself
That it would be all right
Just then the lightning lit the sky
As if it wasn't night

I lay down next to my dog,
His soft fur against my cheek
And with the sound of rain tapping on the window
I gently fell asleep

Brianna Maki, Grade 6
Immaculate Conception School, IL

Summer

S unshine is very plentiful
U mpires are very busy at the baseball games
M owing the lawn is part of my summer chores
M ilk shakes taste great on a hot summer day
E ver think about having a water balloon fight
R iding a bike is something to do while the weather is nice

Brandon Nastepniak, Grade 6
Elwood C C School, IL

Lizard Joe

There was a lizard and his name was Joe.
He likes to eat bugs and play in the grass.
Joe goes crazy when he sees winter snow.
He tugs at the dirt and is very fast.

Joe loves to play outside, in the cold too.
When it is time to come inside, he cries.
He especially likes to play with Sue.
He has a very special friend who flies.

When they see one another they both smile.
They go to the park, and go down the slide.
They like fall, when leaves are all in a pile.
Other times, they like to go for a ride.

When it is time for them to say goodbye.
They cannot wait until they next say hi.

Victoria Groebner, Grade 6
Christian Life Schools, IL

Love

Love
affection, fondness
treasuring, cherishing, admiring
Waiting for Prince Charming
Adore
Shelby Wilson, Grade 6
Rochester Middle School, IL

Mother

M is for the Moments we share.
O is for that she's only growing Older.
T is for the Tears she shed to save me.
H is for the Hysterical laughs we have.
E is for the Eternal love we share.
R is for the Restful nights we enjoy.

Put them all together, it spells *Mother*.
A word that means the world to me.
Emily Layer, Grade 4
Oak Hill Elementary School, IN

My World

The rush of air
as I bring down my sword.
Enemies surround me,
Trapped…Scared…But alive.

Bullets jetting through
the cloudy air.
The thundering boom of guns going off.
An explosion, darkness.

The rush of water
beneath me.
The barrel of my musket,
cold against my bare neck.
The tattered sail
flapping in the breeze.

My imagination
My world
Ben Mair, Grade 6
Linton-Stockton Elementary School, IN

Lost

The waves crash beneath my feet,
The sand is between my toes,
I'm stranded on an Island,
Far away from home.

I don't know where I am,
Or where I'll end up,
The only thing I do know,
Is that I seem to be out of luck.
Brandon Marshall, Grade 5
Bell-Graham School, IL

State of Mind

Fantasy
Wondering, soaring
Vast, colorful, vibrant
Fairies, dragons, science, discovery
Factual, knowledgeable, true
Learning, searching
Reality
JonZachary Forbes, Grade 6
Belzer Middle School, IN

Snow Day

Bright, white, fluffy snow
Shooting down in my backyard
My gosh is snow fun!
Steven Brzowski, Grade 5
Our Lady of Peace School, IL

Dad

Dad
Strong, helpful
Holding, yelling, helping
Holding me at the best of his ability
Hurting, tackling, attacking
Intelligent, popular
Father
Dean Barnes, Grade 6
Stanley Clark School, IN

Dogs Are

Dogs
Hyper, playful
Barking, digging, moving
Loyal, cuddly, fluffy, stubborn
Scratching, licking, purring
Silly, picky
Cats
Alex Sikora, Grade 5
Our Lady of Peace School, IL

Happy Valentine's Day!

This letter is for Mommy
You are my finest buddy
For me, you are always there
Mom, you are the golden key

I love how you run a daycare
Some of the kids call you "Aunt Mar"
Oh won't you be my valentine
Mom, you are as bright as a flare

Mommy? Will you be mine?
Mrs. Benson is fine
You are the very best
To me you always shine
Catherine Benson, Grade 6
St Colette School, IL

The Color of Silver

Silver is like a river,
it sparkles in the light.

Silver is like air,
it is tasteless.

Silver performs in battles,
of the Middle Ages.

Silver is like a rock,
it thuds when dropped.

Silver is the color
of gloomy days in winter.

Silver is as smooth,
as a baby's bottom.
Darcy Andis, Grade 6
Linton-Stockton Elementary School, IN

Benji

Benji
cute, powerful
loving, caring, running
Makes me feel better when I'm sad.
Brother.
Abigail Riggenbach, Grade 4
Robein Elementary School, IL

Lighthouse to Apartment

Light House
Enormous, dull
Gleaming, beaming, lighting
Bright, calm, small, roomy
Cleaning, caring, washing
Colorful, warm
Apartment
Kaileen Hendle, Grade 5
Neil Armstrong Elementary School, IL

The Thing I Sat On

I sat upon the thing I saw
It was very, very hairy.
But as it looked at me,
I thought it was kinda scary.
It was tall, fat, and brown;
I swear I'll never tell my mom,
That today I brought him to town.
I'm sure it's not a fairy,
Because at the front of this poem
I told you it was hairy.
I'm telling you I swear,
That this thing is a bear.
It is quite a scare!
Madi Webster, Grade 4
North Daviess Elementary School, IN

I Don't Want to Play Soccer

I don't want to sit out in the hot boiling sun.
I don't want to sit out I want to have fun.
I don't want to be goalie; Coach don't put me in.
I don't want to be goalie I'll get kicked in the shin.
I don't want to be ball girl, Coach don't make me.
I don't want to be ball girl I'll get hit in the knee.
I don't want to play midfielder; Coach please not this time.
I don't want to be midfielder, I don't get paid a dime.
I don't want to be back wing I'd rather sit here with you.
I don't want to be back wing or I'll cry boo-hoo.
I don't want to play forward I don't want to play back.
I don't want to play forward 'cause speed's one thing I lack.
Please not the retriever, please not that.
Please not the retriever, I'd rather play with cats.
I don't want to play soccer, Mom don't make me go.
I don't want to play soccer, I promise I'll mow!

Shelby Sneed, Grade 5
Floyds Knobs Elementary School, IN

I Know I'm Not a Poet

In class today, we're writing poems
But I know I'm not a poet,
My teacher says to give it a try
But I know it won't work
I know it,

I can't put words together
To make rhythm or a rhyme,
I might be an artist
A scholar
A leader
But I couldn't make poems on a dime,

I couldn't write about withering trees
Or valleys that are breezy,
But now I look back at my poem and think,
"Wow, that was easy!"

Bradi Heaberlin, Grade 6
Clark Pleasant Intermediate School, IN

Slashed Skies

The skies were stabbed, slashed, and beaten
Treated like hostages, living non-existently
The skies so tall and strong
But so weak, and wrong
Swoosh! The plane cut right through
A burning knife, right through butter and glue
Destroying, the untouched cloud
Destroying, what was once so proud
Hope, is what will keep this poor cloud alive
Hope, is what will let this cloud survive
Hope, carries on those who are sad and mourn
Hope, with hope, a new cloud is born

Joe Fagan, Grade 6
St Pius X Catholic School, IN

New York

When I was born
I smelled the first drift of air.
I saw my hands and touched them.
I heard people speaking.
Then I got a bottle of milk that tasted well.

Petar Milisavljevic, Grade 4
Haugan Elementary School, IL

Alone

Alone in the blue sea,
Waiting for someone to save me.
Becoming weak and sinking,
I see all of the colorful fish beneath me.

Suddenly, something rams into me.
I black out, a bright light appears.
Up, up I go…
Out of the cool water, and into the cloudy sky.
Looking up to see the gates of Heaven,
God…waiting, waiting for me to go with Him.

Walking with my Savior, I go on through and see…
Everything I ever thought it would be.

Courtney Barnes, Grade 6
Linton-Stockton Elementary School, IN

Home

Home is where the heart is.
Home is where you spend most of your days.
Being with your family.
That is home to me.
Home is where the heart is.
If your heart is there it's home.

Allison Kinkelaar, Grade 6
Rochester Middle School, IL

Hope Is

If hope could be a color
it would be blue as bright as the sky

If hope could be a taste
it would taste just like fresh-baked cookies

If hope could be a smell
it would be like a home-baked apple pie

If hope could be a sound
it would be the sound of a nice breeze

If hope could be a feeling
it would be a hug from a dear friend

If hope could be an animal
it would be a fluffy puppy

Nikolas McCoy, Grade 4
St Agnes School, IL

The Stormy Night
Thunder lightning, boom crash!
The deep dark night engulfs my room
The tree branch falls and hits a wire
Then something!
A flash of light then nothing!
My door flies open a…
boggart flies out then,
rain hits the window, and I faint.
Ben Drake, Grade 4
Lincoln Elementary School, IL

Homework
H orrifying!
O h so wrong!
M eddling into playtime!
E at my homework Max!!!
W ork
O h how can it be!!!!!!!
R eading
K ill homework!!!!!!!!
Michaela Shelton, Grade 5
Morgan Elementary School, IN

Friends
Friends are funny.
They're like a sweet bowl of honey.
When you mix them all together,
They're as good as perfect weather.
Everybody needs a friend
'Cuz they'll be with you 'til the end.
Julia Zmuda, Grade 5
Seton Catholic School, IL

Sun and Moon
Sun
bright, big
shining, blinding, watching
yellow, rays, white, craters
revolving, exploring, rotating
small, cheesy
Moon
Erick Seaver, Grade 6
Milan Middle School, IN

Cheese
Cheese
I like cheese
But not with peas
People eat it overseas
There are many different kinds
This is one that comes to mind
Cheddar cheese
Pepper Jack Cheese makes you sneeze
Aa-choo
Meranda Jester, Grade 5
Lincoln Trail Elementary School, IN

Brains
Smart
Hardworking, intelligent
Studying, reading, writing
Honor roll, summer school
Whining, failing, uncaring
Lazy, unintelligent
Stupid
Matthew Bauer, Grade 6
Sacred Heart School, IL

Garden
Leaves of velvet,
Roots of silk,
Flowers pure,
White as milk,

Apples red,
I never tread.
My trip to the garden
Mariah said,

Trunks of might,
What a sight,
Berries blue,
Saying "pick me too."

The rain does drop
The sun does shine,
But the garden,
It is not mine

It is for anyone
Who does stop by,
I hope they'll feel
The same as I.
Mariah Sitler, Grade 5
Tri Elementary School, IN

True Friends
What is a friend?
Is she someone who is there for you?
Someone encouraging and kind?
Is she someone who helps you?
Will she lift you up when you're down?
Is she understanding and forgiving?
Someone advising but not critical?
Yes. A friend…
Advises but is not critical;
Understands and forgives;
Lifts you up when you're down;
Helps you;
Encourages and is kind;
Is there for you…
My friends are true friends.
Anna Green, Grade 6
Rochester Middle School, IL

My Dogs
Boomer is his name
He likes to play with Bandit
Bandit is so fat
Alex Bromberek, Grade 6
Heritage Grove Middle School, IL

A Wolf's Life
Wolves are ferocious.
Wolves eat many kinds of meat.
Wolves are lightning fast.
Kevin Hessenauer, Grade 5
St Jacob Elementary School, IL

My Fantasy World
I am alone in a field,
Just outside of an old town.

A white horse is next to me,
Grazing in the tall grass.

Here it is peaceful,
Like being in heaven.

A cool storm rolls in,
A noisy train goes by.

Then, everything gets quiet,
A rainbow covers the sky.
Ali Swiger, Grade 6
Linton-Stockton Elementary School, IN

Shooting Star
A shooting star falls
Through the sky
It always makes me wonder why?
Why you walk right by
My side?
You comfort me when
I cry
I don't want to
Say goodbye…
And I'll never tell
You a lie.
Tia Rogers, Grade 6
GCMS Middle School, IL

Cars/Trucks
Cars
Fast, cool
Zooming, speeding, zipping
Gas, wheels, men, work
Hauling, working, towing
Big, tough
Trucks
Phillip Litchfield, Grade 6
St Mary Elementary School, IN

Rainy Night

Drip, drop, drip, drop,
I hear the rain getting closer.
Boom, bang, boom,
Thunder and lightning appear.
The TV goes blank.
I'm so scared I scream!
Boom, bang, boom, drip, drop, drip, drop
Kaboom!
Crick, crack, crick, crack
Hail is coming.
Ding, dong, ding, dong
Spring is at the door.

Rebecca Lepant, Grade 4
Country Meadow Elementary School, IN

Got Milk?

My mom made some French toast
Of course I would get the most
Once it's done, put some sugar on top
Carry it to the table, make sure it won't drop
It will go great with a tall
Glass of milk for all
Got Milk?

Paige Price, Grade 5
Levan Scott Academy, IN

Christmas Wishes*

M ay you
E njoy the show
R ewind a lot of movies
R ead over Christmas
Y ank your gifts open

C reate a snowman
H ave heavy gifts
R ide your four-wheeler
I nherit lots of money
S uck on candy canes
T oss snowballs
M ake hot chocolate
A ttack your family with snowballs
S ing many songs

Zachary Fiechter, Grade 4
Adams Central Elementary School, IN
*Dedicated to my pen pal's Christmas break

Love

Love is a game, a play, an illusion.
Love can be strong, and weak.
Love can come in many forms,
Love can merrily mean, compassion for one another.
But, one thing I know is everyone deserves it.
But sometimes,
they don't receive it

Frances Foley, Grade 6
Jefferson Jr High School, IL

Death

What is death?
Does anyone know?
I guess it's a part of life's flow.

People must come and go.
People must go away.
That's what happens each and every day.

It's hard to break apart.
But there comes a time when you have to depart.

There will be pain sorrow and tears.
But you have to stay strong for the remaining years.

What is it death does?
Does anyone know?

I guess the answer is just stay strong and let go.

Iyesha Ferguson, Grade 4
Universal School, IL

Puppies

Puppies can be big or small,
They like to frolic in your house.
Throw it, and they will fetch a ball,
They have even been known to chase a mouse.

When someone calls,
They do get wild.
Mouth wrapped around the ball,
Ungracefully running, they're quite riled.

Puppies do get dirty,
You will probably get mad.
But, with their lovely eyes so flirty,
Even on bad days, you'll not be sad.

They have a precious little face,
Wagging their tail all the time.
They're as tender as white lace,
They grow into man's best friend when they reach their prime.

Drake Robert Royal, Grade 5
GCMS Elementary School, IL

The Last Shot

The shot goes up as the ball trembles around
The other team rumbles the ground aloud
As it hits the rim and it bounces down
The other team falls to the ground
Screaming and crying goes down on the court
Too bad that one shot was just a little too short
As they get their trophy and swallow their pride
The other team congratulates and puts their differences aside

Blake Pasley, Grade 6
Rochester Middle School, IL

The Beginning of Winter

Winter is a dream
That dances through my mind
Surrounding me, enfolding me
In the softness of the white.
It can only mean winter is finally here
To cover me again.

Winter is a wild animal
That bucks and throws its white mane.
Ferocious it is, untamed it is,
Thundering blizzards and feral winds
That toss and turn
Till it finally gallops away.

Winter is a blanket of white
Covering me.
Its gentleness
Wrapping me, hibernating me
To my safe home.
Till spring shall I wake my
Thoughts once more.

Stephanie Wang, Grade 5
Steeple Run Elementary School, IL

Basketball

Basketball is my favorite sport
I like to dribble up and down the court
I can do a finger roll
And I can take it to the hole
I may be a little short

But I'm good on the court
I don't argue, I'm a good sport
Basketball is in my soul
Basketball is something I'll never let go
I protect the hole like I'm a fort.

Isaac Nasseem, Grade 5
Floyds Knobs Elementary School, IN

Sweet Dreams

This is my bed.
It comforts me at night.
When having a bad dream.
It helps me through the fright.

This is my bed.
So pretty and so clean.
My bed is a comfort to me.
I walk in my room and smile with glee.

This is my bed
Amazing as you can see.
I slide under the covers.
Trying to catch some zzz's.

Francesca Navarro, Grade 5
Our Lady of Peace School, IL

Piano Recital

Sitting nervously in the small, cramped room behind the stage,
Going over her piece in her head for the millionth time.
Straightening her dress and taking a deep breath,
Then finally walking out onto the brilliantly lit stage.
She sits down on the piano bench,
Closes her eyes,
Takes a deep breath,
And begins to play.
Slowly at first, then faster and faster,
Her fingers flying over the keys.
The music filling the room with joy, happiness, and peace,
Lifting the hearts of all who are listening,
Then gradually getting softer and slower until that beautiful music ends.
As she stands to take a bow, the audience applauds enthusiastically.
She walks back through that small, cramped room she left moments ago,
Experiencing inside herself a feeling of serenity and gratitude,
That no one can ever take away.

Elizabeth Michael, Grade 6
St. Matthew School, IL

What Happened to Summer?

The cold, the wind, its back
Last week I thought we skipped spring and went to summer
But walking to the bus stop today, I thought, "COLD, what a bummer!"
The trees and flowers were ready to bloom
But now I'm looking for warmer clothes in my room
One can only hope that it will warm up soon.
Otherwise my dad says he'll be barking at the moon.

Daniel Wiitanen, Grade 5
Bell-Graham School, IL

Ode to My Piggy Bank

You hold all my money, and sometimes you look funny.
When I put my money in you, you make weird noises like old people snores.
When you get full of my money I crack you open and it's extremely funny.
Then I will buy one of your brothers or sisters, but you will always be my favorite.
When I break them I'll just get another one, but I will only remember one — you.
That's my ode to my piggy bank.
P.S. Don't tell your brothers or sisters.

Brendon Meek, Grade 5
Morgan Elementary School, IN

Haley

Haley
Caring, funny, smart
Sister of Austin, daughter of Brian and Tracy, owner of Shania
Who loves Derek Jeter, to read mysteries, and dogs
Who feels happiness, sadness for the elderly, and excitement when I see Derek Jeter
Who fears spiders, violence, and snakes
Who needs to be confident, lose weight, and stop worrying
Who gives help to Mom and Dad, support to Austin, and time to Shania
Who would like one million dollars, a new house, and more clothes.
From Haubstadt
Wolf

Haley Wolf, Grade 6
Haubstadt Community School, IN

The Back Lake

There is one place I go with my Papaw.
Snakey Point
no sound, nothing, just us talking together.
It's a special place where we go,
when we're sad, happy, or mad.
Us catching fish always gets us in a good mood.
Grandpa shares this place with me
I hope someday I can show it to my kid or grandson.

Will Niederhaus, Grade 6
Haubstadt Community School, IN

Tricia

Tricia has always been there for me.
To be like her is all I want to be.
She is my cousin and my godmother too.
She used to ask, "Who do you like best?" and I'd shout "You!"
She used to put make-up on me and do my hair.
I can count on her to always be there.
She lives in Bedford which to me is far away.
I wish I could see her every single day.
Tricia is married and has a daughter, Elle.
When Tricia sings her voice is clear as a bell.
When I don't see her I make a big fuss.
I know nothing will ever come between us.

Mackenzie Etienne, Grade 5
Perry Central Elementary School, IN

Ode to Cayden*

He'd always make me smile,
Oh how I miss him so,
I'll always think of his cute little face,
No matter where I go.
I still miss him and I never will forget,
How he'd always smile when we put on his outfit.
The only reason I won't cry forever,
Is because I'll go to Heaven and we'll live together.

Cassidy Logsdon, Grade 5
Morgan Elementary School, IN
*Dedicated to my nephew, Cayden.

The Viper

My favorite snake is a viper.
It is as fast as a sniper.
If you run into the snake,
Make sure you can take
The ferocious bite
That gives you such fright.
Its head looks like a leaf.
Beyond your belief,
It will attack
Behind your very back.
That's why you need to look out,
Because it's lurking about.

Caleb Brown, Grade 5
North Intermediate Center of Education, IL

The Fall

Down the slide zoomed the tool man, Paul;
Funniest guy I've ever seen fall.
Off the slide he feel hard;
To the hospital I went with a card.

Chandler Klauer, Grade 5
Seton Catholic School, IL

Springtime

Winter turns from a lion ready to roar,
To springtime, a lovely bird ready to soar.
From sweet-smelling flowers and vegetable plants,
To all the scampering, scurrying animals, even the ants.
These are all signs that springtime is here.
Beavers, badgers, bluebirds, and bears,
Will come out of hibernation,
To create a new springtime sensation.
Having a ball playing in the yard with your friends,
Even riding your bike around some bends.
These are all signs that springtime is here.

Abbie Gerth, Grade 6
St Philip the Apostle School, IL

Books

Books are full of wonderful things.
Knights and dragons or shoes with springs.
Kicks your imagination into gear.
And then you soon will finally hear.
The wonderful words of books alike.
Even if you're just a tike.
Songs and pictures all are fine.
But books will give you that sort of chime.
That gets you going through the day.
Even if you're in utter dismay.

Parker Wilkinson, Grade 5
North Intermediate Center of Education, IL

If Hope Is…

If hope could be a color
it would be orange as bright as the sun.

If hope could be a taste
it would taste just like a coconut.

If hope could be a smell
it would smell just like the salty ocean water.

If hope could be a sound
it would be the ocean waves washing against the shoreline.

If hope could be a feeling
it would be a palm tree blowing at you.

If hope could be an animal
it would be a fish swimming in the sea.

Alexis Jaeger, Grade 4
St Agnes School, IL

Butterfly
Pretty butterfly.
Butterfly fly, fly away.
Up, up in the sky.
Chelsae Daily, Grade 4
Marine Elementary School, IL

Queen
There was a queen who lived in a castle.
On her coat was a tassel.
The tassel was red,
so was the hat on her head.
Now she rides and uses a lasso.
Bridgett Hamilton, Grade 5
Freeburg Elementary School, IL

Monkey
I saw a brown monkey.
He sure was fat and chunky.
He had a banana.
He lives in Montana.
He sure was a funky monkey!
Nicole Empson, Grade 6
ROWVA East Elementary School, IL

Pets
I searched the land of Bozo
for my own little pet
I found a giant Calozozo
and then a mean Muloset

The Crackle kept on blowing
I swear I flew away
The Slobby ate my Capowing
and I stepped on my Calaway

My Tolinko bit my arm
The Kippo found a barn
My mom's kicked me out of the farm
I think I like my Calocarn

Now I'm with my animals
Living in my nice barns
Snuggled against my animals
Loving all my pet charms
Aileen Chu, Grade 5
Countryside School, IL

Laughter
Laughter is in the air
Laughter is everywhere
Laughter is in the sea
Laughter is there to be
Now you can see,
Have a happy good evening
Allison Johnson, Grade 4
Martin L King Elementary School, IL

In the Summer
Ice cream melts
Kids get sun burnt
There is no homework
People go on vacation
Kids are free from teachers
Everyone likes to go swimming
Everyone likes the sand
Kids go crazy
Parents want school to start again
Kids don't want summer to end
People love to shop and sample things
Most people go to the beach
I prefer to go to the lake all day
That's my opinion
What's yours?
That's what Summer is all about
Elysa Stout, Grade 6
Rochester Middle School, IL

Burning Fire
The burning fire
It burns hotter than the sun
Burning the dry grass
Sam Lawson, Grade 5
St Jacob Elementary School, IL

My Little Snowflake
One snowflake came into my life.
Shortly after, six more snowflakes
Came into my heart.
They were all so
Furry, but, bloated looking.
I couldn't bear to wait
Till they got big like her.
I was proud of her
For being such a wonderful mom.
But then one big snowflake
Left my life early
But not my heart.
I will always love
My Siamese cat, Phoebe,
And all of her little
snowflakes…forever.
Nikki Rogers, Grade 6
Staunton Elementary School, IL

Football
Colts
Fast, awesome
Catch, throw, run
Manning, Super Bowl, defense, Urlacher
Tackled, intercept, turnover
Big, aggressive
Bears
Steven Boggs, Grade 6
Rochester Middle School, IL

Monkeys
Monkey
Brown, tiny
Swinging, squealing, eating
Loves to climb branches
Banana.
Kenzi Crowell, Grade 4
Cynthia Heights Elementary School, IN

Grandparents
Grandparents
Sweet, generous,
Loving, caring, sharing,
Extravagant, grateful,
I love my grandparents.
Kalah Reed, Grade 5
Cloverdale Middle School, IN

What Shall Happen to Thee?
As I look up in the sky
With the heavens above,
And on the ground,
A sea full of hatred and love.
I ask to thy lord,
"What shall happen to thee?"
For I should not know what will
Become of me.
Should I cling on
And hope for the best?
Or should I lay down
And take the eternal rest?
I should now know what will
Happen to me,
But I hope you live up to what you
Want to be
Khristian Jones, Grade 6
McHenry Middle School, IL

Dranadon
In the land of Dranadon
Where the fairies will dance
With a green leprechaun
Where dragons fly forevermore
When you open the door
You might see an ogre
When bugs fly
And birds sing
Where fairies can fly
On a dragon's wing
Where glorious wolves
Howl at the moon
And giant flowers
Are in bloom
In the wonderful land
Of Dranadon.
Skylar Fox, Grade 5
Tri Elementary School, IN

Is Love Really Love?

A little crush can be considered love.
You are never sure about your first crush.
Love is as gentle as a white dove.
When you have your first kiss it makes you blush.

Looking in the eyes of your desire.
When you wish to spend your whole life with him.
Make sure you're not trusting a liar.
Your love says, "You don't trust me, Kim?"

Always loving him you don't back away.
He says he loves you but you're not sure.
When he calls you, all you can say is, "Hey."
He brings you a present, a teddy bear.

You say you're not in love, ever, never.
In the end you are in love forever.

Erica Joyce Patterson, Grade 6
McHenry Middle School, IL

I Wonder

I wonder why there are wars.
I wonder how many planets are in a whole galaxy,
I wonder why people kill,
I wonder where the real dinosaurs went,
I wonder why we can't live more than 200 years,
I wonder if there are aliens,
I wonder why we can't fly,
I wonder how big the sun really is,
I wonder why we can't breathe under water,
And I wonder why volcanoes blow up.

Ihor Omelyan, Grade 6
Norman Bridge Elementary School, IL

The Flower's Troubles

A flower sits so sadly,
Her friends are wilting away.
Because they are annuals,
Never again will they play.
Now her petals turn bright brown,
The only direction she'll go is down.
Down to the soil,
Down to the earth,
Down until she gets a new birth.
But her friends will never start anew,
For yes their budding is quite through.
Her mother always loved her perennial life.
She never said it came with strife.
She didn't mind when she was hauled away,
To a vase where she would wilt someday.
So the flower decided on that sunny day,
That next year when friends came to play,
She would make a new perennial friend.
She hoped their friendship would never end.

Ellerie Baer, Grade 4
South Adams Middle School, IN

The Cabin

On a cool, damp, windy night
I lie in front of a snapping fire
I can smell the fragrance of cinnamon
I can taste the sweetness of sugar cookies
I can hear the quiet voice of the rain
Pittering and pattering on the rooftop
The marshmallows sloshing around as I
Taste the steamy chocolate touch my lips
In the cabin of peace and warmth
I suddenly drift off to sleep.

Danielle Orman, Grade 6
Linton-Stockton Elementary School, IN

Ode to a Rubber Chicken

A rubber chicken is really cool,
but when you hang around with it
you look like a fool.

When it lies around it looks dead,
but when your brothers are annoying,
you can use it to hit them upside the head.

That's why I like rubber chickens.

Cameron Smith, Grade 5
Morgan Elementary School, IN

The Fast and the Furious

I am long, thick, and chunky,
I am fat and hunky.
I live on a truck as red as an apple.
My job is very wet.

On go the lights and up goes the door.
When we arrive they open the drawer.
Out comes me to save the day.
Pull the lever twist the knob. *Shhhhhhh*

Out go the flames with a crash.
On the truck we go within a dash.
Back to the station we go in a hurry.
On goes my job with a scurry.

Matthew Ladniak, Grade 6
Our Lady of Peace School, IL

Ode to a Dodge Charger

A Dodge Charger can be black or red.
It can go so fast it throws me out of bed.
It is awesome and very loud.
If you drive one it will make you proud.
It has a noss system and uses lots of gas.
It passes through the motor and makes the cars go fast.
I hope I get one someday,
and drive it far away.

Brandon Allen, Grade 4
Morgan Elementary School, IN

A Monkey Named Bob

There once was a monkey named bob,
Who liked to eat corn on the cob.
He liked it with butter.
It made his heart flutter.
When it was gone he began to sob.

Josh Voignier, Grade 5
Floyds Knobs Elementary School, IN

Be Yourself

Do what you do,
Be what you want to be.
These are the things,
I feel inside me.
Dress how you want to dress,
Wear what you want to wear.
I would not be mad,
If you have ugly hair.
I don't care if you are short and fat,
Or tall and skinny.
No matter what you look like,
You will always be pretty.
So as you can see,
Do what you do,
And be what you want to be.

Allison Ernst, Grade 6
Westchester Middle School, IL

Frogs

Frogs are very green.
Ponds and lily pads are home.
Ribbit is the sound.

Jared Lambrecht, Grade 5
Seton Catholic School, IL

Love

Love is forever love is for all
if you don't love them they
don't love all.

Jaime Barrón, Grade 6
San Miguel School, IL

Tooth Fairy

Roses are red,
Violets are blue,
Someone is flying, but it's not you.
It is the Tooth Fairy,
with money for you.
Oh no!!!
She has broken a wing!
Somebody must sing.
Great!
Also she has some bling bling,
she brought me a new ring,
Now she is a queen!

Yazmyne Franklin, Grade 4
W E Wilson Elementary School, IN

I Am

I am an eagle
swooping down on prey
flying high above
waiting for the moment to strike
protecting my chicks
swaying where the world takes me
I am unpredictable.

Eric Pearson, Grade 6
Norman Bridge Elementary School, IL

Bees

Bees
Black, yellow
Buzzing, stinging, flying
Always working for their queen.
Busy

Jenine Abuzir, Grade 4
Universal School, IL

Goodbyes

See ya later alligator
After awhile crocodile
Bye bye butterfly
Give a hug lady bug
Be sweet parakeet
See ya soon raccoon
Take care polar bear
Out the door dinosaur
So long king kong
Adios amigos

Allie Ishmael, Grade 6
Rochester Middle School, IL

No One Knows

No one knows that inside this girl
a broken heart lies.
That behind her eyes no one knows
she cries.

She wants to believe
that they are still here.
She wants to believe that they
did not die.

The truth hurts
her so much.
She missed their
soft gentle touch.

No one knows that inside this girl
a broken heart lies.
That behind her eyes no one knows
she cries.

Mackenzie Onan, Grade 6
St Anastasia School, IL

Leah

She is nice and sweet
She had 11 children
She was Jacob's wife

Selena Rios, Grade 6
San Miguel School, IL

What Is Chocolate?

Creamy
Rich
Light brown
Makes me happy
A bar of joy
A yummy treat
Sometimes dark brown
Delectable
Sometimes in cakes
Heaven sent

That is chocolate!!!

Kelsey Chinn, Grade 5
Morgan Elementary School, IN

Sports

S occer
P owerful
O utdoors
R ough
T ough
S uper

Cody Hickey, Grade 6
Rochester Middle School, IL

She and I

I am a boy
And, she is a girl.
I like to play with toys.
She likes to play with curls.

Curtis Miller, Grade 4
Lavizzo Elementary School, IL

Grandparents

Grandparents
Special, graceful
Caring, sharing, loving
Healthy, delightful
That is why I love my grandparents!

Lindsay Robson, Grade 5
Cloverdale Middle School, IN

Swaying Pink Roses

Beautiful flowers
Swaying in the breezy wind
Pool of pink roses

Kirsten Vancura, Grade 5
Our Lady of Peace School, IL

My Mom and Dad

M y mom can help me with every subject.
O nly my mom is the best.
M y mom can take me to the park.

A ll of us go to the park.
N o one is left behind.
D oing projects is so much fun.

D ad is the best too.
A lways you are here for me.
D ad can help me with many things.

Natalia Kalamarz, Grade 4
Norman Bridge Elementary School, IL

Loved Ones

Grandparents are as funny as a bunny.
Grandparents are as grand as a duke and duchess.
They're like a bright blue balloon.
They sound like a beautiful song played by a harpist.
They love me like pie,
Grandparents are great to be by.
They smell like a bottle of perfume.
Grandparents are great.
Grandparents are great to have by my side.

Kim Vitale, Grade 5
St John of the Cross Parish School, IL

A Twinkling Memory

I twinkle above all my friends.
I can be red, purple, or clear.
It's great to see smiling faces.
I only show up once a year.

I'm always placed in the same spot.
I symbolize something Christians believe in.
I'm full of light, and very bright.
I like to make you grin.

I am as pretty as a flower.
I am a beauty.
I am a great friend with a Christmas tree.
I am a star, truly.

Anna Krcek, Grade 6
Our Lady of Peace School, IL

S P Cuddly Animals

Cuddly animals want you to hug them,
Kiss and play with them
Make them feel special
And do you know what else they like to do?
Play catch the Frisbee
They have love for you
That's why I want a cuddly animal

J.W. McBee, Grade 4
Martin L King Elementary School, IL

The Codes of Da Vinci*

The world of his own,
Shrouded in Mystery.
Made it his own.
Of Ancient History.
Left clues for his own,
On the very front cover.

The clues lead forward,
To an upcoming book.
The secrets we know,
And the secrets that hurt.

To find out what's in the next book,
You must stare at the very first hook.

Those are the only clues I can give you for now,
As I have yet to find the secret and don't know how,
But always make sure the Mona Lisa gives you a smile.

Ming Quek, Grade 6
British School of Chicago, IL
*Inspired by the book "The Da Vinci Code"

Hope

If hope could be a color
it would be blue as the ocean waves.

If hope could be a taste
it would be as tart as fruit punch.

If hope could be a smell
it would be home-baked cookies.

If hope could be a sound
it would be as joyful as a trumpet.

If hope could be a feeling
it would be like winning a championship.

If hope could be an animal
it would be a tiger as strong as steel.

Jordan Benavides, Grade 4
St Agnes School, IL

Summer

When school is out,
Kids run about,
They play all different sports,
They play on big courts,
At night kids catch bugs,
When they are tired they lay on rugs
They may not have homework,
but kids may have yard work,
When school is in,
the children play again.

Kyle Kieffer, Grade 5
North Intermediate Center of Education, IL

My Parents

I love my dad
He is so rad
I love my mom
She is the bomb
My parents are so cool
They're better than school
When I pretend to be sick
They know it's a trick
So they still send me to school
Even though it's not cool
Then later on
Around dawn
They give me cash
If I take out the trash
I love my parents!!

Veronica Garcia, Grade 6
San Miguel School, IL

Popcorn

P owerfully good
O verwhelming
P opping
C asual
O utstanding
R eminds me of good times
N eed for it

Sullivan Friebus, Grade 4
Lincoln Elementary School, IL

Basketball Rocks

Basketball so
FUN!
But you
RUN!
You can be
fast or
you can be
last.

Rachel Bilau, Grade 4
Marine Elementary School, IL

Sister of Mine

You are my sister,
You are my friend,
I look up to you,
When I need a hand.
I look up to you,
And what do I see,
A beautiful face staring back at me,
You are always there for me,
I am always there for you,
We're two of a kind,
And I am just like you.

Krista Jost, Grade 6
Haubstadt Community School, IN

Music

The soft melody fills my ears,
Her voice is singing on key,
This song is my favorite,
It fills me with glee.
The band plays the notes smoothly,
As if the notes are gliding across ice,
One note is held for eight beats,
The grand finale.

Beth Condon, Grade 5
St John of the Cross Parish School, IL

Time

Time goes fast
Twenty-four hours
Never last
The Big Ben tower

Time flies
When you're having fun
It ascends into the sky
The day is done.

Ryan Valesh, Grade 5
Bell-Graham School, IL

Buzzing Bees

Bees
Mean, little,
Stinging, buzzing, flying,
Busy bee's produce honey
Colorful

Hana Khatib, Grade 4
Universal School, IL

Football/Beach Volleyball

Football
Fast, challenging
Punting, throwing, tackling
Helmet, pads, sunglasses, hat
Spiking, diving, serving
Fast-paced, hard-to-keep-up
Beach volleyball

Dalton Gee, Grade 6
St Mary Elementary School, IN

Secret

He had a secret
Oh yes he did
A little secret
I did not know
Until that day
He did not tell
A single person
Except myself

Ben Carter, Grade 6
St Pius X Catholic School, IN

Fish

A fish in the sea
Having lots of fun today
How perfect is life

Sophia Spyker, Grade 5
Tri Elementary School, IN

Christmas Celebration

Christmas
Joyful emotional
Caring sharing forgiving
Music mistletoe wishes love
Lasting expecting never ending
Peaceful dreaming
Celebration

Patric Hruswicki, Grade 4
Norman Bridge Elementary School, IL

Spring

The sun is shining
The snow is crying
Winter's gone
The shiny ice on the pond is gone
The bears are yawning
They are clawing
The snow is going
The grass is growing
School is out
You won't hear me pout

Spencer Graham, Grade 4
Chrisney Elementary School, IN

Seashell

A small patient seashell,
Crying, waiting for the tide to come in
To come and cleanse his skin
To come and take him off this shore
For he cannot bare it anymore
Hoping the tide will come soon
Before, out comes the moon
So he can find his family and friends
This is how the poem ends

Dash Holland, Grade 6
St Pius X Catholic School, IN

Forests

Pine trees and rose bushes.
Leaves and a bud.
Big tall pine trees.
Animals playing in the mud.
Raccoons and skunks.
Squirrels need food and gather the best.
No cars. No cars.
In the forest animals never rest.

Jessica Barton, Grade 4
St Robert Bellarmine School, IL

Charred Marshmallows

Charred marshmallows smelling like smoke,
A gooey monster once stuck in the flame,
Riding rigorously right from my stick,
Going to get gooey if not gone,
Charred marshmallows are not yummy.

Michael Sullivan, Grade 6
St Pius X Catholic School, IN

Summer

I can't wait for summer
When school days are all done
There will be no more homework
The days will be filled with fun in the sun.

We will hang up the backpacks
Put the home links away
And just enjoy each and every day

Swimming in the summer beats homework any day
Put me on a tennis court and watch me play

On cloudy days my favorite time is spent
With my grandpa and a fishing line
When I need to feel the wind in my hair
I will hop on the jet ski and have not a care

While summer is the best of times
Fall will come and school bells will chime

I guess a new school year is not so bad
Considering all the summer fun I had

Chris Lucatorto, Grade 5
Bell-Graham School, IL

Sisters

Sisters, sisters, sisters
Tall sisters
Short sisters
Mean sisters, annoying sisters, out of this world sisters
Loving sisters, awesome sisters, caring sisters
Last of all, best of all my sister!!

Taylor Wong, Grade 5
St Jude Catholic School, IN

Books

Everyone likes books,
Books can be fun
Books can be adventurous
Books are much more.
In a book you can float in a hot air balloon
Or you can hunt for buried treasure.
The number one thing you can't forget
On all your reading adventures,
Is your imagination!

Natalie Schaeffer, Grade 5
St John of the Cross Parish School, IL

Battles and Ballads

The knights in shining armour
Rode down on noble steeds
To fight and win the battle
On one midwinter's eve.

With the battle won with not one loss
They decided to take their leave
As the snow began to fall around
On one midwinter's eve.

They marched on by the teller-of-tales
To hear a ballad of their knightly feat
With words meant to be seen and be heard
As the listeners caught on to the beat.

Sara Heiny, Grade 6
Belzer Middle School, IN

Black

Black is the color of my fingernails.
Black is the color you see when everything else fails.
Black is the color of some people's souls.
Is black a color? No one really knows!
Black is the color of blackberry things.
Black's the color when a blackbird sings.
When you buy something Nike, the sign's usually black.
If you want life insurance you should call Aflac.
The chalkboard is black. It writes very well.
My favorite color is black. I think it's swell!

Savannah Dickerson, Grade 5
Staunton Elementary School, IN

Scaring, Slithering, and Sliding

My fangs are as sharp as knives.
They are always filled with poison.
I strike fear into all wives,
For the children she doesn't want me to bite.
I slither on my belly,
Looking for food.
When I eat my prey, I have my own deli.
My scales aren't slimy, but smooth.
When I open my mouth, it's a gaping hole.
I eat my prey live,
My mouth opened like a bowl.
Soon I will have a large lump.
I strike like lightning.
The mouse does not know,
He is in my sighting,
And soon he will have to go.
I strike fear into everyone,
People big and small,
People fear me by the ton,
Thinking I'll attack them there,
There, and there.

Bill Martinello, Grade 6
Our Lady of Peace School, IL

Dog

I love my dog.
My dog loves me.
We play together
with a ball
and my dog always falls
when we play with the balls.

Andrew Sliger, Grade 4
John Simatovich Elementary School, IN

Pizza the Greatest Food Ever

I love Pizza
At the fair
Give me anything I don't care
Pepperoni, sausage, mushroom more
Just don't drop it on the floor
I love pizza every day
I eat it like a horse would with hay
Give me money it's not cheap
pile it all in a heap
Pizza is the greatest of them all
Order me some but not a small

Gabe Ferguson, Grade 6
Rochester Middle School, IL

Hockey Stick

This is my hockey stick.
It is very tall.
So if you want one.
Give it your all.

This is my hockey stick
So get your own.
It is orange and black
So don't ask me to loan.

This is my hockey stick.
When I shoot
And when I score,
I give a big hoot.

Patrick Boniecki, Grade 5
Our Lady of Peace School, IL

The Graveyard

I see tombstones,
And under them are bones

Trees blow in the breeze
And falling leaves

I don't like going there
Because I get very scared

One day I know I'll be in a casket
And my heart will still be lit

Grace Tally, Grade 6
Rochester Middle School, IL

Ode to My Freckles

You're tiny you're on my face
Sometimes you're a disgrace
I wash my face you're still there
As if you're taunting and haunting me at the same time.
My mom and dad say they're so adorable.
If they're so adorable why do people make fun of me why!
I wonder why we have freckles.
Are they just there for decoration or maybe for admiration who knows?
What I do know is that
I hate my freckles!

Jordan Stewart, Grade 5
Morgan Elementary School, IN

Wela/Grandma

Looking out my window I see nothing but the rain.
Trying not to forget the memories,
    Trying to forget the pain.

My window looks real gloomy because there is fog in the view.
Still trying not to forget your image,
    Trying not to rid me of you.

I know you think I lie,
    But what I say is true.
And if it takes the rest of my life,
    I'll never forget the memories of you.

You helped me through life's ups and downs,
    You turned my frowns upside down.
And though you may not be here with me,
    I'd like to thank you for everything that you have done for me.

Victoria Santiago, Grade 6
Michael Grimmer Middle School, IN

Life as a Designer Vuitton

I am high quality, expensive, and cute
I carry all of your loot.
You will find me at the mall, or at a fine purse store,
And when I carried too much, I was tore.

I travel all day, and sometimes all night
I carry all of your things, but that's all right
I am so smooth at your touch,
But my back hurts from dropping, and such.

I love being carried around
I love the massage I get from the vibration of a cell phone sound.
When I finally get to relax,
I know yesterday is over, and another day's passed.

My life is critical, clumsy, and crazy,
But then it's relaxing, like the sweet smell of daisies
And since I am the best of them all,
You will always see me glistening in the window, at the mall!

Becky Pavesich, Grade 6
Our Lady of Peace School, IL

Exercise

Why? Why don't people exercise as much as they should,
What does the word "exercise" mean when it comes to mind?
Well if you really think about it this helps us stay alive.

To exercise you can walk, jog, run, skip, anything that will keep you on your feet.
But another thing to help you exercise right is to eat the right type of food.

In my definition "exercise" is a way of keeping a healthy brain, heart, and muscles in your body.
Can you ever have too much exercising?

To answer this question yes, but then again no. Too much exercising can hurt your muscles.
But it can also help your muscles become stronger.

I love to exercise personally because if I don't exercise while I'm young
my body will be weak and I won't be able to do as much.

My opinion is that people should do this more often than watching TV,
sleeping more than necessary, eating chocolate that is a type of junk food
which refers back to eating healthy.

I love to exercise.

Alleah Moore, Grade 6
Delphi Academy of Chicago, IL

Ambrosia

Ambrosia
Happy, nice, kind
Sister of Austin, step-sister of Ryan
Daughter of Richard and Patricia, step-daughter of Ricky
Master of Garfield and Dutches.
Who loves to read murder and mystery books, rock climbing, going to the movies, loves all animals, and loves math.
Who feels compassion for Chinese foods, hyperness, and loves kittens.
Who fears failing subjects, heights, and waking in the dark.
Who needs helps in literature, new clothes, and a new blue nano iPod.
Who gives things away, Garfield and Dutches new toys, and helps people in math.
Who would like more Japanese and Chinese things, a Shih Zue puppy when I grow up, go to Hawaii, China, and Japan some day.
Haubstadt
Ambrosia

Amber Blaize, Grade 6
Haubstadt Community School, IN

Nature Girl

The doors of the school swing open and the sun reveals the outside world. A cool wind wafts through the school yard making my hair swing into my mouth. The irregular shaped puddles gleam in the sun's ray to resemble an attractive painting professionally painted and is transferred into the hands of a child who wildly splashes blue paint upon it. Trees turning green in the budding process, flowers opening their beauty as well as their scents, and the shrubs' renewal from a long winters rest paint a picture of spring. My feet skid across the sidewalk while the cars vanish through puddles as the engines roar so the birds sing. Each wind whistles a melody. Harmony has created nature's song. Sit still and listen. The ground squishes as I enter onto the grass. After a long shower the earth withdraws a fragrance of damp air mixing with the earthy tone. Drops of rain slide and slip off the leaves where they now reside. Alone in nature's blanket reminds you of two things. Peace and freedom. Gazing at the freedom flag that's waving so high. Red white and blue colors flap lightly in the calm breeze now stirring. Knowing that you can do whatever you please while others sit. Sit and wait for the day to come when they can do what they please. For some, they'll never see the day. A faint breeze still blows which fills my body with a refreshed joy. Everything is growing and returning from the dead. My attitude reflects the outside world.

Meghan McHugh, Grade 5
Ranch View Elementary School, IL

Boys and Girls

Boys
Cool, bigheaded
Playing, running, laughing
Football, baseball, basketball, softball
Watching, skipping, joking
Funny, smart
Girls

Alyssa Vodacek, Grade 6
St Matthew School, IL

My Kitty, Katie

I have a kitty,
her name is Katie.
And if you ask,
she walks like a lady.
I love her so much
she's kind of tubby.
But that doesn't matter
because she's my BUBBY!

Bailey Carpenter, Grade 4
Marine Elementary School, IL

4 X 4 Relay

I am the last handoff
It is up to me to be the big shot
Running on the track
Against five other people
I fight for the win
Coming around the turn
I am in first place
Through the finish line.

Jesse Wooden, Grade 6
Rochester Middle School, IL

Indiana

A state that grows corn and beans,
Has Indiana beach and Lake James,
Has lots of sight and sounds,
Campgrounds and fancy hotels,
The Indy 500 and go cart races,
Snow and sun, 90° F and -9° F,
But most importantly,
Both black and white,
Live freely in Indiana!

Anna Finley, Grade 5
Hendry Park Elementary School, IN

Kites

Kites
Red, colorful, diamond
Blowing, flying, soaring
Always up in the air
Blowing

Abdalrahman Kort, Grade 4
Universal School, IL

Willy

There once was a boy named Willy
Who always gave me wet willes
He'd say hey come here
I'd be filled with fear
And I'd say are you crazy or silly

Zach Whittaker, Grade 5
Arlington Elementary School, IN

The Messy Desk

The desk is messy.
It's so messy nothing's found.
So keep your desk clean.

Riley McClenning, Grade 4
Coal City Intermediate School, IL

Christmas

Christmas
Happiness joyful
Giving playing sharing
Freedom family forgiving loving
Caring remember memories
Awesome careful
Wonderful

Joshua Santos, Grade 4
Norman Bridge Elementary School, IL

Riddle of Nature

Many colorful suns
Shining in velvety luminescence
Only as tall as a candle
Opening with no reticence

Delicately bending
Along with the wind
Possessing a sweet scent
Which it likes to lend

The power of their color
Which cups toward the sun
Attracts bees and other bugs
And cheers everyone

What is it?
(A daffodil)

Chelsea Edwards, Grade 5
Countryside School, IL

Insects

Insects
Fuzzy, wuzzy
Crawling across the ground
Stretching their tiny little legs
Creepy

Karly Prichard, Grade 5
Adams Central Elementary School, IN

The Forest

The forest is nice
It has lots of animals
Like deer and nice mice

Olivia Robinson, Grade 4
Goodfield Elementary School, IL

Science versus Social Studies

Science
Interesting, fun
Experimenting, studying, learning
Animals, plants, people, culture
Exploring, researching, learning
Adventurous, exciting
Social studies

Natalie Lopez, Grade 5
Our Lady of Peace School, IL

Fading Fantasy

My smile fades…
A tear rolls down my cheek,
I can't speak as I see them
Strolling hand-in-hand.
Together. Forever.
And there's nothing I can do about it.
I bury my face in my hands,
My friends shake me by my shoulders.
Their voices sound so far away…
I'll get over him.
Won't I?
Won't I?

Sarah Broad, Grade 5
Steeple Run Elementary School, IL

Pant Trouble

I went to school one day
But, something was horribly wrong
It seems that I've forgotten,
Something very long

All the children laughed at me
All the teachers stared
I don't know what it is
But can it be repaired?

So I asked my friend what happened
And then she pointed down
I had forgotten my pants!
I felt like a clown

So here's the thing my friend
I've stayed away from school
I study in my room
Where I can't be such a fool

Abby Stombres, Grade 5
Bell-Graham School, IL

My Dogs, My Best Friends

My dogs are always there when there is nobody.
My dogs, my best friends.
They are always there when I am mournful.
My dogs, my best friends.
They are always there when I want to frolic.
My dogs, my best friends.
Lets just say they are going to be here until the very end!
My dogs, my best friends.

Rebekah Greer, Grade 6
Perry Central Elementary School, IN

Drug Free

Stand up against drugs for you and me.
Drugs can hurt you even if you have a few.
It is no joke if you smoke.
Your body will dry out just like a drought.
If you're smart, you won't start.
So just say no to your friend or foe.
If you stay drug free, just think how much more you can be.
If you wear red, you won't turn out to be dead.
So be a rookie; instead of drugs have a cookie.
Drug free is the way to be!

Jorie Bollman, Grade 6
St Thomas the Apostle Elementary School, IL

Nature at Night

The moon appears over the trees
Beavers sleep and so do bees
The cool night mist comes settling down
And covers everything on the ground
The owl's silhouette blocks out the light
Scaring everything in the night
Coyotes howl up to the moon
For dawn will be coming quite soon
Up to the moon the coyotes howl
Just before the midnight prowl
The rabbits get scared and hop into their dens
And stay there until the night hunt ends

Abigail Steck, Grade 6
Rochester Middle School, IL

Fast Food

Why do you want a large fry?
I feel hungry.
Why do you feel hungry?
I didn't have breakfast.
Why didn't you have breakfast?
I was driving to Florida.
Why are you driving to Florida?
I'm going on vacation.
Why are you going on vacation?
I feel like it. Why do you want this information?
Fine, here's your food.

Alex Cecchi, Grade 5
Bell-Graham School, IL

Be One with the Horse

Be one with the horse be one with the sky.
Be one with the horse and you can fly.
Be one with the horse
While flying through space.
Be one with the horse
And you can race.
Be one with the horse
Don't stay on the side.
Be one with the horse
And you can ride.
Be one with the horse
Then splash in the bay.
Be one with the horse
And you can play.
Be one with the horse
Be one with the sun.
Be one with the horse
And you can have fun.
Be one with the horse be one with the sky.
Be one with the horse and you can fly.

Mattie Eckerstrom, Grade 4
Central Elementary School, IL

Ode to My Mom

She's always right beside me.
I can always count on her on basketball season.
She jumps and yells. She's always nice.
She disciplines me when she should.
But at night she kisses me good night.
But she will always be my best buddy.

Grant Kelley, Grade 5
Morgan Elementary School, IN

The Sorrow

One chilly fall night while sleeping
My Aunt Jamie got a phone call
Her caring husband had died
Aunt Jamie knew her love was gone
My Uncle Tim left this earthly world
Her heart sank

When I hear that story
I just want to break down and cry
When I hear that story
I can see the sorrow in everyone's watery eyes
I wish he was still here today
But now he is up far, far away

In a special place called Heaven
Driving his favorite truck
I never got to meet him
But I wish I would have
The stories that I have heard
Make me think he was a 10 on a fun day

Jackson Bohnert, Grade 6
Linton-Stockton Elementary School, IN

Grateful

Tears don't feel no more like the skies burst open.
Tongue no longer bleeds from biting back words unspoken
And it seems to me that life could finally be turning for the better.
Seems to me that in changing for the better, as I read old letters from the past
I have to sit and wonder how long to last.
This period of finally being free, so blissfully happy.
Not questioning powers that be for I have not reason to doubt myself anymore.
There's no reason to question what's in store for you or me.
It's possible that God has finally seen how sorrowful life has been for a city full of lost teens.
With no hope, no minds, and no hearts left to give and nothing but empty faces and souls full of cold dark places.
Who while paying for their parents' sin by the age of ten Do realize that there is nothing here but pipe dreams left to live.
Has someone finally given us all a break?
What have I done to deserve this? What have you done to deserve this? Could it be a mistake?
Then again what has anyone ever done at all to deserve such fates?
Maybe I'm just lucky, maybe you're just lucky.
I'm grateful — are you?

Jaila Watson, Grade 6
St Catherine of Siena School, IN

Summer Dream

Sitting on the porch swing listening to the birds sing
Sun shining in on me then all the little birdies flee
And then silence arrives it makes me feel so alive
I smell the sweet freshness of the air the wind is getting stronger blowing through my hair
The birds come back and fly around then the sun decides to go down
Purple, orange, red, and pink it makes you really, really think
As darkness closes in on you you don't think what to do
You just look up at the sky wishing you could fly
To touch the stars see what they are
Sit on the moon ah, you must go in soon
So you take one last look take everything you took
The night sky fades and goes and you do the same as you close
The screen door behind you you're gone too

Rachel Mason, Grade 5
Hendry Park Elementary School, IN

Summer

Can you feel the wind blowing through your hair as you race across the grass in your bare feet?
The beautiful green leaves on the trees glisten overhead; flowers bloom in gardens nearby.

This is summer: with the warm sun beating down on you,
Diving into the pool when you become too hot, drinking cold water as you escape into the air-conditioning.

Doesn't winter leave you hanging out in the cold? You wait for long months and never seem to reach warmth,
Thinking that on the other side of the Earth it is warm as sunlight streams through the windows.

Why does winter have to last so long as summer seems to pass away like the minutes of your birthday?
Can't they switch and let us sit in the warmth of the sun? Why can't we just capture summer and make it stay?

At least it's not winter all year, and fall and spring are not too bad.
But what is a year without summer? I can't even imagine.

If we believe, we can keep the warmth in our hearts and minds, just not our bodies.
Just think through winter that summer is coming; it's just a few months away.

Ali Julian, Grade 6
Immaculate Conception School, IL

Let Your Mind Run Free!

Run through the meadow, run through the trees
so then everybody may see that you are running free.
The meadow shall be your cover
and the trees your lover,
but I shall always believe.
I do have have a free mind, I do believe in you,
but sometimes I think you should just love me too.
I love the way you think of letting your mind run free,
but if you ever get lost remember to just believe in ME!
Remember to be careful when you let your mind run free!

Briana Lampert, Grade 6
St Lawrence School, IN

Sneaker

Shoes come in many different sizes and colors.
You can get new or old
You can get heel sneakers or sandals
You can have stripes and flowers and so much more
So have a great day

Donasia Tolliver, Grade 4
Martin L King Elementary School, IL

Lacrosse

L ots of fun!
A lways hard, but good exercise!
C ooperating with your team is important!
R unning is a huge part of the sport.
O utside or inside is where you play.
S hooting is essential to the game!
S cores don't really matter if you are having fun!
E ventually, you will become a great player!

Hope DiPaolo, Grade 6
Sacred Heart School, IL

Yogi/Jo

Yogi
Playful, swift
Licking, begging, guarding
Stuffed rabbit, kennel, fake duck, food bowl
Sleeping, barking, smiling
Curly-haired, slobbery
Jo

Ben Tackett, Grade 6
St Mary Elementary School, IN

Tinker Bell

You flutter and fly
In Neverland's sky
You're small but oh so feisty
And your enemy is Captain Hookie
You're funny and look adorable at the same time
And you help people fly
With just a little fairy dust
Anyone can fly

Mary Grace Gehm, Grade 5
Morgan Elementary School, IN

Real Warmth in Winter

Red is the color of warm wool slippers
on little feet,
running down the stairs.
Shiny red ornaments,
peppermint candy canes, above a fire.
Big red bows
and crumpled up wrapping paper on the floor.
Red is the color of mittens, and homemade scarfs,
sleds sliding down big hills,
and shovels clearing driveways.
Little red noses and cheeks
wrapped in a blanket
by a hot fire.
Red is the color of big heavy boots sitting in a puddle
by the door.

Anna Pezanoski-Cohen, Grade 6
Alexander G. Bell Elementary School, IL

What a Night

What a night
My brother and I had a fight
And now my lamp will not give light
Such a fight that dark night,
Made me wonder why my lamp will not give light
What a night.

Hillary Hubert, Grade 5
Perry Central Elementary School, IN

The Person I Love

My mom is so nice.
She doesn't like mice.
She always makes me dinner.
She is happy when I'm a winner.
My mom loves me so much.

She also makes me lunch.
She sometimes makes brunch.
When I take a shower,
She doesn't want me to take an hour.
She loves me so much.

She sometimes gets mad,
Or she is sometimes glad.
She likes to relax in pools,
Because it cools her off.
I love my mom so much.

When I am sick
She takes care of me.
When it's my birthday she buys me presents.
She sometimes takes naps.
She sometimes claps.
I love my mom so much.

Garrett Bundy, Grade 4
Hoagland Elementary School, IN

Name

C ool and weird
H as lots of hair that makes me a hippie.
R eally annoying
I nteresting
S uper cool

B uddy to everyone
E njoys playing football
L ikes the show *Full House*
L ikes to play guitar.

Chris Bell, Grade 5
GCMS Elementary School, IL

Alarm Clock

This is my alarm clock
It is digital and black
It plays the radio stations
It keeps me on track

This is my alarm clock
It wakes me up on time
It will never be out of style
I'll always wake up to the chime

This is my alarm clock
It stares at me with eyes
Every day I rely on it
I just hope it doesn't tell lies

Melissa Steinken, Grade 5
Our Lady of Peace School, IL

Baseball

I like baseball. It is fun!
It makes my body jump
into a bun.
It's not easy.
It's not hard.
Baseball will
make you want
to run a yard.

Tristan Daily, Grade 4
Marine Elementary School, IL

My Special Day

Today is my special day
I want all my way
If I don't get what I like
I might need to pick a fight

OK maybe I don't want to pick a fight
It's all right if I don't get what I like
It doesn't all have to be my way,
Even though it's my birthday.

Brandon Huff, Grade 5
Bell-Graham School, IL

At the Circus

The smell of cotton candy
Floats through the air
The clowns running around on stilts
Give me a little scare

I'm feeling a little dizzy
Those rides go really fast
I really love this feeling
I hope that it lasts

I hear talk and laughter
People are all around
Over there, a lost bracelet
Has been found

Now it's growing dark
Everyone is going away
Even though I leave
I wish I could stay

Haley Schueler, Grade 5
Butterfield School, IL

Winter

It is the season of delight,
My favorite time of year.
Snowflakes are falling in the night,
Snowdrifts I do not fear.

I bundle up, outside I go,
To play and run around.
Rolling big balls of snow,
That has fallen onto the ground.

Building snowmen is so much fun,
I'll need a big black hat.
We hope they don't melt in the sun,
We like them round and fat.

I like to drink hot chocolate,
After I play outdoors.
I go in my warm cozy house,
And finish doing chores.

Tanner Butler, Grade 4
Adams Central Elementary School, IN

Mrs. Cox

M y best friend
R ocks my world
S o totally cool

C razy
O riginally great
e **X** cellent

Abby McGuire, Grade 4
GCMS Elementary School, IL

The Friend I Wish I Knew

My friend is now in heaven
I miss her very dearly
She's died of cancer
She used to be a dancer
Though now she prances in heaven
My friend is now in heaven
I'm glad I know she's there
I wish I knew her better
'Cause now I'm wetter than ever
My friend is now in heaven
When I received a letter in the mail
inviting me to her funeral
I prayed and cried thinking Why
My friend is now in heaven
It's Christmas time
I'm at school thinking of her
and how I didn't say a word
My friend is now in heaven
I know it's time to just let go
and think
at least I know she's now in heaven

Heather Knight, Grade 6
South Spencer Middle School, IN

My Dog

My dog likes to wag his tail.
When he plays with a shovel and pail.
When he played in the sand,
I said, "Here, take my hand."
But, he was too busy eating a snail.

Taniesha Dukes, Grade 4
Lavizzo Elementary School, IL

Cardinal

Cardinal
Beautiful, small,
Flying, landing, eating
A wonderful state bird
Singing, perching, standing
Amazing, colorful
Redbird

Justin Rusk, Grade 4
Dixie Bee Elementary School, IN

Red Rocks

Red is the flag
That waves in the air.
Red is the 4th of July
When fireworks are in the sky.
Red is Santa's suit on Christmas Eve.
Red roses bloom in the spring.
In the fall red leaves fall.
Red is the best color of all.

John Batchelor, Grade 5
Staunton Elementary School, IN

I Am

I am a boy who loves basketball.
I wonder if I will make it to the NBA.
I hear I will make it to the NBA.
I see myself in the NBA.
I want to go to the NBA.
I am a boy who loves basketball.

I pretend I can slam on Yao Ming in the NBA.
I feel I will make it to the NBA.
I touch the NBA rim.
I worry about the NBA.
I cry if I don't make it to the NBA.
I am a boy who loves basketball.

I understand the NBA rules.
I say I will make it to the NBA.
I dream about going to the NBA.
I try to make all my free throws.
I hope I make it to the NBA.
I am a boy who loves basketball.

Derrick Tennant, Grade 4
Levan Scott Academy, IN

Basketball

I love basketball.
It's my favorite sport.
It's cool doing ticks up and down the court.
When I dribble I feel the adrenaline rush.
People say I'm so good.
I wish I could go to the NBA I wish I could.
And that's how I feel about basketball.

Alanté Massie, Grade 4
Lincoln Elementary School, IL

Wildfire

Poisonous flowers like vivid leaves of fall,
climbs up trees like a naughty child,
leaving behind nothing at all.
Carried by the wind and grasses,
through the prairies, through forests.
Leaping gracefully over the stream and passes,
growing larger, bursting with pride.
An enemy on nature's side?

Robin Wang, Grade 6
Thayer J Hill Middle School, IL

My Favorite Sport

I'm up to bat I hit the ball.
I run the bases.
I score a point for my team.
When I hit a home run I run around the bases
And my team wins the ball game.
That's my favorite sport baseball.

Jesse Koonce, Grade 5
North Intermediate Center of Education, IL

Sour/Sweet

Sour
Tart, puckery
Unsweetened, acidic, pungent
Tangy, vinegary, syrupy, candied
Honeyed, saccharine, lovable
Amiable, agreeable
Sweet

Harrison Goldenberg, Grade 5
Frank H Hammond Elementary School, IN

Clay Pots

C lay pots are made by Indians.
L ong ago, they traded them for goods.
A ll of them are artifacts.
Y ou see clay pots at museums.

P ainted pots tell stories,
O range, red, yellow, brown all the colors can be found.
T ens of thousands of pots were made.
S ome are still around today.

Zach Meehling, Grade 5
Freeburg Elementary School, IL

Phoenix

Phoenix
Was angry.
Sneakily flying through the sunset sky.
Which watched him
While guarding it with its ruby red hands
Silence was spread on the land
As it grabbed mouths shut.

Phoenix
Was blood.
A drop of blood falling from the bloody sky.
For it tied him down on the grass.
Darkness rested on his eyes.
A bandage covering the phoenix.
It laid there dead.

Phoenix
Was up.
It sprung in the air.
Phoenix had a new beginning.
Phoenix was a new phoenix.
It flew-flew-flew!

Lily Fayz, Grade 5
British School of Chicago, IL

Halloween

Halloween is when the ghosts and goblins
Come out to play.
Don't let them get your candy
Or else they'll run away.

Cole Hartman, Grade 4
McKenney-Harrison Elementary School, IN

The Light

When your time has come you will know
Because you'll see a beautiful show
The Light you will see just that day
You just have to realize
That that's the way
When God lets you in that golden gate
Look around…

that is your fate.
Aaron Clapper, Grade 5
Bell-Graham School, IL

Basketball

B ounce passes
A lways listen to your coach
S hoot the ball
K eep control over the ball
E veryone do a lay-up
T echnical fouls aren't good
B all hogs aren't fun
A lways try to steal the ball
L ook to pass
L isten to the ref
Mary Kim Tadda, Grade 5
Seton Catholic School, IL

Chocolate

Yummy rich dark chocolate
little bite size squares
put one in your mouth
let the gooey sticky chocolate
melt in your mouth
running down your throat
so you get another.
Faith Valentine, Grade 5
Hendry Park Elementary School, IN

Let's See

Let's see
see the sun so bright
The sun that makes the
water's waves shine
Let's see
see the waves
the waves that splish and
splash on the shore
Let's see
The shore covered
in sand and shell
Let's see
see the sand and shells
The shells that shine
and the sand that
rides the waves
Elizabeth Langefeld, Grade 4
Bright Elementary School, IN

The Forest

The expansive forest is a home for chirping, overjoyed birds
Green, crisp grass popping and poking its way through the dark soil
Moist, slimy frogs leaping and splashing into the clear, clean water
The forest is full of life

Graceful, white swans swimming proudly in the glistening lake
The shy gentle wind rushing through the towering, thin trees
Making crinkled leaves take flight
Tall, thin deer munching on blooming flowers
The forest is full of life
Kyla Graves, Grade 6
Linton-Stockton Elementary School, IN

Spring

The first day of spring is my birthday
I taste sugar cookies in my mouth.
Spring taste like ice cream too.
The first day of spring I feel like a hero.
I feel like a free person.
Spring feels like a new place for me.
The first day of spring I hear the ice cream truck.
In spring I hear laughter too. I also hear the waves on the shore.
The first day of spring is so fun.
I play around with all my friends.
We have barbecues outside.
The first day of spring is so bright.
Everybody's walking around.
The first day of spring.
Caroline Siena Knight Pearson, Grade 4
British School of Chicago, IL

Shining Bright

I am decorated with many ornaments and lights.
In the dark my branches shine bright.
I can be fat and tall or short and small.

Sometimes I shed, but I don't have to be fed at all.
My needles are green and my trunk is brown.
The bad thing is I get cut down.

I am neither bad nor good, but sometimes I am found in your neighborhood.
You can be rich or poor, but buying me you can't ignore.
The things that get put under are one big score for children's glee.
Claire Kiolbasa, Grade 6
Our Lady of Peace School, IL

Inside a Book

Inside a book there is a whole new world
It is like a roller coaster
There are twists and turns, and you never know what is going to happen next
There are sad times like losing a family member, and happy like winning the lottery
It is a mysterious sound coming from the forest
So if you are looking for some extreme excitement, come join me
Inside a book…you'll never know what is going to happen unless you take a look!
Emily Lux, Grade 6
St Pius X Catholic School, IN

Little Brother

What's mine, is his
what's his, is his
what's gross to me, is a prank to him
what's dirty to mom, is extra clean to him
how awful this may seem…
but he is my little brother,
and there is no way to change that!

Alexis Gage, Grade 6
Rochester Middle School, IL

America!

America is my red, white, and blue.
America is my free country.
America is where I live.
America my home sweet home.
America where I go to school.
America where I come home.
America where my family and I were born.
America where my friends are.
America my pride and joy.
America where I am so glad to be free and an American.
America is one nation under God.

Crystal Hubbartt, Grade 6
First Baptist Christian Academy, IL

I Will Definitely Win!

One day I entered a poem contest
To see if I could win,
I think it is pretty good,
Because I have a massive grin.
I have a lot of ideas so listen well
I have a book full of poems to tell!
I have ideas like a dog flying a plane.
No! No! That is too hard to explain.
I got it, a moose on a train's caboose!
No that's not right,
Maybe I should call my friend Dwight
O well, I think I can write a great poem for the contest,
That will certainly be better than the rest.
I say all of this while I am scratching my chin,
Thinking of a poem for that contest
That will certainly win!

Stephen Bola, Grade 5
Fredrick Nerge Elementary School, IL

The Monsters Are Coming

Ghouls and goblins, witches on brooms
Werewolves that howl at the moon.
Tonight is the night that they come for you.
The witches are making potions.
Werewolves are sharpening their claws.
Ghouls and goblins are making a commotion in the parade.
They're coming closer and closer and then Bam!
Happy Halloween!

Alora Swafford, Grade 5
Country Meadow Elementary School, IN

Bold Color

Red is…
The taste of the juiciest,
Most delicious apple on the tree

Red is…
The POP when you open a cold coke

Red is…
A soft velvet curtain,
Friendly and inviting

Red is…
The smell of campfire, s'mores,
And the summer breeze

Red is…
The fire in your heart,
When you struggle for something you love.

Ethan Lannan, Grade 6
Linton-Stockton Elementary School, IN

Dolydedoo

Have you ever seen a grasshopper talk?
Have you ever seen a whale talk?

If you ask me how I know that they do,
I'll hop on one foot and say, "Dolydedoo!"

Have you ever seen a cat playin' pool
Have you ever seen a T-rex play pool?

Jacob Gaham, Grade 4
Churubusco Elementary School, IN

I Am

I am cool and nice.
I wonder if I am really cool.
I hear that I am nice.
I see that I am.
I want to be a superstar.
I am cool and nice.
I pretend I am a singer.
I feel awesome.
I touch high notes.
I worry I lose my voice.
I cry then I am happy.
I am cool and nice.
I understand that I am not that cool and nice
But just cool and nice.
I say I am Hanna Montana.
I dream I am on a stage.
I try to sing like Hanna.
I hope to win an Emmy.
I am cool and nice.

Steffanie Cisco, Grade 6
Heritage Grove Middle School, IL

The Happy Clown

One day I met a clown.
On his face was a big frown.
He is very handy,
And then he met Mandy,
Then his frown turned upside-down!

Kaitlyn McQueen, Grade 6
ROWVA East Elementary School, IL

Parents

What are parents?
Parents are loving,
Caring people
Who watch
Over you.
They take
You places and
Work hard to get you
The things that you want.

Parents are people you love.
That's what parents are.

Mackenzie Flamion, Grade 5
Perry Central Elementary School, IN

Dog

Dog
Loving, caring
Trotting, running, walking
Furry, spots, spotted, little
Listening, scratching, running,
Cuddly, cute
Cat

Rebecca Rachke, Grade 6
Elwood C C School, IL

Poetry Is Me

P oetry is my passion
O n rainy days. It is also
E ndangered love on
T hose sad, calm days. It
R eels me to a nice place to write.
Y ou would love it, I know I do.

Nathan Striegel, Grade 5
Floyds Knobs Elementary School, IN

Friends

F un to be with
R espectful
I ntelligent in many ways
E nergetic
N ever has to be perfect
D ear to me
S omeone to depend on

Jordyn Byrd, Grade 5
Perry Central Elementary School, IN

Skateboarding

Skateboarding, skateboarding.
Skate in a line.
Skateboarding, skateboarding.
Don't fall on your behind!

Skateboarding, skateboarding.
Hurt my head.
Skateboarding, skateboarding.
Fall on your bed.

Riley Ebl, Grade 4
Marine Elementary School, IL

Running Back

Rumbling through people
Unified against the other team
Never dropping the ball
Integrity in action
Nagging about your run
Gettin' the ball
Brakin' tackles
Attacking the middle
Catching for points
Kinetic energy on the field.

Dylan Post, Grade 6
Rochester Middle School, IL

Emma Leigh

E ver so cute
M y little angel
M y baby girl
A nnoying sometimes

L oving
E xciting to be with
I ntelligent
G ood person to talk to
H ilarious

Alexandria J. Masterson, Grade 5
Morgan Elementary School, IN

Fountain

Fountain, Fountain
Flowing so peacefully
Into the river it goes
Trickling, trickling
What a peaceful sound
From a spring
In the hill
The artists made
It a peaceful place
For people
Like you and me
To go

Jonathan Wrobel, Grade 5
Maplebrook Elementary School, IL

Green

Green is the color of the grass
Waving on a windy day.
Green is the color of leaves
Swinging in the tall trees.
It's the color of apples,
Tart and juicy in your mouth.
The beautiful garden in my yard,
That's the color of the
Beautiful green summer.

Rachel Wilson, Grade 5
Staunton Elementary School, IN

The Apache Clay Pot

Apache is the Indian tribe.
A pot like the morning sky.
Buried a thousand years ago.
Found on a sunny day.
Bright like the sky.
Broken now.

Ben Lauritsen, Grade 5
Freeburg Elementary School, IL

Animals

A lligator	N ice cat
B at	O tter
C at	P arrot
D og	Q uail
E agle	R ats
F ish	S tar fish
G oat	T iger
H og	U nicorn
I guana	V ery nice
J ack rabbit	W hale
K itten	X -ray fish
L ion	Y oung animals
M ouse	Z ebra

Angel Alsman, Grade 4
Shoals Elementary School, IN

Pants

My pants
They live in France
They are dyed red
They never go to bed
And they like to dance.

Brandon Pendley, Grade 4
Shoals Elementary School, IN

Bear

The bowlegged, brown bear
Broke the brittle branches
To battle the buzzing bees to get
The bountiful honey.

Bryce Butler, Grade 5
Staunton Elementary School, IN

My Room

My room is green like the jungle
It's dark like the night sky
It's as comfortable as heaven
It's quiet like a shy person waiting for you
It's one of my favorite places besides Florida
It is my room.

Dominick Figliulo, Grade 5
St John of the Cross Parish School, IL

Summer Swimming

Prodigious water slide
Strong scent of chlorine
Screaming laughter of children
Frigid water against my skin
Crisp water all around me
Summer

Tiffany Troumouliaris, Grade 5
Frank H Hammond Elementary School, IN

My Friend

When I needed a friend
Like a brother you stand with me 'til the end
Helping me to see light I've been in the dark too long
Giving me love and hope reasons to carry on
Giving me your courage smiling now when I rise
From wisdom you shared sparkle returned to my eyes
Your shoulder I lean on you're my shining star
You lend me your strength lifting me up from afar
How do I thank you for what you've given me
Words do not seem enough for what you made me see
So just for you alone my arms do extend
Giving you all my love forever my brother, my friend

Joel Leon, Grade 6
St Joseph School, IL

My Favorite Season

The birds singing their endless song
The ripples in water go on and on

New born kittens and ducklings and chicks and guppies
New born calves and bunnies and cute little puppies

The patter of rain on a moonlit night
Singing me to sleep 'til morning bright

The garden outside that had once been bare
Now filled with beautiful flowers in need of love and care

These are all signs of my favorite season
These are all hints and these are all reasons

My favorite season; if you guessed right
Is the season spring when the sun's always bright

Brittney Suits, Grade 5
Norris City Omaha Elementary School, IL

Reading

Reading is like a movie with words,
It's like the color sky blue.
Reading feels like a calm feeling,
It's like a cloud high above.
Reading tastes like my favorite food,
When it has so much detail.
Reading smells like a calm ocean breeze,
When you can't get your mind off of it.
Reading can be like anything you want,
As long as you use your imagination!

Rachael Schopp, Grade 5
St John of the Cross Parish School, IL

Orange

Orange is a pencil that you write with.
Orange is a fruit that you eat.
Orange is the sunset, bright as could be.
Orange is a crayon that you color with.
Orange is a folder that you use.
Orange you glad I didn't say orange again.

Chad Carbo, Grade 5
Staunton Elementary School, IN

Vacation

Undulating lake
Misty air
Cries of seagulls
Water against my face
Gritty sand
Stress blowing away

Allison Mudro, Grade 5
Frank H Hammond Elementary School, IN

The Fraidy Cats: A Poem for Two Voices

Whenever we're asked

    Why we don't swim

We answer

    It's suicide

Insane

    Quite crazy

Quite true

    Whenever we're asked

Why not? The dogs do it

    We answer

Because they're crazy

    Suicidal

Quite true   Quite true
We would drown

    Down to the sea floor

Very scary
Quite true   Quite true
We will not go swimming

    So

Give up!   Give up!

Nick Czarnowski, Grade 5
Maplebrook Elementary School, IL

Happy

H ave fun.
A very good time.
P eople and places.
P ositive times.
Y esterday or any day!

Natalie Ogle, Grade 4
Robein Elementary School, IL

My Poems

I am a dancing poet,
My poems are my ballet shoes.
Who move across the floor,
Like a bird in the sky.

I am a cheerleading poet,
Who's poems are the pom-poms.
They shake and spin,
And make the game worthwhile.

I am a learning poet,
Who's poems are what I learn.
Everything I learn,
Is a new thing to explore.

I am a swinging poet,
My poems are the swings.
Up and down they go,
Until they're finally gone.

I am a volleyball poet,
My poems are the ball.
I serve, bump, set, spike my poems,
Until they hit the floor and win.

Heidi Cusack, Grade 6
St Barbara School, IL

Autumn

Autumn leaves are falling,
Turning yellow, red and orange,
Wrapping the World in Earth,
Animals creeping over them,
All so peaceful when the leaves fall.

Kaylee Poole, Grade 6
Rochester Middle School, IL

Grandma

G rand
R espectful
A lways spoils me
N ot trouble
D arling
M y favorite
A lways loves me

Winston Glenn, Grade 4
Morgan Elementary School, IN

I Am Quilliam

I am **Q** uiet
I am **U** nnecessary
I am **I** ntense
I am **L** earnful
I am in **L** ove with Rosalina
I am **I** nsane
I am **A** musing
I am **M** anly

Quilliam Johnson, Grade 5
Amy Beverland Elementary School, IN

My Own Room

Cramped into one place,
Not enough space to put all of my things.
It's like I live with a pig that never
Gives in to the idea of cleaning.
Don't get me wrong.
My sis and I have a unique bond,
But it drives me nuts having
Two live in one messy space.
But now I am happy
That I have my own room!

Hannah Schneeman, Grade 5
St Anthony's School, IL

Life

Some people have hopes
Some have dreams,
But things are never as they seem.
Someone is crying on the inside
But laughing on the out.
Is that really what life is about?
Cry when you're hurt,
Laugh when you're not
It won't put you on the spot.
Only one person can judge who you are,
It's the one person driving in your car!

Kayla Hickey, Grade 6
Rochester Middle School, IL

Mornings

The sun awakens me
to a brand new day
It's golden light shines
like it will never go away
The bacon sizzles
crackling and popping
And crunchy toast
with my favorite topping
Mornings are great
in every way
Now if only it wasn't
a week day!

Kira Yelinek, Grade 6
St Pius X Catholic School, IN

Cars

Cars
Fast, aerodynamic
Zooming, winning, racing
The grand prize trophy
Skyrocketing, speeding, jouncing
Victorious, sleek
Vehicle

Nick Guy, Grade 4
Norman Bridge Elementary School, IL

Grandpa Eurton

G reat man
R esponsible
A ngel
N aturally
D oes so go with us
P retty
A lways there for me

E ver so nice
U nusually kind
R eally kind
T here for me
O ne of my family members
N ever alone

Brittany Knight, Grade 5
Morgan Elementary School, IN

Wasting My Time

Top
People are
Wasting
Their time
Seeking solutions
For everything
Many obstacles
Drag people
Down in
Their lives
Time to abandon
Seeking solutions
And get back to my life.

Joseph Dean, Grade 5
Twin Branch Model School, IN

Waters

Pond
Mucky, still
Calming, relaxing, reflecting
Warm, paradise — creature, island
Flowing, shining, shivering
Rocky, muddy
Creek

Jessica J., Grade 5
Bell-Graham School, IL

Friends

A udrey	**N** ice
B est buds	**O** n the run together
C aring	**P** illow fights
D aily laughing	**Q** uiet
E asy to talk to	**R** unning
F unky	**S** inging
G iggling quietly	**T** ogether
H yper	**U** sually fun
I mportant	**V** ery fun
J umping rope	**W** ise
K ylee	**X** tra special
L oud	**Y** elling
M onkeying around	**Z** in queens

Holly Self, Grade 4
Shoals Elementary School, IN

Thanksgiving

Pumpkin pie, apple pie,
Uncle Larry, Aunt Carry,
Cherry tomatoes, sweet potatoes,
Cousin Pete with smelly feet,
Ham and turkey,
Pam and Cam,
Grand old stuffing, green bean something,
Grandpa Dean, Grandma Jean,
Whipped cream, and sweet dreams,
So many things to be thankful for,
Thanksgiving!

Katie Hamlin, Grade 5
Country Meadow Elementary School, IN

Shopping

Into the mall,
Across the lobby,
Through the crowd,
Past the food court,
In front of Claire's
Across from Hollister,
With bags holding me down,
Toward Abercrombie,
Beside Gloria Jean's,
With only Dad's credit cards,
Like I care,
Down the escalator,
Since the day is over, it's time to go home.

Alexa Rainbolt, Grade 6
Michael Grimmer Middle School, IN

Blue Jay

Blue Jay, Blue Jay flying in the sky over here over there you fly.
You're the mascot of the Blue Jays,
You're the very best bird of all.
You're ziggin and a zaggin from tree to tree,
You're as fast as a hawk but as gentle as a fly.

John Wietbrock, Grade 4
Oak Hill Elementary School, IN

Fruity

Orange
Sweet, juicy
Tongue-tingling, mouthwatering, satisfying
Juicy and sunshine
Refreshing, puckering, juicing
Sour, juicy
Lemon

Wil Keesey, Grade 5
GCMS Elementary School, IL

I Am Everything

I am a pencil, waiting for a break.
I am a bird, flying everywhere.
I am the smallest button on a remote, so don't touch!
I am a pillow, always wanting to go to sleep.
I am a blanket, not wanting to get up.
I am a turtle, taking it slow.
I am a dog, waiting for someone to play with.
I am a flock of geese, never alone.
I am a lightbulb, full of ideas.
I am a remote, searching for a TV.

Mandi Krecik, Grade 5
Churubusco Elementary School, IN

This Place Is So Heavenly

I see the beautiful, yellow bright light
The clouds take me up
Like marshmallows,
But hold the stickiness.
I start to hear the hallelujah chorus.
Seeing all my family and my friends,
Don't forget Adams, my cat.
Meowing, greeting, and smiles are upon me.
Angels fly by,
Guardians are protecting their man.
This place is so…heavenly.
Death might seem scary but it's not,
It's a new state of the world,
And it's definitely not the end,
It's the beginning.
A beginning of happiness, playfulness, wonderfulness,
And most of all, heavenliness.
This place is different,
This place is grand,
This heavenly place called heaven,
Is so heavenly.

Katie Ronzio, Grade 6
McHenry Middle School, IL

Rainbow

Rainbows over high.
Rainbows sparkle in the sky.
Cool, pretty colors.

Hannah Walls, Grade 4
McKenney-Harrison Elementary School, IN

Snow

Snow
Cold, wet
Laying, falling, creating
Little, wet
I love snow!

Beth Slicer, Grade 5
Cloverdale Middle School, IN

white

a blank piece of paper
a wall not yet painted.
cumulus clouds floating in the sky.
one of the lightest colors.
a water bottle cap.

Jennifer Ashdown, Grade 4
Erie Elementary School, IL

Friends

Friends
Nice, trustworthy
Talking, playing, shopping
Mall, school, competitions, school
Teasing, fighting, bickering
Mean, annoying
Enemy

Sarah Bermingham, Grade 6
Rochester Middle School, IL

Mamaw and Papaw

M arvelous
A lways there for me
M akes me happy
A mazing
W onderful

A perfect grandma
N ever yells at me
D oesn't be mean

P lays games with me
A lways will love me
P erfect
A lways by my side
W onderful grandpa

Hannah Elliott, Grade 4
Morgan Elementary School, IN

The Cat and Dog

The dog has very long fur.
The cat always purrs.
The dog always tugs.
The cat lies on the rug.
The dog chews on a bone,
While the cat would rather be alone.

Betsy Zahringer, Grade 5
Seton Catholic School, IL

Stacey Marie Lawalin

S tacey is my mom
T aking care of me every day all day long
A fter school she meets me in the office every day
C alling me at my friends all the time to see if I'm O.K.
E very day she takes me everywhere, she's always on the go
Y ou probably wish you had my mom

M om is the best, she is so fun
A lways on the go
R unning here and there
I n the days that she has to work she is tired, but she still takes her time to have fun
E very day I can count on her to be there right by my side.

L aughter goes on all day long in the Lawalin house.
A fter school mom takes me out to eat
W hether it is just McDonald's or Taco Bell I always have fun
A bsolutely every day my mom is loving and caring
L oving and caring all day long my mom is always
I love my mom so very much
N ever will she not be there by my side. I love her so very much.

Breyan Underhill, Grade 5
Perry Central Elementary School, IN

Score!

Running from the half court towards the three pointer line.
Walking to the right of the three pointer scouting back down just a bit.
Crossover two players. Grabbing the ball with one hand.
Get clear, with no players in my face grab the ball with two hands.
Shoot a three and make it. Everyone screaming, SCORE!

Sophie Vivero, Grade 5
Cortland Elementary School, IL

True Best Friends

A true best friend is there for you,
They'll let you laugh and cry,
A true best friend will care for you,
And won't tell a single lie,
When you're hurt, they'll make you grin,
When you lose, they'll make you win,
When you're confused, they'll understand,
And give you a strong helping hand,
When you're gone, they'll wish you were there,
And think of some stories, that when you're back, you could share,
When you can't go outside to play,
Your true best friend will find a way,
For both of you to keep in touch,
They'll never tell your secrets,
Not one, not two, not three,
You won't have to change yourself,
Just be the person you want to be,
And if you have to move to another state,
So very far away,
The truest of best friends will not call once a year,
But every single day.

Pauline Esman, Grade 5
Decatur Classical Elementary School, IL

Day Dreamer

Sitting and staring blankly into space,
As the hands of the clock slowly revolve around its face,
Slipping away into a fantasy land,
Where the secrets it holds is in the palm of your hand,
You're not the same kid from your neighborhood,
You could be King Arthur or maybe Robin Hood,
Or you could be a brave night riding a white stallion,
Defending the castle and leading your battalion,
Or maybe a pirate sailing the seven seas,
Finding buried treasure and going where you please,
Or even a secret agent on a new mission,
Just like the one you saw on television,
There's no limit on what you could achieve,
All you need is time and a passion to Day Dream.

Sam Hanauer, Grade 6
St John Evangelist School, IN

Snowflakes

Snowflakes, snowflakes,
Are all I see.
Snowflakes, snowflakes,
All around me.
Snowflakes, snowflakes,
In the sky.
Snowflakes, snowflakes,
Way up high.
Snowflakes, snowflakes,
Pile on the ground.
Snowflakes, snowflakes,
In a mound.
Snowflakes, snowflakes,
Cold not hot.
Snowflakes, snowflakes,
I like them a lot.

Corey Worman, Grade 4
Country Meadow Elementary School, IN

Lightning Speed

I race around the track.
My tires came from a rack.
But when I hear a crack.
I know there is a crash.

I have many bright colors.
I am very fast like lightning.
I like to live in the fast lane.

My driver drives as fast as lightning
I have many fans
They scream out my number because they want me to win.

A transport truck brings me to race tracks.
I've been to many race tracks around the world.

Andrew Hawken, Grade 6
Our Lady of Peace School, IL

Softball

Softball is fun for all.
Hitting, pitching, catching that little white ball.

Hit then run 1st, 2nd, 3rd base,
Try not to get hit in the face.

When you're in the outfield try to catch a pop fly,
After you win time to say good bye.

Maddie Adams, Grade 5
North Intermediate Center of Education, IL

Give Me

Give me courage.
Give me perseverance
And I will help the sick people.
Give me determination.
Give me power
And I will stop all the crime in the world.

Brooke Sparks, Grade 6
Norman Bridge Elementary School, IL

My Birthday Party at North Beach

We arrived at North Beach with anticipation,
The invites had been sent for the celebration.
I'm now turning eight and I just can't wait!!
My friends come in and make a din,
The birthday bash starts to begin.
We go to the sandpit to run and have fun,
We run to get pizza to fill up our tums.
Now the cake comes for our taking,
We've been waiting.
We saved the best till last,
We went to the moon walk really fast.
My party ended but it was a blast.

Arpad Neale, Grade 4
British School of Chicago, IL

Diving

Swimming past animals unimaginable
Watching dolphins herd fish to fishermen
Hearing the buzzing of jellyfish
Feeling the smooth surface of a turtle shell
Diving, the wonderful world of water revealed

Jason Weber, Grade 5
Bell-Graham School, IL

Light/Dark

Light
Bright, warming
Living, securing, heating
Heaven, day, shadow, night
Dying, falling, shading
Gloomy, murky
Dark

Trenton Blake, Grade 5
Frank H Hammond Elementary School, IN

That Night

Silver and white flashed in the night
Flying in the moon light
Swishing and swirling
Dipping and twirling
Trying not to fight
The moon light
That magical
Night
I took a magic carpet ride
Levi Schulz, Grade 5
Lincoln Trail Elementary School, IN

What Is a Friend?

Someone who cares about you,
Never lies to you, plays with you
When you are down,
Makes you feel good inside,
Always waits for you,
Shares when wants to,
Gives presents whenever they want to,
Brings us together to have fun,
Yep, those are friends!
Sidney Gieselman, Grade 4
Morgan Elementary School, IN

Purple Martins

Purple Martins
Majestic, purple,
Flying, swooping, hunting
Wonderful bird to watch
Eating, nesting, hatching
Interesting, skilled
Swallow
Cory Stephens, Grade 4
Dixie Bee Elementary School, IN

Deep Darkness

This deep darkness
Makes me feel scared
Depressed
It takes me to a dark
Damp, cold house
I look in the window
Find a child
Scared to death
Crying
He sees me in the window
Runs
Afraid of me
The unforgiving darkness
Of the black clouds
Gathering around me
Deep Darkness
Tyler James, Grade 6
Linton-Stockton Elementary School, IN

Wrestling

Wrestling
fun, tough
hardworking, awesome, wrestling moves
single leg, Pederson, hitting, running
pitching, catching, bunting
home run, strikeout
Baseball
Ben Kaehr, Grade 5
Adams Central Elementary School, IN

I Am

I am a tornado
destroying everything I see
ripping out trees and plants
frightening everyone
leaving people homeless
I am powerful.
Dominika Duda, Grade 6
Norman Bridge Elementary School, IL

Winter

A fierce wind begins to blow
Harsh, cold, and bitter
Blinded by the bewildering snow
The icy white season is here
Numbness in the fingertips
Shaking, shivering, rosy cheeks
Unrelenting, piercing, blustery gusts
Springtime not for numerous weeks
Mariah Cherry, Grade 6
Rochester Middle School, IL

A Loyal Companion

This little funny puppy
His name is Rusty.
His coat is soft and furry
He is always in a hurry.
He's white and brown
And barks throughout the town.
As he walks on by
With his great big eyes
He'll win any prize.
When we get out his treats.
He is at my feet,
Wagging his tail.
To his own little beat.
He is my four-legged friend,
Who likes to have fun.
Who plays all day in the sun.
What he does best is run, run, run.
At the end of the day
It's all said and done.
He is at my feet fast asleep.
Julianne Epperson, Grade 6
St John Evangelist School, IN

Something Strange

There's something
strange
running around my house.
I don't know what it is!
It's tall
and skinny,
and it's carrying a skateboard.
It's scaring me to
death!
Oh, no! Here it comes!
1, 2, 3, run
Oh…!
Wait…! It's just my brother.
McKenzie Behrends, Grade 5
Tremont Elementary School, IL

Peyton Manning

P asses the ball
E nergetic
Y ells a lot
T ouchdown
O ffensive line
N ever gives up

M y favorite football player
A wesome
N ice
N ever lets the other players down
I ndianapolis Colts
N oble
G ood player
Anna Russell, Grade 5
Morgan Elementary School, IN

Water and Fire

Water
blue, cool
relaxing, soothing, refreshing
sea, ocean, sun, fireplace
hurtful, dangerous, colorful
hot, red
Fire
Daniel Kinsella, Grade 6
Rochester Middle School, IL

Favorite Sports

Basketball
Fun, fast pace
Bouncing, swishing, fouling
Hoop, court, touchdowns, field goals
Tackling, kicking, running
Physical, hard-hitting
Football
John Russo, Grade 6
St Matthew School, IL

Silent

The night was silent
So sad and still
There he lay,
So peaceful and ill.
My eyes grew heavy,
And began to wail
We left that night
With death on mind,
Not knowing this would be the last time,
Gave him a kiss and left the room,
Turned around one more time,
To see the ruin.
So deathly ill, it gave me a chill.
The next morning death was our fear.
Left the house to go to his room
Got to his room with Earl on mind
Doctor said "He went to Jesus last night"
Now cancers gone, have no fear.
We went to his room to see the chill.
There he lay so peaceful and still
There through the window a ray of sunlight shone through.

Katelyn N. Christ, Grade 6
Good Shepherd Lutheran School, IL

St. Patrick's Day

S o much fun for everyone!
T he color green everywhere!

P eople buying almost everywhere you look.
A t home we celebrate.
T oday's the day
R oya! In Gaelic that means, "celebrate."
I rish love this holiday.
C ome and play!
K eep believing!
S o, are you celebrating?

D o you believe in leprechauns?
A t Irish dances there is lots of fun.
Y ou will have fun!

Cody Nicholson, Grade 5
Fredrick Nerge Elementary School, IL

Snowflakes

S is for the beautiful snowflakes that make the land white
N is for the nice patterns that bring a wonderful sight
O is outside, where the snowflakes fall
W is for wonderful snowflakes that bring joy to us all
F is for falling, that's what snowflakes do
L is for laughing when children have fun, it's true
A is for asking mom to go out and play
K is for the kids that play all the day
E is for everyone that explores and has fun
S is for snowflakes that are fun for everyone

Makeda Winfield, Grade 5
Benjamin Franklin Elementary School, IN

Sky

Big and blue
background
white fluffy cotton candy
day by day the sky can rotate
mean gray when it rains
bright lights when the sun comes and plays
dark as a cave at night
with little twinkles of light
the sky
the sky
with different moods every day

Channing Wenger, Grade 4
Bright Elementary School, IN

Why

Why is there violence
Why do we watch the news to see
The horrifying stories
Why don't we see the positives
In the world
Why do we only hear about global warming
Instead of a successful cause
Why do you cry
Why do we worry
Why can't we just calm down
Because we are human
We are not perfect
But why are there wars
If we can help it
Because we aren't always thinking
Why is used an awful lot
But why

Hayley Roets, Grade 6
Thayer J Hill Middle School, IL

Monster Minnow

Tike was a minnow who could eat a whale.
Tike would eat a whale and lick his mouth clean.
After tike had a whale he had some ale.
People can't think of Tike as very lean.

Tike was the strongest minnow of all-time.
His pecs were the size of some people.
His guns were bigger than one whole wind chime.
He could bench weights the size of a steeple.

Tike's favorite sport to play was football.
Tike could level other football players.
Tike was 15 feet 9 inches tall.
Tike does not like to dog pile in layers.

In Tike's dreams he dreams of being Darth Maul.
But, sad to say, he is just simply tall.

Alec Swan, Grade 6
Christian Life Schools, IL

Stinky Feet

Hairy and muddy, really dirty.
I think the smell, killed a birdie!

Smells terrible, is really bumpy.
Sticky, slimy, and very lumpy!

Icky and yucky, really rough,
I think these feet, have had enough!
Emily Neuhauser, Grade 5
Floyds Knobs Elementary School, IN

Volleyball/Kickball

Volleyball
Fun, energetic
Spiking, hitting, diving
Teams, leather ball, rubber ball, bases
Kicking, yelling, running
Exciting, intense
Kickball
Rebecca Edwards, Grade 6
St Mary Elementary School, IN

White-tailed Deer

White-tailed deer run fast
Big, brown, active, beautiful
Bucks have big antlers.
Samantha Jordan, Grade 5
St Jacob Elementary School, IL

Christmas Time

Presents and decorations
Santa Claus and family
Snow so cold
Waiting for toys under the tree
Making angels in the snow
Baking our holiday cakes
Getting off of school
Christmas this makes
Jenna Walaszek, Grade 5
Our Lady of Peace School, IL

What Is Church

Church is praiseful
Church is fun
A joyful inspiration
There are good people
There is so much singing
The people are respectful
You talk about God
Church is helpful
You take offering and communion
You praise Jesus
That is my church
Jalisa Jones, Grade 5
Morgan Elementary School, IN

She Is

She is a cloud in the sky
She is a song to sing
She is a sly cat
She is sweet candy
She is the soft breeze on my face
She is a move on TV
She is Hannah Montana on her DS
She is my awesome sister
Jessica Coryell, Grade 5
Floyds Knobs Elementary School, IN

Spring

Rain is falling
Flowers are blooming
The wind is blowing

The sky is bright
No one's in fright
The bugs bite

The grass is green
Nobody's mean
The weather is warm
People are in swarms

Everyone is happy
Because it's spring.
Jordan Cheesman, Grade 6
Rochester Middle School, IL

Sox

Two years ago the Sox were the best,
That year they beat all the rest.
Last year wasn't as fun,
Only ninety games they had won.
With Konerko, Pierzynski, and Dye,
The home runs sure will fly.
White Sox with be back, we have no fear,
Hopefully they will win it again this year!
Alexis Cannistra, Grade 5
Fredrick Nerge Elementary School, IL

Books

Books bound in leather,
Strings,
All sorts of things.
In books, on books.
Always a good read.
Take time to sit and read,
A good book,
From your shelf.
The world's greatest treasure.
Books!!!!
Samantha Sims, Grade 4
Cynthia Heights Elementary School, IN

Zesto

White, white, white as snow
Yum, yum, yum, that frozen dough.
Brr, brr, brr, cold as ice.
The dough shaped like ice.
A Cookie Dough Blizzard in summer
Couldn't be funner.
Cody McCoy, Grade 5
Levan Scott Academy, IN

Clay Pots

Cherokee was their name.
Laughed and worked all day.
A clay pot they made.
Yes, they were real.
Jacob Wiskamp, Grade 5
Freeburg Elementary School, IL

War

Desire, passion
Fear, anger, hatred, courage
Stress, shame, regret, lack
Arras Korogluyan, Grade 6
Sacred Heart School, IL

Food

I like burgers and so do you.
They are great and awesome too.
You'll have some, and I will have more.
After I get home from the grocery store.
Corey Fields, Grade 5
GCMS Elementary School, IL

The Hill

Extremely nervous,
as I board The Voyage.
Going up, up, up,
the unbelievable slope.
Almost there.
My stomach flipping,
like an acrobat.
Up high,
in the cool dense air.

I wish I could…
turn back around.
Even though,
I love roller coasters.
But…oh no…
I am at the top of the hill.

When I finish,
the enormous ride.
Will I ride again?
Ramsey Ferree, Grade 6
Linton-Stockton Elementary School, IN

Hope

If hope could be a color
it would be white as soft as a lamb

If hope could be a taste
it would be just like a juicy apple

If hope could be a smell
it would be just like pumpkin pie

If hope could be a sound
it would be tweeting birds in the morning

If hope could be a feeling
it would be a big hug from an old friend

If hope could be an animal
it would be a soft and cuddly bunny

Alex Langbartels, Grade 4
St Agnes School, IL

Mrs. Steffel

Mrs. Steffel is the best!
Now don't be a pest!
Listen with two ears not one.
Do you have your work done?
There are a lot of things to hear during the year.
Shh! She's almost here,
The year is almost done.

Brianna Cody, Grade 5
Hendry Park Elementary School, IN

The Only One I Needed

Someday you will find the place
It's the place where love takes over hate
And you'll see all the things you do
Affect everyone around you
Then you'll see there no fear at all
You held my hand we took down that wall
As I looked at you with nothing to say
Now I understand why you pushed me away
I looked far and now I see
That the only one I needed was me

Brianna Campos, Grade 6
Milan Middle School, IN

Gloom/Pleasure

Gloom
Melancholy, somberness
Depressing, breaking, hating
Dislike, pessimism, optimism, rejoice
Dancing, jumping, laughing
Delight, joyfulness
Pleasure

Akhilesh Mishra, Grade 5
Frank H Hammond Elementary School, IN

Grandpa's Gone

I felt a tear run down my cheek
As I watched them close the lid.
"Grandpa's gone now. Let's leave," sighed Mom.
I didn't want to leave his side
So many good memories with Grandpa.
So many I cannot say
Grandpa's gone now
It's time to pray.

Whitney Haecker, Grade 6
Laketon Elementary School, IN

Friends

Friends mean a lot to me,
When we're together we're filled with glee.

When we are separated we are sad,
When we're together we are glad.

We stay together through every trial,
We walk together through every mile.

And every friend means everything,
because we all have joy to bring.

Kelsey Mayberry, Grade 5
North Intermediate Center of Education, IL

Winter

W inter is a grand old time;
I t's a time of laughing and singing,
N ever have I ever had a bad winter;
T o everyone we wish a merry Christmas
E ven dear old Mr. Evers who buys everyone and everything a
R oast for their fire.

I love winter so much.

L ake, ahh! You're frozen over, how does it feel to be solid?
O ur fire is popping and cracking.
V isiting everyone on the block,
E veryone has something for us.

I 'll remember Christmas no matter what
T o everyone I wish a merry Christmas!

Lane Turner, Grade 5
First Baptist Christian Academy, IL

Let's Go Shopping

Imagine you can buy anything
The clothes you buy are as cute as a puppy
The salespeople are kind like parents
They treat you like royalty
Store names are as odd as a platypus
Buying whatever you want is like a fairy tale
Shopping is fun and exciting!!

Anne Carden, Grade 5
St John of the Cross Parish School, IL

Books/Television
Books
Exciting, fun, entertaining
Reading, learning, looking
Convenient — portable, loud, distracting
Watching, waiting, listening
Big, expensive
Television
Diana Hass, Grade 6
Sacred Heart School, IL

The Classic and the Modern
Book
Old, classic
Reading, drawing, shushing
Imagination, adventures, shows, movies
Laughing, acting, advertising
Modern, amazing graphics
TVs
Johanna Kerber, Grade 5
GCMS Elementary School, IL

By Myself
When I'm by myself
And I close my eyes,
I'm so tall I can touch the sky,
I'm so light that I can even fly.
I'm so strong I can lift a boulder,
I'm running with it over my shoulder.
I'm sailing across the Black Sea,
I'm listening to my new CD.
And when I open my eyes,
All I want is to be me.
Thomas Jackowski, Grade 6
Norman Bridge Elementary School, IL

Pets
Pets are so much fun.
They're cheerful and warm like the sun.
Maybe a fish, dog, or cat,
Or even a gerbil, lizard, or rat.
You really should have a pet;
You would love it I bet!
Alexandra Kerr, Grade 5
Seton Catholic School, IL

Kittens
K ind and cute
I ndependent little cats
T oo cute for words
T errorizes furniture
E xcellent pets
N eat and nice
S mall and furry
Heather Mix, Grade 5
Seton Catholic School, IL

Birds
Beautiful birds sing
While fluttering in the wind
Migrating again
Julia Beardsley, Grade 5
Stanley Clark School, IN

Ice Cream
Ice cream
I like it
Ask me why
Because it's cold
Because it makes my feet tingle
Because it has Reese's Cups pieces in it
Because it gives me a brain freeze
Because, because, because
I like ice cream
Richard Lucas, Grade 5
Staunton Elementary School, IN

What Is a Big Sister?
She's always on the phone.
She bothers me.
Always in the shower for 10 minutes.
She loves animals.
She's nice and pretty.
Her favorite color is purples.
She makes me feel good.
She lives in my house.
She loves chocolate ice-cream.
She loves to go shopping at the mall.
That is a big sister!
Kimberly Chiquito, Grade 4
Morgan Elementary School, IN

Grandma and Papaw
L ove
I nstead
S illy
A lways funny

B uilder
I nto cars
L oves
L uck
Michael Ford-Bowman, Grade 4
Morgan Elementary School, IN

Spring Flowers
Daisies
Sweet, beautiful
Springing, blooming, shimmering
Flowers are the most beautiful plants
Flowers
Aminah Zegar, Grade 4
Universal School, IL

The City
Chicago City
Moaning groaning
People sitting
Top floor
Amazing height
Banging keyboards
Buzzing elevators
Sears Tower
Andrew Hallet, Grade 5
Bell-Graham School, IL

Shopping
Go to the mall
You'll have a ball.

You will have fun
When you get your nails done.

You can buy clothes
And make-up and shoes.

Oh! Look at that shirt
It surely will do.

But no it is time,
Time to go.

But I will come next time
To buy eye shadow.
Allyson Barnes, Grade 5
GCMS Elementary School, IL

Beautiful Peace
The gently fluttering snow
is beautiful,
cascading down gracefully
in soft, white flakes,
with a single,
unchanging,
tone
singing out.

The moon is bright,
with the comforting glory
of the darkness,
and silent,
heartbeat of night.

A face I know is beautiful,
like the soft,
white, snow,
with the peace
of a bright moon.
Chelsea Wang, Grade 5
Steeple Run Elementary School, IL

Pheasant Hunting

Lying low, lying low, lying low, now!
Here comes the dog with his nose to the ground.
He stops. He points. The command is to go.
The pheasant takes flight. It is a frenzied sight.
I bring up my gun and fire with a bang!
The pheasant still flies. I fire again, bang!
The dog looks at me with much disgust. "What?"
The pheasant flies to live another day.

Kenny Fiantago, Grade 6
McHenry Middle School, IL

People

People here, people there.
Hey, there's people over there!
People see and people hear.
Hey, do you know they have two ears!
People work and people play.
They say hey, may, and lay!
People touch and people taste.
They love to use paste!
People are small and people are tall.
Some people are thin and little,
And some are plump an big!
But one thing is for sure…
There are people all around!

Alyssa Conrad, Grade 4
McKenney-Harrison Elementary School, IN

The Storm

A thundering crash, a flash of light
Makes me shiver like a new born fawn.
Outside the window,
Shadows are made
Rain pelting down
The window panes.

The storm,
Like my sister in a tantrum
I did not like the storm.

Outside the window
A rumbling noise
Creepy, scary, flashing

The storm,
Like a booming giant turning electricity on and off.
I did not like the storm

Running, beating, lashing, crashing
Pelting, scary, creepy, flashing
Booming, screaming, humid puddles

My dog is panting and trembling.
He did not like the storm either.

Mira Tiwari, Grade 4
British School of Chicago, IL

You Don't Always Get What You Want

I wanted to go on a hike
But my brother was still a little tike
So my parents said no
In a voice very low
And to cheer me up they let me ride my bike

Danielle Swinford, Grade 6
Rochester Middle School, IL

Jalysse

I know a three year old named Jalysse.
I know her very well because she's my niece.
She's quite a talker as three year olds are.
She especially talks in the car.
She likes chocolate donuts and chocolate cake!
And oh, what noise she does make!
Then it becomes quiet.
You can bet her head and pillow have met.

Jaxyn Jones, Grade 5
Center Street Elementary School, IL

Tomorrow

We lost our last basketball game yesterday.
We worked hard until the last shot.
My coach said, "Guys it's okay!"
But my stomach was tied in knots.

I walked away and started to cry.
"Good game!" called one of their girls.
"You too!" I kind of had to lie!
On the way home, I spun my hair in twirls.

I was angrier than a boar.
I was filled to the top with sorrow.
But, I have to remember,
There is always tomorrow!

Jackie Banet, Grade 5
Floyds Knobs Elementary School, IN

Football

Football is a very tough sport
You don't play in a gym or on a court

All you need is to want to play
Plus it's best on a sunny day

By the time the game was over they were beat
It was all because we train in the intense heat

When we were done it was all the same
Beating players and taking names

The Fightin' Irish is the one
Playing hard and having fun

Joseph Kennedy, Grade 6
St John Evangelist School, IN

My Dog Molly

M elissa's Golden Retriever
Y ippy (not really)

D avid is the owner (my brother)
O utstanding dog
G oes on walks a lot

M outh full of tennis balls
O utgoing with us a lot
L oveable
L icks people a lot (gives kisses)
Y is Molly so scared of everything?

Melissa Molohon, Grade 6
Rochester Middle School, IL

Murphy

Around my house he runs.
Against my leg he brushes.
Beside me he sits.
Upon the counter his paws lay.
Through the glass door he looks.
Beneath the table he sleeps.
Over the bone he walks.
Outside running around,
Toward the water bowl he runs.
By the chair he chews his toy.
Without a clue he's being bad.
Since he's mine, I love him.

Kaitlyn Weis, Grade 6
Michael Grimmer Middle School, IN

Mustangs

Mustangs
Strong, brave
Galloping, riding, grazing
A four-legged spirit.
Wild horse!

Lexi Barnett, Grade 5
Staunton Elementary School, IN

Snow

S oft as a feather
N ever not fun
O ften when I play with you I get cold
W hen you fall from the sky it is beautiful

Sierra Layton, Grade 4
GCMS Elementary School, IL

All About Me

S mart
A thletic
L oving
E nergetic
H appy

Saleh Ahmed, Grade 5
Hendry Park Elementary School, IN

The Moment of Magic

Have you seen the starry night skies when they're filled with gleaming stars?
As they twinkle and glow in the crisp chilly night air dancing across the sky,
As the sun starts to set and the stars start to glisten
Is when you need to seize the moment of magic,
What an unbelievable stunning experience, such a beautiful breathtaking sight,
When you're filled with joy and start to smile as the heavens sing
And people rejoice, is the moment of magic.

Graham Novak, Grade 4
Ranch View Elementary School, IL

The Ride of My Life

I'm going for a ride in the dark woods
My horse is ready I am too.

I pretend I'm in the rodeo the bell rings.
We shoot out the gate the crowd rises as we win.

All of a sudden we hit a tree!!
I fall off and my horse falls to the ground.

I went over to my horse; she had her eyes closed.
It looked like she broke her nose so I grabbed her by her halter.

She got up for me; we started walking home
When we got home my mom helped me clean her up…soon she was better.

Another day we went for a ride in the dark woods
My horse is ready. I'm ready too…for another rodeo.

Cheyanne Hinds, Grade 6
Rochester Middle School, IL

Basketball

Basketball is fun to play,
my friends and me practice night and day.
We learn how to dribble, we learn how to pass,
win or lose we do it with class.
The position I play is small shooting guard,
in order to get better I practice real, real hard.
There are many people who come to the game,
boys, girls, moms, dads, it doesn't matter they cheer for us all the same.
I hope we get better the longer we play,
because when we win the crowd cheers hey, hey, hey!

Meghann Krone, Grade 6
Prince of Peace Catholic School, IL

Music

A feeling so jubilant builds up in your soul.
It lets you express yourself in ways nothing else can.

You can hear the clacking of heels and the tapping of toes on the tile floor.
It's a wonderful sensation that carries you to a world all your own.
Lose yourself in song and dance.

Be a part of that fantastic moment when you listen to music.

Rita Orazi, Grade 6
Zionsville Middle School, IN

Valentine

With you I have lots of fun
I know you are number one
To me you are very true
Mother I love you a ton

Roses are red and violets are blue
No matter what I will always love you
When my days get sad I know you are there
Loving you is easy like tying shoes

You help, cook, and clean and show you care
You are more lovable than Pooh Bear
You love me so much which you intend
When you have something you always share

To you this card I will send
Because you are my best friend
Will you be my valentine?
I know we will never end

Kezia Orofeo, Grade 6
St Colette School, IL

Valentine's Day!

Valentine's Day comes once a year.
And on this day these words you will hear,
"I love you!" people say to each other.
To your father, mother, sister, and brother.
Kids pass out cards, and adults go on dates,
On this holiday nobody hates.
The Christmas lights have been taken down,
Now pretty colors are hanging around,
Like red and pink, but you won't see blue.
Happy St. Valentine's Day to you!

Lauren Mantei, Grade 6
Rochester Middle School, IL

Grandma Come Back

Walking down the lonely, old street
Makes my heart beat faster
Up above me is a green blanket of branches
Protecting me from the cold rain
Freshly cut grass fills the air
Smelling so wonderful

There is a house, surrounded by yellow and red flowers
It's Grandma's house!
Inside, the air smells like chicken and noodles
That makes my stomach growl
Chocolatey baked cookies makes my mouth water
On the round table, lays a white note

The sad note says, "Wake up it's all a dream
You know I am in a better place now."

Breely Carpenter, Grade 6
Linton-Stockton Elementary School, IN

Hope

If hope could be a color
it would be the color of my mom's pink roses.

If hope could be a taste
it would taste just like my grandma's homemade applesauce.

If hope could be a smell
it would smell like fresh cookies.

If hope could be a sound
it would sound like the ocean waves.

If hope could be an animal
it would be a black cat.

Alee Turk, Grade 4
St Agnes School, IL

Sun

The sun is like an orange,
rolling up and down,
back and forth,
like a boat rocking on the waves.

Hunter Hantz, Grade 4
Country Meadow Elementary School, IN

The Teacher's Class

The teacher's class is really fun.
Mrs. Moody, our teacher, she's number 1.
She teaches math and all other things.
Until the lunch bell rings.

She sits and eats her lunch as she
munch, munch, munch.
As we go along we sing our favorite song.
Sometimes we eat cake and ice cream in our class.
Most of us say no thank you I'll pass.

We get ourselves packed and sometimes we get a snack.
All of us say hip hip hooray! We push and play.
School is almost out.
Let me hear you give a shout.

Ashlei Taylor, Grade 4
Summit Elementary School, IL

The Things Money Can't Buy

There are a few things money can't buy
Like soft silence
Or a long rest
Or a true friendship
Or a desire to do something kind
Or good advice
Or fun times
Or love
Money can't buy things you can't live without.

Camille Morrow, Grade 5
Terre Haute Adventist School, IN

The Wild Ones

I've been waiting all day long,
Just to sing one simple song.
And at the crack of dawn,
The wild ones sang their song.

It's here they cried!
The time has come!
It's time to have all of our fun!

So the wild ones danced,
And they pranced.

And they sang their merry song!!!

Kaitlin Mckernan, Grade 4
Butterfield School, IL

My Cat Baby

M y favorite
Y ou make me laugh

C ute
A wesome
T he best cat

B aby
A wonderful pet
B ad sometimes
Y owls at me

Lacy Brown, Grade 5
Morgan Elementary School, IN

Siblings

Sisters
Friendly, Beautiful
Smiling, Thinking, Talking
Best Friends, Worst Enemies
Teasing, Destroying, Tormenting
Bold, Careless
Brothers

Katie Dieckman, Grade 5
Bell-Graham School, IL

By Myself

When I'm by myself
And I close my eyes,
I'm shining high like a star,
I'm looking down from afar.
I'm flying high like a balloon,
I'm trying to reach the moon.
I'm as dark as the night,
I'm as brave as a soldier, ready to fight.
And when I open my eyes,
All I want is to be me.

Natalia Chmiel, Grade 6
Norman Bridge Elementary School, IL

Cat and Dog

Cat
Sly, soft
Pouncing, purring, scratching
Mouse, fish, leash, bone
Running, panting, begging
Playful, lazy
Dog

A.J. Adams, Grade 5
Seton Catholic School, IL

Bill

There once was a frog named Bill
who drove his car down a steep hill
he hit a brown bear
and flew into the air
when he landed he said, "what a thrill"

Kenny Christian, Grade 5
Arlington Elementary School, IN

Joe's Toe

There once was a boy named Joe
Who tripped and broke his toe
He screamed and cried
And help finally arrived
And off to the hospital he goes.

Cody McKennedy, Grade 6
Rochester Middle School, IL

I Am

When I'm by myself
and I close my eyes…

I'm as tall as the sky
I'm like a beautiful butterfly

I'm as bright as the sun
I'm having lots of fun
I'm as colorful as a flower
I'm full of Power

And when I open my eyes
All I want to be is me

Jazmeen Rivera, Grade 4
Norman Bridge Elementary School, IL

Volleyball/Kickball

Volleyball
Hard, complicated
Diving, serving, hitting
Ball, positions, field, bases
Running, kicking, tagging
Fun, enjoyable
Kickball

Bernadette Mock, Grade 6
St Mary Elementary School, IN

Triumphant Trees

Trees truly triumph
Trees provide helpful products
Leaves blow in the wind

Jeremy Strom, Grade 5
St Jacob Elementary School, IL

Home Is…

Home is the place
where I get that
warm touch.

Home is that place
where I smell and
taste what is
cooking.

It is that place
where I see and hear us
laughing.

It is that place
where we like to
be!

Ndeyiah Corneh, Grade 4
Haugan Elementary School, IL

A Long Walk Home

A long walk home,
here on my own,
a long walk home,
I walk alone.

The sun shines bright,
on my way home,
I hear the wind,
as I walk alone.

My shadow walks by me,
on my long walk home,
so I'm not really,
on my own.

When the sun goes down,
I'm back on my own,
but until then,
I walk alone.

Jordan Allen, Grade 6
Northwood Elementary School, IN

Leaves

Leaves are attractive
The leaves are enjoyable
Leaves fall from the trees

Hunter O'Dell, Grade 5
St Jacob Elementary School, IL

Beautiful Sea

O Beautiful sea,
How I doth miss thee,
With thee's foam, soft as silk,
Alas, how thou doth bilk.

Our family — mothers, fathers, sisters, brothers all
Still, we stand tall
United by brotherhood
And love, and joy, and all things good

Victoria Martin, Grade 6
Rochester Middle School, IL

Wind

The wind blows across your face
Like a bird, calm and graceful
It blows as if it were a chameleon
Always changing
On windy days, it blows with the strength of a man
Wind is everywhere
People love the wind
As they love each other

Colin Pitt, Grade 5
Countryside School, IL

Queen of the Court

Playing basketball was her game,
She was sure to earn some fame,
When she played she felt no shame,
Her game was not lame.

During a big game she does not choke,
When she stepped on the court it was not a joke,
She left the other team broke,
Her team would celebrate by all having a Coke.

All of her friends like to go to the mall,
But not her, she would rather play ball,
It was a good thing she was tall,
So she could block all the basketballs.

All of her friends like to play in a fort,
but she would rather have a wart,
Don't think of her as a sorry sort,
We all know she is Queen of the Court.

Maggie LePage, Grade 6
Wauconda Grade School, IL

Capone

My dog, Capone, was the coolest dog EVER,
I wish that I could have kept him forever,
He was the best dog I ever had,
And when I gave him away it made me sad,
he was like a really close friend,
I wish that I could have him again.

Adrian J. Kyles, Grade 4
Creekside Elementary School, IL

Snowboarding

The drifts were deep, the snow was cold
Our boards raced down the slopes so bold.

Just as the wind brushed my face
I didn't want to break my pace.

Snowboarding is a sport I love
Because I am on the snow sailing above.

Mark McLaughlin, Grade 5
Seton Catholic School, IL

Emily

E njoys collecting dolphins
M any talents but I don't let it show.
I like playing sports.
L oves every animal.
Y oung and restless

E njoys getting new things especially dolphins
L oves playing basketball
D rumstick is my nickname
E vil Emily is what my teacher calls me.
R anch goes on a lot that I eat.

Emily Elder, Grade 5
GCMS Elementary School, IL

Water

Clear as a crystal,
moving up and down.
Gliding everywhere,
surrounding me in a soft silky blanket.
Showing a new pathway
to a new world.
It's a free world to enjoy.
Living in the water is a great thing.
Being underwater is the best thing.
Living like a mermaid in my fantasy.
I dream of this stuff on my special nights,
wishing it was true,
that's why I like to dive into my swimming pool.

Alyssa Lewis, Grade 5
Twin Branch Model School, IN

Common Time

Books are laying side by side,
Kids working one by one,
teachers drinking coffee,
bathroom passes flying by,
kids singing American Pie,
coats hanging inside out,
an inconvenient truth happening now and then,
spelling bees being done,
and no one listening to what is being said.

Luke Matulewicz, Grade 6
St John the Baptist Elementary School, IN

Roses

Roses
Smelly, prickly
Growing, picking, smelling
Bees buzz by collecting nectar
Flowers
Corbin Bowen, Grade 4
Norman Bridge Elementary School, IL

Tornado of Destruction

WHOOSH!
Everything
goes by —
as you
watch
the sky.
The day
before
you
dreamed
of flying.
Today
you
got
in
the
air!
Tony Acinelli, Grade 4
Marine Elementary School, IL

My Mom Knows It All

My moms knows it all
If I make a mess
If I do something wrong
If I do anything at all
My mom knows it all

If I break the lamp
If my brother gets mad
If I let the dog in the house
If I run in the hall
My mom knows it all

If I scratch the kitchen floor
If I break down the door
If I get mud everywhere
If I rub paint off the walls
My mom knows it all

If I put a hole in the couch
If I blow up the oven
If I knock over the grandfather clock
If I trip and fall
My mom knows it all
Nathan Schulz, Grade 6
St Theresa School, IN

Ode to Pizza

Pizza can be good.
Pizza can be bad.
Sausage is the best.
Mushrooms are the worst.
Anchovies are the worst of the worst.
Cheese is second of the best.
Still my pizza is sausage.
Wesley Haub, Grade 5
Morgan Elementary School, IN

The Bear

Bear in the forest
Late at night
Fire in his eyes
Fire in his bite

Where is he going?
Where has he been?
Late at night
In his dark den

There he will stay
All night long
He will go to sleep
With a snore like a song

He will awake and be again a
Bear in the forest
Late at night
Fire in his eyes
Fire in his bite
Megan Kornesczuk, Grade 6
Immaculate Conception School, IL

Give Me

Give me skills.
Give me friendship
And I will help those who need it.
Give me talent.
Give me bravery.
Give me loyalty
And I will be loyal to the world.
Filip Czarnik, Grade 6
Norman Bridge Elementary School, IL

Boys and Girls

Boys
Rough, rowdy
Running, climbing, jumping
Male, lad, female, lassie
Giggling, primping, talking
Prissy, dramatic
Girls
Bryant Cope, Grade 5
GCMS Elementary School, IL

Making Mondays Memorable

It's a Monday morning,
I wake up, as always,
As I walk down the hallways,
I start to reach in my pockets,
Now where is that locket?!
I start to yawn,
But it's all gone,
I want to go home,
I'm sure not alone,
I'm in my first class,
I'm thirsty, so I use my last pass,
Today there's a sub,
I want to get out,
We all scream and shout!
He tells us to stop,
He gives us some candy,
We all felt so dandy,
He tells us, "Okay,"
"What did you do yesterday?"
We tell him we're done,
Let's go have some fun!
Kevin Celmer, Grade 6
Three Rivers School, IL

Mouse

There once was a mouse.
Who liked to play house.
And when the son got home.
They'd play house all alone.
And when the dad came over.
They all played Red Rover.
When the cat got in.
The boy said run away from him.
And when the mouse got away.
He ate cheese the rest of the day.
Hunter Konopasek, Grade 5
Center Street Elementary School, IL

I Am

I am the moon
looking at everyone
thinking at night
singing with the wind
shining in the dark
I am sparkling.
Diana Herrera, Grade 6
Norman Bridge Elementary School, IL

Baseball

Baseball is so fun
My team is number one
I love to play
Day after day.
Nicholas Van Atta, Grade 4
St Robert Bellarmine School, IL

My Lake House

I feel…
the wet sand sinking between my toes
the soft wind flowing through my hair
the sun burning my back

I hear…
my friends and family talking all around me
the birds singing their morning song from in the trees
the waves washing bits of rock onto the shore

I smell…
Dad cooking hamburgers on the grill
the lovely flowers in Grandma's garden
the seaweed being washed up onto the beach

I see…
my brother riding his dirt bike in the open lot
my younger cousin trying to catch a frog
my little sister fishing on the beach

I remember…
reading a book in the hammock
doing puzzles in the family room
flying across the water on my skis

Katie Garelli, Grade 6
Immaculate Conception School, IL

Beast from the Deep

Down in the ocean
Down in the deep
A creature sleeps with glowing eyes
Anyone who finds it is sure to get a nasty surprise

Don't wake it up,
You'll be eaten alive!
Not two, not four, but tentacles galore
Beast from the deep, there is danger in store!

Brandon Schumacher, Grade 5
Delphi Academy of Chicago, IL

Spring

A time when nature comes back alive
Possums come looking for fruit
Bees have awoke and working in their beehive
Birds are sounding like flutes
Trees start turning green
Flowers start blooming
Many wonders I have seen
Natures work is resuming
The winter is gone
Snow has disappeared
Worms pop out of lawns
Warm weather has interfered

Mario Ezra, Grade 6
Aurora SDA School, IL

Death

The last summer my parents got a divorce
My grandma was unwell
When she passed away
I heard her say good-bye

When I said my good-byes
I felt her say, "I love you"
It looked as if she was frozen
Because she was motionless

I tasted the harsh salt of bitter tears
I felt the soft side of me
Get ripped out of my soul
I have been alone since

My hard side took over
Helped me through my pain
I was with friends again
I felt happy again, after death

Dominick Thompson, Grade 6
Linton-Stockton Elementary School, IN

Winter

Winter,
So quiet, so silent
You can hear the wind whispering to the trees,
The soft footprints visible in the pure white snow
Trees are whispering back to the wind:
Winter, I think it's time to go.

David Ross, Grade 6
Rochester Middle School, IL

Wolf

I am a wolf. A little scary wolf.
I eat, I sleep and I howl all night
and I feast and attack with all my might.
I can smell from a distance and run after a deer.
I can see you from a home and eat right here.
I look dangerous and can be really shy.
You can see me in books and see me in zoos.
I am an animal that can be everywhere.

Michael Espinoza, Grade 5
Neil Armstrong Elementary School, IL

Tractor

It is very loud
When you hear it, you know it's a tractor.
It's fun to drive.
It is very powerful.
The huge thing can pull about anything!
It can be orange, red, green, or even brown,
They can be big or small,
There are ones with roofs or ones without roofs
But no matter what kind of tractor it is, they are loud.

Evan Dyer, Grade 5
Arlington Elementary School, IN

President's Day

President's Day we celebrate,
All the great presidents.
Our presidents are very good,
Even for our residents.

A president is good to have.
They pick the cool state tree.
A president works very hard.
He helps my friends and me.

They live in a big special house.
It is immense and white.
It is in Washington D.C.
He can stay up at night.

You should believe me about them.
They have lots of power.
They will control a lot of things.
They set the state flower.

Blake Lewis, Grade 4
Adams Central Elementary School, IN

Beautiful Butterflies

All butterflies fly
That butterfly made me sigh
They are beautiful.

Jennifer Schreiber, Grade 5
St Jacob Elementary School, IL

Winter

I saw the beautiful sight,
Of white flakes in the night.
So I looked outside and saw,
The dog got ice in her paw.

As afar as the country bound,
I saw paper flying around.
The silver string was frozen,
The trucks were bulldozing.

Everywhere there are bare trees,
As far as I can see.
You can smell the burning wood,
Come and see the sight if you could.

Kira Telford, Grade 4
British School of Chicago, IL

Bad Winter

Winter is not very fun
If you like it you're a son of a gun
Winter is so very cold
It doesn't make me very bold
Winter hurt my little toes
It also hurts my poor little nose

Louis Berardi, Grade 4
Goodfield Elementary School, IL

In My Dreams

Ever since I was little I dreamed of many things,
such as princesses, princes, and just plain weird things
But the thing I dreamed about the most was me on a horse
all my own! galloping I was as fast as the wind could go!
I had a beautiful dappled thoroughbred with the
bright yellow sun glistening in her hair
while she runs swiftly in the pasture!
when I jump on her back we explore the beautiful world
and all of its contents!
but then when I wake up it is all just a dream and wish it wasn't over!

Josephine Binette, Grade 6
St John Evangelist School, IN

The Beauty of the Beach

Oh, the beauty of the beach
The wonderful, wonderful beach
I see many shades of blue in the water.
I can hear the crash of the rough waves beating against the rocks.
The many seashells of the seashore are glistening in the warm sun.
I can feel the sand squishing between my toes
As I walk along the beach.
As I walk the sun beats down upon me,
Warming my body inside and out
Making me tingle.
Seagulls dive into the water gulping down small fish
When they reappear.
Beautiful swaying palm trees line the beach
Creating shade for beach lovers.
Oh, how I love the beautiful, beautiful beach.

Brittany Ogden, Grade 6
Laketon Elementary School, IN

Snow Day

Waking up to a world of snow, you mom telling you NO SCHOOL
you jumping up and down in pure excitement
but then calming yourself down to think about what to do today,
you see your dad getting ready to shovel the snow off your driveway
you dig through your closet to find your snow pants
you rush towards your coat, gloves, and hat, you tighten your boots so no snow gets in,
you rush outside to bitter coldness,
you make a snowball to throw at your brother
direct hit right in his face, he chases you down and tackles you,
your dad tells you to help him with the shoveling, but you don't listen and keep playing
you go back inside and take your snow gear off
you find a cup of hot cocoa waiting for you
you call your friends, first you play football, then you have a snowball fight
after that you go sledding at the biggest hill you know of
you race down the hill knocking each other off their sleds
you then arrive home at dinnertime, you eat a homemade meal
at the table you talk about what happened during the day
you tell the best part to your parents and they laugh in return
then your mom says time for bed, you argue with your mom and she says fine
thirty more minutes so you go downstairs and watch some TV
you finally go to bed wishing tomorrow will be a snow day too.

Michael Shannon, Grade 6
Immaculate Conception School, IL

Bad to the Bone

I am not good, but bad,
My range is from a D to an F,
When kids see me, they are usually very sad.

Teachers try to keep me private from other students
So they won't see how bad I really am
As you hand me in, the teachers put a frown on their face, no one knows when I will come
Although I am not as silent as a lamb.

As you gaze upon me, I am covered with red,
You wish that you can redo me.
Sometimes when kids see me they wish that they could run home and go to bed.
Most kids hide me in their expandable files and wish that I am not even there

I am strong, stainless, and steel
With a heart the size of a pen
I am bad as you can see
But that is just the way I really do feel.

Emma Wilkinson, Grade 6
Our Lady of Peace School, IL

The Steady Beat of the African Drum

The African drum has a steady beat like the people on New York street
The chocolate hands hit the drum in a steady beat so we move our body and feet
The African king tells the prince that the spirits play their holy drums so they can bring out the sun
The other village comes to visit as they play their drums I feel my soul and the song become one
The drum is the sound of my brothers and sisters back in Africa
I listen to the drum as if I'm listening to my heart beat
On the seven days of Kwanzaa I wear my African dress
It symbolizes how far my people have come and how me and the spirits of the African drum are one
Our people carve the drum from the spiritual tree
And we take hide from a sacrifice that the gods give to us for the top of the drum
Rap is the child of the African drum it forms my attitude
Rap is an untamed lion but the African drum is a formal flower
The African drum is the mother of all music and music is attitude
And attitude sets us free and shows our true colors

Peniel Love, Grade 6
Belzer Middle School, IN

The Lake of the Ozarks

My friend is calling me. The blue jay is singing peacefully. The motor of the boat is relaxing. The lake is crashing against the wall. My moms mushy brownies are the best. The chicken is crunchy. Our boat is lovely. Party Cove is a little crazy. I smell the fresh fish. The fish are slimy.

Mary Chapman, Grade 4
Erie Elementary School, IL

Colors of the Rainbow

R ed: Love. Is the feel of roses surrounding you. The feel of chocolate running down your throat.
O range: Glory. The gleam of a medal, shining brightly. When you slap the hands of your opponents after winning the game.
Y ellow: Joy. The blazing sun on your face. The sight of shining items in the sand.
G reen: Envy. The sight of green eyes, staring long and hard. Longing for an object that belongs to someone else.
B lue: Sadness. The sight of the ocean; deep, cold, and never ending. Big tears rolling down someone's cheek.
I ndigo: Aloneness. The smell of an empty house standing by itself. The sound of the night with nothing to hear.
V iolet: Calm. The sight of the morning pond when the fisherman casts his nets. The sound of crickets in the night.

Becca Carpenter, Grade 6
St Joseph Elementary School, IN

Beautiful Song
Birds sing in a tree
Singing their beautiful song
Tweet tweet the birds say
Ambrionna Alexander, Grade 6
Christian Life Schools, IL

The Little Princess
This is my guinea pig.
She is small and very cute.
Every time I pet her,
I'm glad I don't have a newt.

This is my guinea pig.
She is silly and funny.
Every time she sneezes,
Her nose must be runny.

This is my guinea pig.
She is soft and cuddly.
Every time she takes a bath,
She makes it very bubbly.
Samantha Duffy, Grade 5
Our Lady of Peace School, IL

Spring Has Sprung
Spring has sprung
It has officially begun
There are flowers and bees
And birds in the trees
They sing happy songs
For winter has come and gone
Summer is on its way
Hip-hip-hooray!
Natalie Sheehan, Grade 6
St Mary School, IL

Ice Hockey Rocks
I cy
C old in the rink
E xtraordinarily fun to play

H ot on ice
O utstanding
C osts a lot of money
K ey play
E xciting
Y elling people

R eady for hard hits
O utstanding players
C hecking hard
K icking the other teams' butt
S kating hard
Jake Jauch, Grade 6
Thayer J Hill Middle School, IL

Peaceful
The sun is shining,
your sister is laughing,
you're sleeping,
all is peaceful.
Birds are chirping,
flowers are blooming,
all is calm.
People sleeping,
animals scurrying,
into their homes to sleep,
all is quiet for the world to sleep.
Katie Roe, Grade 6
St Scholastica School, IL

Snow
White, chilly
Freezing, chilling, snowing
Fun, numb
This makes snow fun.
Andrew Beatty, Grade 5
Cloverdale Middle School, IN

Brother's Habits
J ared is his name
A real pain in the neck
R eal silly
E rodes away
D rives me crazy
S o special

H as a gold fish
A lways talking
B oring
I think he's weird
T hinks he's tough
S melly
Kylie Trantina, Grade 4
GCMS Elementary School, IL

The State Fair
My brother threw up on every ride
I got ice cream in my eye
I spent all my money to win a stuffed cat
The wind blew away my favorite hat
Somebody screamed in my left ear
I sure do hope we come back next year
Margaret O'Mahoney, Grade 4
St Matthew School, IL

The Frog
I sat by the pond
I saw a big, fat, green frog
SPLASH! He jumped away.
Nate Meinders, Grade 4
Robein Elementary School, IL

Benjamin
B all sports I like
E very game I make a tackle
N ever hates to mow the yard
J ake is one of my best friends
A nd my favorite color is blue
M y favorite sport is football
I like circle noodles
N ever will play soccer again
Benjamin Johnson, Grade 4
GCMS Elementary School, IL

The Cutest
They are the cutest
Everybody should have some
Cats are so fluffy
Alexis Barrera, Grade 4
Martin L King Elementary School, IL

Homework
Homework is Too Hard!
I'd like to throw it out,
My teacher gives me too much,
I'd just like to pout.

My mom does all my homework!
She still doesn't get it,
She is up all night,
While throwing a fit.

All the parents say it's too hard!
My kids are going to quit school,
If this homework keeps up,
The kids will feel like fools!
Connor McCadam, Grade 5
Bell-Graham School, IL

My Brother Jacob
J ust arrived.
A dorable face.
C ries a lot.
O ut of the ordinary.
B rings joy when he smiles.
Lauren Kusbel, Grade 4
Liberty Elementary School, IN

Friends and Enemies
Friends
Caring, comforting
Laughing, talking, shopping
Honest, loving, mean, cruel
Gossiping, lying, cheating
Unkind, dishonest
Enemies
Isabella Conrad, Grade 5
Adams Central Elementary School, IN

Legos

There is a great craze that is sweeping the nation.
It's Legos and you use your imagination!
Enjoy and play with your favorite creation.
What ever is your fascination!
They're fun! They're cool!
They rock! They rule!

Michael Gerard Majerczyk, Grade 6
St Daniel the Prophet School, IL

Heather

You are great at basketball
It helps that you are so tall
On the court you are steady
So you will not ever fall

Whenever I need you you're there and ready
Like when I get hurt you're there with a teddy
On my birthdays I can always tell you care
You never get me gifts I have already

They're two peas in a pod, Heather and Clare
I know for each other they're always there
I have heard many people say these things
Next to you, Heather dear, no one compares

Clare Koehler, Grade 6
St Colette School, IL

Moms

Moms are funny,
Like a silly bunny.
They are always so bright and sunny.
Like a big pot of Pooh's honey.

They are there to give a helping hand.
Always, forever, until the end.
Guidance and love throughout the land.
Moms will always be your best friend.

Ashley Downs, Grade 5
North Intermediate Center of Education, IL

Daniel's Poems

I am a sky poet sitting on big fluffy clouds
Writing white poems.
My poems glide through the huge vivid sky.

I am a night poet growing darker and darker
Every few minutes writing pitch black poems.
My poems give the moon and stars their show time
Painting everything black.

I am an Earth poet blending in with mountains
And oceans writing beautiful landscape poems.
My poems change the format of the world
Producing many elements.

Daniel Kazimierski, Grade 6
St Barbara School, IL

I Got an A!

Last week my class took a test
I really didn't study
I know my grade won't be the best
I bet it will be cruddy
I'll be lucky if I get a B
I'd absolutely love it
But if I end up with a D
I won't hear the end of it
My heart is pounding from the stress
My teacher's coming this way
She puts the paper on my desk
Oh look, I got an A!

Suzana Rodriguez, Grade 6
Benjamin Franklin Elementary School, IN

Summer Fun

I love riding bikes.
I like to swim in the sun.
I love horses.
I will go and play soccer.
But most of all I like playing with my puppies.

Mallory Gores, Grade 4
Cynthia Heights Elementary School, IN

My Pageant

I remember when…
Winning the Miss Indiana National Pre-teen contest
Second youngest
Only one who did well in the interview
I had a good chance
I remember when…
My name was announced in the top five
I was terrified
I answered the hardest question in the world
I thought I bombed it
First runner up again
I remember when…
The first runner up wasn't me
I was so excited
I was the new Miss Indiana National Pre-teen
And I was going to Florida for the Nationals

Jasmyne Milheiser, Grade 6
Haubstadt Community School, IN

Fire

Fire! Fire! Light and bright
Through the forest of the night
You give us light in the dark
But why thy heart of burning coals?

Though you help us night and day
Your ever swinging pattern may slightly sway
And cause living things the light of day.

Hanna Brown, Grade 4
Creekside Elementary School, IL

The Legacy of the Stooges

Moe
The toe
Pointing the way
Larry
The hairy
Sticking up in fright
Curly
The girlie
Just not up to the fight
The three
Have taught
Us so much in life
The process
Of planning
And trial and error
Thinking
Interdependently
Disseminating duties among each other
Do you doubt
My opinion?
The Stooges have taught us
Exactly how not to act.

Sunny Zhao, Grade 5
Steeple Run Elementary School, IL

Steven Burbank Pelcha

My step dad
Went to the hospital
I was terrified
I thought…
He was not going
To make it,

I was right

When mom told me,
I did not
Want to believe her…

I checked everywhere…
He was nowhere to be found

Then…
I started to sob
Timothy Wilson, Grade 6
Linton-Stockton Elementary School, IN

The Sky

Bright sky
Friends say good-bye
The bright sky turns to night
Every light gets turned off so people
Can sleep.

Jacob Short, Grade 4
Robein Elementary School, IL

Me

I have a heart.
I have a soul.
I'm full of dreams
Through which hope flows.
I'm full of courage,
Love, true.
Bending down to help you
Smiling,
Frowning,
Happy,
Sad,
Sometimes angry,
Sometimes mad.

What do you see in me?
Amelia Glueck, Grade 5
Tremont Elementary School, IL

Autumn

Wind through my fingers,
Jacket around my back,
Squirrels gathering food,
I know it's Autumn.
As I watch the trees,
I notice falling leaves,
With cold growing colder,
I know it's Autumn.
As I with knees shaking,
Sit down reluctantly,
by my freezing pond,
I know it's Autumn.
Too cold for sports,
Too warm for sledding,
I walk silently,
I know it's Autumn.
Plants dying,
Animals hiding,
School starting,
I know it's Autumn.

I know it's Autumn.
Brent Johnson, Grade 6
Oak Prairie Jr High School, IL

Diamonds

D azzling and sparkling
I s a girls best friend
A mazing shapes
M oms love diamonds
O oooo! So pretty
N o fake ones, please
D ads spend lots of money
S uperbly perfect

Emy Lutchka, Grade 5
Seton Catholic School, IL

What Is a Brother?

What is a big brother?
A big brother is so…
Annoying
Weird
Mean
Doesn't listen
Not helpful
Funny
Be active
Smart
Playful
He's in 5th grade
He's boring
That's my brother Zeb!

Elley Levell, Grade 4
Morgan Elementary School, IN

My Poem

I am a flag poet
Sitting on the
Red and white stripes
As I write my poems
They flap in the breeze
And my poems fall to Earth
Gently and quietly

I am a bird poet
Soaring through the air
Gliding gently
Letting all my poems soar
Behind me

I am a cloud poet
Bouncing from cloud to cloud
Watching my poems glide to the ground
Lawrence Nisivaco, Grade 6
St Barbara School, IL

The Untold Story

Watch me weave my tales…
Tales of finches, monkey, ducks
Rhyme away on whales
Who listen, awestruck

The fine music of this song
Is too fine to be heard
So listen to that distant gong
Instead of to my words

But, with paper, quill or pen,
I unravel tales of gold…
Since you won't listen to them,
They will be left untold

Ruth Kahn, Grade 5
Countryside School, IL

What Am I Today?

I am a football being thrown into the air,
A top spinning that needs to be stopped,
I'm a dancer leaping for joy,
A marker being used on a whiteboard,
I feel as a picture being cut apart,
I am the sun larger than life,
A mouse, small, too small to be heard,
I'm a bright red box hiding all of my secrets,
A dolphin swimming from all fear,
I feel as a divorce pulling everyone apart,
I am a sunset glowing purple and orange,
A frozen icicle gleaming and sparkling,
I'm a math book with all of the answers,
A song playing that everyone knows and sings along with,
I feel as waves crashing on the sandy beach,
I am a book with too many words to read,
A cookie being baked in an oven,
I'm a trumpet with a broken key,
So, what are you going to be today?

Maggie I. Kitt, Grade 5
Churubusco Elementary School, IN

Angel

I closed my eyes to go
to sleep, but there I felt something by my
feet. I fell asleep early that night and awoke
wondering if it was a rat running by my toes.
Early that morning I opened my eyes and there it
floats; it's not a shadow or a ghost, but an angel
watching me with every hope.

Alexandra Vela, Grade 6
St Anastasia School, IL

Summer

Summer's here again,
All warm and nice.
Children run and play with joy throughout the day.
Instead of winter's icy breeze
The days are long and warm with laughter.
The grass is green, the flowers rich with color,
Every leaf, every gust of wind is filled with life.
Summer's here once again.

Gwendolyn Huth, Grade 5
Maplebrook Elementary School, IL

Movies and Books

Movie
Fun, long
Sitting, looking, listening
Epic Movie, Ghost Rider, Redwall, The Lightning Thief
Reading, attention, focus
Interesting, great
Book

Amadeus Garcia, Grade 6
Rochester Middle School, IL

Skateboarding

I love skateboarding I love the feeling of it
I love the sound the wheels make on the pavement
The wind in my face to go so fast I can't stop

I love learning new tricks.
Also the detail of learning them
Landing them gets me excited and makes me feel good
Flip tricks, Grabs, Grinds, Manuals.
I like them all.

I love going up things, ramps, kickers, etc.
Going down things, ramps, staircases, hills.
Over things, chairs, benches, rocks, sometimes even people.
Also grinding on things, rails benches, tables, parts of ramps.

That's why I love this sport.

Carlos Skenandore, Grade 6
Thayer J Hill Middle School, IL

Bunnies

Bunnies are funny,
the way they hop
because their ears go
flop, flop, flop!

Keziah Lehman, Grade 4
Country Meadow Elementary School, IN

The Old Man

There once was a man with a book.
He told his wife that he was a very bad crook.
He went to jail
For burning people's mail,
And now the man thinks that he can cook.

Taylor Roberts, Grade 6
ROWVA East Elementary School, IL

A Puzzle Piece of Learning

Teachers teach so many things
Topic to topic to topic
Teacher can be fun at times
But are usually cranky
Mean, happy, surprised, or full of laughter
If we do bad on a test,
We get a lecture
That goes on and on and on
If we're too loud
We get in trouble
And stay sad for the rest of the day
Some have style,
Others are funny,
Some get behind
And some are always ahead
But without teachers,
We'd all be clowns.

Paulina Niebrugge, Grade 5
St John of the Cross Parish School, IL

American Flag

Look at our flag flying high
The red and white stripes
The blue and white flying
When we see the flag tears are wiped

We fight for it
We live in the stars
To think it was made out of bits
It's all thanks to those bars

Aleka Seneca, Grade 5
GCMS Elementary School, IL

Paintball

Despite the pain,
Toward the bunker,
Among teammates,
Across the field,
Past the enemy,
Without cover,
By a tree,
Along the river,
About the gun,
Beyond the gun's capacity,
In spit of the danger,
Out of the fear I win paintball.

Jake Melcher, Grade 6
Michael Grimmer Middle School, IN

My Mom

My mom is like the sun.
My mom likes to have fun.
Although she can be a bum.
I love my mom.

My mom is like the sun.
She can be a bit boring
Once we were soring sick.
But she pulled a little trick!

My mom is like the sun.
My mom appreciates what I do.
She loves me and cares about me.
I love my mom.

My mom is like the sun.
I have the best mom I could have.
My mom encourages me to do stuff.
I love my mom

My mom is like the sun.
When I was a baby she loved me.
And fed me and she still does.
I love my mom a lot.

Esmeralda Martinez, Grade 4
Hoagland Elementary School, IN

Sports

Sports are awesome sports are great
Soccer is the only sport I hate
It has no point it is not fun
Because you are always on the run
Kicking the ball up and down
Looking like a weird clown

Jocelyn Matsen, Grade 6
Rochester Middle School, IL

Mrs. Overman

M elvin, Gibson City, and Sibley
R uns our school
S weeter than apple pie

O ver the intercom
V ery funny
E lementary is where she rules
R ight on top of things
M om at home principal at school
A lot of energy
N ice, nice, nice, and nice

Mallory Bauer, Grade 4
GCMS Elementary School, IL

Miranda

There once was a girl named Miranda.
Her best friend was Amanda.
They always walk to school,
And sometimes the outside is cool.
They like to look at the trees,
Especially the ones with colorful leaves.

Karli Anderson, Grade 5
Seton Catholic School, IL

Darkness

Darkness
Scared, blind,
Falling, yelling, dreaming
No one is responding to me, screaming
Stopping, calling, hearing
Visible, audible
Blackness

Demetre Stavros, Grade 6
Stanley Clark School, IN

Red-tailed Hawk

Red-tailed Hawk
Accipiter, buteos
Soaring, shining, mesmerizing
Searching for their prey
Diving, feeding, tearing
Swooping, gliding
Hawk

Matthew Gonzalez, Grade 4
Dixie Bee Elementary School, IN

Skateboard

Skateboard
Dangerous, scary,
Flips, jumps, turns,
Hurts when you wreck
Knee buster

Thomas Light, Grade 5
Staunton Elementary School, IN

Storm

Splash! I jumped into the pool
It was so warm and cool
The hot tubs were so bubbly and warm
Then blew in a big, gigantic storm!
I grabbed my shoes and my towel
Before the storm began to howl

I ran into the wooden clubhouse
I sat in there as quiet as a mouse
Until I heard no sound
Then I started to dance around

Brittany Lord, Grade 5
Bell-Graham School, IL

Chocolate

Chocolate melting in front of my face
I want to have it with me my whole life
You can buy it at a store in a case
You can cut it at the end with a knife

Taking a huge bite out of the middle
Ripping the wrapper off it carefully
Sometimes the chocolate can be little
People think it is so chocolatey

Sometimes people think it is funny
People like it to swirl in their belly
People think it looks like a bunny
I once got chocolate from the deli

I save it and close it up with my bands
Holding it preciously in my big hands

Korey Partenheimer, Grade 6
McHenry Middle School, IL

Step Dad

S o you're talking about your dad
T ough guys tough guys
E very day he's mad
P eanuts are his favorite

D o you know him well enough
A t lunch he has pizza
D ude I hope I live

Devyn Roesch, Grade 4
GCMS Elementary School, IL

Shoes Are Accessories for Your Feet

Shoes are accessories for you feet,
they make your feet feel pretty and neat.
You can dress them up all nice and sweet,
or dress them casual and upbeat.
You can wear heels, you can wear flats,
you can even wear sandals that have no backs.
But whatever you wear just remember,
that…
Shoes are accessories for your feet.

Natalie E. Bengert, Grade 6
Haubstadt Community School, IN

Got Milk?

I went to the store to buy
some flour, eggs, milk, sugar, butter,
vanilla, peanut butter! Then I went
home and got out a cookie sheet,
fork, measuring cups, spatula, mixer, and
bowl, and turn on the oven! Next
thing I did was hear the tick,
tick, ticking of the timer! The
cookies are fresh!
Got Milk?

Kendra Goins, Grade 5
Levan Scott Academy, IN

The Whispers of the Sea

I am the sea
I haul my current along the shore
My bridge poles are stable as they can be
I have so much waste as the eye can see
So come on out and I'll tell you a story
From my disgraceful times

Kayla Mayberry, Grade 5
Norris City Omaha Elementary School, IL

Nature

The sounds of nature float about the air
Animals, insects, and trees lay about
The den of wolves and the beautiful mare
Love is all around in the nature route

The smells of fresh trees enlighten my day
Green bushes and red roses look pretty
Nature will hurt sometimes while on the way
But the view is better than a city

The cute frogs look exotic in the fog
The sun stares down until the moon rises
The ants lay around in some special log
The forest friends hide in their disguises

Nature has more feelings than words can say
Even if you're at the dunes or the bay.

Emily Herne, Grade 6
McHenry Middle School, IL

Where Is Green?

Where is green?
Green is nature sitting in soft grass
Where is green?
Green is an apple falling off a tree
Where is green?
Green is a watermelon sweet and juicy as can be
Where is green?
Green is a frog jumpin' and leapin' around
Where is green?
Green is a lime sour and sweet
Where is green?
Green is Tinkerbell's color of dress
Where is green?
Green is the color of St. Patrick's Day
Where is green?
Green is inside of me

Rebecca Feliciano, Grade 5
Norman Bridge Elementary School, IL

Winter Wonders

The crystal white snow is a fantastic sight
Snowing in the day, snowing in the night

But snow storms like a blizzard could start
Yet it truly is a piece of nature's art

Every day in the winter we see snow
The snow on some mountains can be very old

But a bad thing is that the winter's cold
And we often have to shovel snow

A fun winter game is the snowball fight
Snowballs flying in the air day and night

We also see snowy trees, standing with might
Seeing those snowy trees is a breathtaking sight

Let's not forget that holiday fun
Which makes winter a season for everyone

And when the winter's finished, the snow is too
But you'll never forget the joy it brought you

Hector A. Quinones, Grade 5
Benjamin Franklin Elementary School, IN

Cupid's Heart

Love floats around in the air like a fluffy cloud
It spreads like dandelion seeds blowing in the wind
It's red and pink like a big, lacy Valentine
Love is a puppy licking with affection
Love is God welcoming you into His reaching arms
I have never-ending happiness when I feel love.

Anna Rafanelli, Grade 5
St John of the Cross Parish School, IL

Spring

Spring is smelling flowers,
Playing outside for hours and hours,
Colors all around,
Lots of bugs, lots of sound.
Spring is the best season all year round.
Morgan Alewelt, Grade 6
Rochester Middle School, IL

Brandon

B randon
R ear-ended
A
N on-smart
D ork
O h, did I say
N on-smart!
P.S. His name was Austin!!
Kylee Hardwick, Grade 4
Shoals Elementary School, IN

What I Don't Like

I don't like mice
And I don't like lice
I don't like peas
And I don't like cheese
And now you might think
I don't like pink
Prairie Boschulte, Grade 4
Goodfield Elementary School, IL

People

People aren't judged
By the color of their skin
People aren't judged
By country or religion
Everyone is equal
Frank Kalisik, Grade 6
Elwood C C School, IL

Dog

I once gave a dog a milk bone.
A hole he then did dig.
He planted it right in the ground,
And did a little jig.
Benton Griffiths, Grade 4
Adams Central Elementary School, IN

Eagle

Eagle
Graceful, powerful,
Diving, flying, soaring
Searching for fresh fish
Nesting, hatching, feeding
Young, needy
Eaglets
Evin Fisher, Grade 4
Dixie Bee Elementary School, IN

My Four-legged Friends

My four-legged friends have spots that are brown, white, and black
My four-legged friends have hooves, a tail, and a mane
My four-legged friends eat hay, oats, and treats
My four-legged friends need clean stalls and water
My four-legged friends you can ride
My four-legged friends are horses of course
Kehlee DeKeyrel, Grade 6
Illinois City Elementary School, IL

If Hope Could Be A...

If hope could be a color
it would be pink as bright as a rose.

If hope could be a taste
it would taste just like a sweet watermelon on a hot summer day.

If hope could be a smell
it would be my mom's floral scented perfume.

If hope could be a sound
it would be the crackling of wood in a fireplace.

If hope could be a feeling
it would be the feeling of being loved.

If hope could be an animal
it would be a new-born puppy.
Karina Ayala, Grade 4
St Agnes School, IL

Room Two (A Poem for Two Voices)

(Voice 1)   (Together)   (Voice 2)

Room two

Is a terrible classroom!

A terrible, horrible, awful room

The teacher snores as loud as an elephant.

Like a roller coaster.

Kids throw paper airplanes all around,

Like pure white snow falling from the sky.

Room two.

There's gum under the table.

Spitballs fly,

From their naps, by and by.

Sleepy heads awaken

For kids, a happy time.

Pie in the teacher's face.

Graffiti on the walls,

Room two.

Writing

Paint,

Everywhere.

Dancing ballerinas, in funny little shoes

Pets make silly noises, like hip-hop, jazz too.

Room two. What a horrible classroom!
Emily Martiens and Marisa Voos, Grade 5
Tremont Elementary School, IL

The City

All the beautiful things I can see
All done for you and me
Everybody's screaming from this crowd
Oh my gosh it's really loud
Some are running some are walking
Some are whispering some are talking
There are so many stores
I even get surprised when I enter the doors
All the restaurants where I can eat
Everything is always really neat.
Well what can I tell you this is the city.

Jocelyne Muñoz, Grade 5
Peck Elementary School, IL

America Is…

America is the state of love,
America is the state of power,

America is…
Well, no one can tell about America,
because America is so famous that no one wants to leave,

Everyone is coming to America,
America is the state of …nature,
America was made for "freedom."

Ronisha Brown, Grade 6
Emmett Louis Till Math & Science School, IL

Colts vs Bears

This Sunday is the Super Bowl.
And I must confess,
I'm cheering for both teams.
They are both the best.

My dad is from East Chicago,
so he likes the Bears.
My mom likes the Colts.
What a game this will be!

I can hardly believe what I'm about to say,
I might watch a whole football game!
Then who will I cheer for?

I must confess,
I'm cheering for both teams.
They are both the best.

Good news and bad plays,
it doesn't matter anyway.
Don't get me wrong because it's true.

I must confess,
Both teams are the best!

McKenzi Sidor, Grade 4
Snacks Crossing Elementary School, IN

Peace

Peace is more powerful then some people think.
To get peace all wars and problems would end.
People would start to care about one another.
Nobody would lie, cheat, murder, or steal.
We would look into each others eyes
with love and passion not hatred.
We would help everyone,
and everything that needed help.
Most of all we would have warmness and love in our heart,
like those who are deeply in love have today.
That's my definition of peace.

Jessica Bulinski, Grade 6
Rochester Middle School, IL

Shooting, Scoring, Soccer Cleats

These are my soccer cleats
They're white, red, and black
At the bottom there are a lot of little spikes
With an Adidas sign on the back.

These are my soccer cleats
With them I can spike the ball
It always goes in the net
Except in indoor it sometimes hits the wall.

These are my soccer cleats
Sometimes they wait in my mom's convertible
They help me get a lot of speed
They're also very comfortable!

Michelle Morefield, Grade 5
Our Lady of Peace School, IL

Living in a Watery World

I fly through the air like a bird,
Kerplunk!
I shatter the calm blue world with a plop.
I am the Earth in a vast blue universe.
Then comes the waiting, wishing, and wondering,
If a monster will come.
I feel it coming now, but I can't see it yet,
I spot it now!
It's my arch nemesis, the swordfish.
He swims up close, he bit! Hooray!
Then down I go into the home of fish.
I now feel my master's tug;
I'm in a tug of war.
Then up, up, and away.
I soar into the heavens,
I feel the wind slap my round face.
Now I'm plunging back down to Earth.
I see my master lunging for his net,
This is going to be close.
Then three cheers!
He caught the fish!

Stephen O'Neill, Grade 6
Our Lady of Peace School, IL

My Babysitter

My babysitter is a wreck.
She is such a pain in the neck.
She makes me mow the lawn.
She tells me to clean the house 'til dawn.
I beg her not to do it on my knees,
But she refuses even if I say please.

Mathew Nuguid, Grade 5
Seton Catholic School, IL

Jim

There once was a boy named Jim
Whose father never taught him to swim
He slipped off the dock
And sank like a rock
And that was the end of him

Megan Handa, Grade 4
Beebe Elementary School, IL

Imagination

Can you hear that grand whistle,
coming closer in like a missile,
squinting your eyes for a closer look
you see it had come from Stoneybrook,
suddenly you hear glass shatter,
then a few things clatter,
temptation makes you go outside,
and you watch birds over you glide,
finally you know what that noise is,
it's your neighbors cat Frizz,
reaching out your hand to pet him,
touching and noticing he's so slim,
taking off your hand quickly,
Frizz suddenly running slickly,
you wake up from your sensation,
and notice it was your imagination!

Batoul Hasan, Grade 4
Universal School, IL

My Skill Helper

This is my volleyball.
It spikes very well.
If someone wants to have it,
I will never let it sell!

This is my volleyball.
It helps me practice my skills.
It makes me much stronger,
It will always do my will.

This is my volleyball.
If it ever went flat…
It makes me crazy
Just to think about that!

Emily Hogan, Grade 5
Our Lady of Peace School, IL

Bright Star

A star is in the sky
Shining very bright
Oh so far up high
Lighting up the night

Maria Voss, Grade 6
Milan Middle School, IN

Reality

I have my moments,
I have my times,
When I wish all moments were mine.

I have this feeling
Inside my heart.
It's not like eating a fresh raspberry tart

It's a feeling called love
That is sent from above

A feeling of truth
That has come from a root.

The tree of life,
The tree that grows,
With magic that nobody knows.

A mystery, a clue
What can you do?
It's reality.

Samantha Campos, Grade 6
St Anastasia School, IL

Walking on Sunshine

The sun is a battery
except the sun will
never run out of energy
Oh, I love to walk in the sunshine
The sun is what keeps me playing
until the sun goes to bed
and the moon comes out
to greet the cool, midnight sky
Oh I think I'll sing a song
"I'm walking on sunshine!
Woah oh! It's got to feel good!!!"

Alec Hurst, Grade 6
Haubstadt Community School, IN

Billy

B eing a loser
I s a
L ittle hard for
L iving like
Y ankee Doodle

Austin Jones, Grade 4
Shoals Elementary School, IN

Sunset Watching

Sunset watching
Isn't so boring you see
You can talk and laugh
Or eat some spaghetti
It's nice to take pictures
And see them later on
You look back and see
What you did with you and me
You can eat your lunch
From some hours ago
Or you can just sit there
And fall asleep you know?
Sunsets are so colorful
And pretty to you and me
Something else about sunsets
If having time for you and me

Jenny Gavin, Grade 6
St Mary School, IL

Florida

The suns in the sky
Like a big ball of fire
The airplane is off
Like a white winged flyer.

The flight has just ended
Although it is night
I can still see
With the moons dimming light

When I wake up
I run down the stair
Put my bathing suit on,
Pull a comb through my hair.

The hot sand and cool water
Looks so appealing
My brothers and I
Are so happily squealing.

We had a good time
But now we're all low
We get on the plane
And downhearted we go.

Maddie Brewer, Grade 4
British School of Chicago, IL

Horse Pasture

H ay is good for them to chew.
O ats are good for them too.
R unning in the pasture.
S itting in the sun.
E ating and seeing what to do is fun.

Peyton Winchell, Grade 5
Floyds Knobs Elementary School, IN

Thinks That I Am Thankful For…

My life, my family,
Friends who are there for me,
Having food on the table at every meal,
Being able to share my talents with others,
That I can go to school, having a healthy body,
Having a dog who I love,
Being able to read a book, and write a letter,
Having my dad be my coach for basketball,
Having a mom when I am sick,
Being able to share Thanksgiving with my family,
The things I have that maybe others don't,
Having a nice house to live in,
People in this world that I can trust,
Being able to see my friends and family every day,
Being able to play sports and be good at them,
Being able to give to others,
Going on wonderful vacations,
Having nice clothes, being able to go shopping,
Being able to go to the movies,
Having a TV, having a computer, having an iPod,
Loving the Lord.

Anna Maria Sikorski, Grade 6
St Matthew School, IL

The Day My Sister Flew Away

There once was a day my sister flew away.
That was the day I could not stay.

I just was too excited,
I was most delighted.

When my sister flew away,
that was the day.

Justice Wrobleski, Grade 5
Gard Elementary School, IL

The Sun

Sun
Beautiful, round
Shining, warming, brightening
Lighting the Earth and making flowers bloom
Important

Amna Ali, Grade 4
Universal School, IL

Friends

Friends are for laughing,
For roasting marshmallows over an open fire,
For camping out in tents,
And for telling ghost stories at night.
Friends are for pillow fights,
For make-overs and slumber parties,
For staying up late and watching movies.
Friends are forever!

Jessi Chambliss, Grade 5
Tremont Elementary School, IL

Genius

Genius
Knowledgeable, quiet
Flying, risk taking, disobeying
Uncontrolled by those pulsing, evil red eyes —
Loving, missing family, learning
Miniature, pleasant
Child

Andrew Yarger, Grade 6
Stanley Clark School, IN

By the Little Creek

Lush emerald plants on the edge of a creek
Crisp maple leaves and wavering pine needles
The creek splashing down on chestnut-colored rocks
Gentle breezes playing with my hair
Flying drops of cool clear water flying from the creek
Spring has begun

Neeta Patwari, Grade 5
Frank H Hammond Elementary School, IN

The Tea Gown Clown

There was a clown who lived in Queenstown
He was large and reddish brown
Wearing an orange and blue tea gown
He stole a king's crown
He did not understand
When things did not go as he had planned
That the people of the town
Felt so letdown
They had to frown
His house they tore down
When they found him way down
Under the ground
He had changed his gown to olive brown
It was his own hand
That caused him to take the stand
And become banned
To no man's land
Where he was renown
As the clown
In the tea gown
Who stole the king's crown

Jared Light, Grade 5
St Peter Immanuel Lutheran School, IN

Baseball

Baseball is a sport of nine.
With four bases and a ball.
With eight in front and one behind.
The catcher sits back and signals the call.

The umpire calls the batter out.
As the fans stand up and shout.

Dacota Schaad, Grade 5
Perry Central Elementary School, IN

My Best Friend

My best friend has pointy ears.
He cries a lot with no tears.
He walks around on all fours.
He even tries to open doors.
He is shiny and black.
Beware he might attack.
He has a brother just like me.
At night, it is my friend you can't see.
He is skinny, not fat.
In fact, he is my cat.
His name is Little Bit.

Byron Starr, Grade 6
Rochester Middle School, IL

Art

Art is like a
Dark lonely heart.
But it's a
Smarter heart of art.

Wade Tomes, Grade 5
GCMS Elementary School, IL

The Person I Love

The person I love the most
Would have to be my mother
Because my mother takes care
Of me and my sisters

She goes to IVY Tech College
She wants to be a teacher
I think she would be
A great teacher some day

She does well in school
She is a responsible mother
I love her very dearly
She is so kind and sweet

She loves cats and hates mice
My mother is truly the best mother
I could ever have
And that is all about my mom

Christine Celeste Marquardt, Grade 4
Hoagland Elementary School, IN

Dogs

dogs
cute cuddly
running jumping barking
protecting me every day
listening obeying entertaining
soft warm
best friend

Dana Rudzinski, Grade 4
Norman Bridge Elementary School, IL

I Remember

I remember,
I remember when
The sky was blue
and my room too.

Where my closet was big,
and my bed real small.
Where I learned to
walk and talk and crawl.

My old school,
my best friend.
I remember we would
laugh for days on end.

They said I'd forget.
I said, "Do not fret,
you are my memories.
I will make new,
but do not argue.
You are all just
like family."

Trisha L. Cosby, Grade 6
Haubstadt Community School, IN

My Birthday

I woke up this morning
I yelled, "Hooray.
Today is my birthday!"
I will have a party.
I will invite Mrs. Hardy.
We will have some cake.
And, go fishing by the lake.
I will have fun, for heaven's sake,
Because, today is my birthday!

Debra Cole, Grade 4
Lavizzo Elementary School, IL

Grace

There once was a girl named Grace,
She always ran at a steady pace,
She came in first,
She had a great thirst,
And drank water by the case.

Megan Adams, Grade 5
Arlington Elementary School, IN

Guitar

Guitar
Fun, cool
Learning, playing, strumming
Is fun to play
Guitar

Frankie Caparula, Grade 5
Seton Catholic School, IL

Monkey

Monkeys are so funky
They love bananas that are chunky
He swings from a vine
And almost breaks his spine
His master is an ape
That wears a crown and cape
His cape is red
It's also used for a cover on his bed.

His crown is gold
As he is bold
His fur is brown
He's sad when he's down
So this is the poem of the monkey

And they are soooo funky.

Blake Connor, Grade 4
Summit Elementary School, IL

Teachers

T hey are helpful
E very day they give too much homework
A lways busy
C onstantly talking
H opes that we get good grades
E very minute they're teaching
R eally nice
S ometimes it is like a never ending story

Tyler Hinshaw, Grade 4
GCMS Elementary School, IL

What Is Tiny?

What is Tiny?
She is cute.
She has hair.
She is playful.
She is kind of weird.
She is funny.
She is not a talker.
She loves to sleep.
She has black and brown hair.
That is my dog Tiny!

Paige Mosson, Grade 4
Morgan Elementary School, IN

The Moon

White light and Swiss cheese
Spaceships and flag
High in the night
Hills and craters
Far from Neptune
Shining down Shining down
That makes the Moon

Matthew Gonzalez, Grade 4
St Robert Bellarmine School, IL

Swimming Tutor

Years ago, when I was three
The time many things happened to me
I had a friend who was sixteen
Who tutored me to go swimming.

The one fateful day that she had crashed
I felt my heart had just been bashed.
And then I took all of the blame
Nothing then was ever the same.

I promised myself we would still be friends
From beginning until the end.
Five years ago when I was seven
I knew she watched high from Heaven.

I knew her spirit was in the air
Every now and then I say a prayer.
I hate to know that she is dead
The pain still rushes through my head.

Brett Vaughn, Grade 6
Linton-Stockton Elementary School, IN

Wild, Wild Hair!

I woke up this morning, when I got out of bed,
In place of my face; I saw a furrball instead!
I ran for the comb, I ran for the brush,
But when they saw my hair, they made a big fuss.
I looked at my clock; it's 8:25,
I gotta leave now, to get to school on time!
When I got there, though, much to my dismay,
Everyone saw my bad hair day!
Nancy screamed; Mia covered her eyes
Suzana shrieked, much to my surprise.
I ran to my homeroom, I sat down really nice,
But when my teacher saw me, she did a double take, twice.
I searched my pack for a comb and a brush,
I found them, and this time, they didn't fuss.
I combed and teased and, "WOW!" I say
"My tamed hair is here to stay!"
From all my friends I get an okay sign,
My bad hair day turned out just fine.
So if you're in a rush,
Grab a comb and brush
Or all day you'll have wild, wild hair!

Evelyn DaSilva, Grade 6
Benjamin Franklin Elementary School, IN

Courage

Courage is a dark yellow.
It smells like freshly cut pine trees.
It tastes like your first bite of asparagus.
It sounds like a lion's roar.
It feels like a feather against rough sand paper.

Heather Wendling, Grade 5
East Elementary School, IN

As Long as That Smile Is in Your Eyes

As long as that smile is in your eyes,
As long as that smile never lies,
As long as that smile never dies,
Every butterfly will fly.
And I don't think I'll ever cry.

Vanitha Raguveer, Grade 5
Ranch View Elementary School, IL

Horses

H onorable animals running about.
O utstanding colors they can be.
R ight out of sight they can jump.
S ee the beautiful creatures.
E ating hay and feed.
S helby's my name and horses are my favorite animals.

Shelby Price, Grade 4
Liberty Elementary School, IN

When I Woke Up Today

When I woke up today
I could almost hardly wait
For my dad to bring the tractor
Around the corner with the planter
And to rev it up
Meaning for me get up
Then we head out to the fields
And we stay till my dad yields
He says that it's time to go on back
So I climb down
On the squishy ground
Then my dad calls me, so I come around
And there by his feet lay a deer sprawled on the ground
So I ran to get some help
He called for help, but I got there too late
A bunch more deer were coming to bait
On the way home
We stopped in the field
To only find another deer!

Alec Scheib, Grade 6
Harding Grade School, IL

TT

She was always by my side when I cried
She made me smile and giggle
She was there to take care of my problems
She always takes my side
That's why I love her

Ashly Martinez, Grade 6
Francis Granger Middle School, IL

Snow

Snow is so fluffy.
It glistens in the moonlight.
Snow is so pretty.

Ryan James Olsen, Grade 4
McKenney-Harrison Elementary School, IN

Will You Be My Valentine?

To you I will send; "cuz" you're my best friend.
And you are not sly; friends until the end.
Together we're soaring high up in the sky; when we are apart I really want to cry.
Together we can really, really succeed; when we're together I can say you and I.
When sad or in need; you do a good deed.
Really rock on gal; when you take the lead.
You are my best pal; you've a great vocal.
Girl you really rule; to me you're royal.
We like to swim in my pool; it helps us stay very cool.
Forever and days it took; it is much more fun than school.
Both of us try to cook; we both like a great book.
Both of us are quite fine; we don't mind how we look.
You are really so divine; to me you so brightly shine.
I write this while you're away; will you be my valentine?
Forever shall this friendship stay; about forever and a day.
You were my best friend from the start; maybe tomorrow we can play.
One, two, stick like glue and never pull apart; this poem I'm not asking you to cart.
And I'm very glad to say you're my best bud; as you can see I've written this from the heart.

Tara Murray, Grade 6
St Colette School, IL

Racism Is Not Fair

Roses and peaches, peaches and roses.
What's the difference?
What's the big deal with all the racism here?
So what!
We may be different colors here,
You can be French, Puerto Rican, Scottish, Irish, Indian, Dominican, Caucasian, Polish, and Mexican.
But so what!
We may have different colors of skin!
But aren't we the same?
Who cares if we have different personalities.
If God made us the same, we would be pretty boring,
Wouldn't we?
You and everybody else knows, I'm right!
You can have your own trial here,
But just letting you hear what I thought!
And hopefully, I didn't waste my breath!
So what's the difference?

Alexis Aleman, Grade 4
Bailly Elementary School, IN

Jenna

Jenna
Nice, aggressive, cool
Sister of Jack, Jason, and Janelle, daughter of Jeff and Lisa
Who loves to read mystery thrillers, play volleyball, watch Hannah Montana, and watch scary and comedy movies.
Who feels frustration when we're losing volleyball games, excitement when we're winning, and lonely when home alone.
Who fears speaking in front of people, staying home alone, the dark, and failing math.
Who needs help in math, a DVD player, and a new TV for my toy room.
Who gives time to play with brothers and sister and time for homework.
Who would like to see my cousins more and less school time
Haubstadt
Robertson

Jenna Robertson, Grade 6
Haubstadt Community School, IN

Red

Red is the color of the stripes of the United States flag.
It is the color mad everyone gets.
Red is the color of a crown and jewels from a queen.
Red is a color of sweet, juicy apples.
It is red around a big bumblebee sting.
Red makes me think of a red lunch box I used to carry.
I think red is for me!

Nikki Wright, Grade 5
Staunton Elementary School, IN

I Am

I am loving and caring
I wonder why people don't get along with animals
I hear rap music
I see cute kittens
I want to fish more
I am loving and caring

I pretend I am a famous fisherman
I feel very happy
I touch kittens
I worry about friends
I cry when something I care about dies
I am loving and caring

I understand a friend is always a friend
I say God is real
I dream there is one day of school a year
I try skateboarding
I hope I have a good life when I grow up
I am loving and caring

Bradley Kies, Grade 6
Heritage Grove Middle School, IL

Revenge Over Christmas

On a snowy Christmas afternoon
A father and his son
Were shopping in a busy mall
Before the day was done.

The father was buying gifts only for himself!
Every object the son admired
The father rejected
While his son reflected.

When they got home, a plan the son hatched.
He was most careful not be catched!
From the bathroom he took his father's hair gel
And replaced it with glue, ignoring the smell.

Behind the shower curtain he waited a while
Until his father came and used the gel with a smile.
Old Dad put on his hat and went out the door.
Now he isn't so selfish at Christmas anymore!

Justin Uppal, Grade 4
Countryside School, IL

My Grandma

My grandma and I
were playing at a park.
My friend came along
and asked if he could play.

We said, "Sure, if you follow the rules."
"If you say it's okay, I will play!"
We played a good game
and went home when it was dark.

At home I asked my grandma,
"Grandma, Grandma, why are you so nice?"
She said, "To make you happy
and give you a good life. That's why."

"Grandma, Grandma, why do you like to teach me?"
She said, "Once I used to teach my daughter,
so now I can teach you one-on-one."
I am happy and I am smart.
I thank my grandma for helping me.

Masashi Azuma, Grade 4
Countryside School, IL

Memories

Everyone has fond memories
Some are good and some are bad.
Me I have fond memories of me and my dad.
Whether hunting or fishing we had good times.
The only bad memory I have is the day that he died.

Steven Thomasson, Grade 5
Perry Central Elementary School, IN

I Am

I am an athletic boy that loves playing games
I wonder if I will start to quit playing games
I hear my feet hitting the solid ground
I see people in front of me
I want to win the races
I am an athletic boy that loves playing games

I pretend to go in slow motion
I feel that some day I will fall
I touch the wind as I hustle through it
I worry that I will lose
I cry out, "Why does it have to be me?"
I am an athletic boy that loves playing games

I understand that no one can be perfect
I say that if you lose or if you win you still had fun
I dream that I will be champion
I try to win all the races
I hope to be the champion
I am an athletic boy that loves playing games

Wes Kamp, Grade 5
Hiawatha Elementary School, IL

The Mountains

The mountains
Enormous and majestic
Reaching and spreading
Skyward
Rocky

Jonah Maynard, Grade 5
Seton Catholic School, IL

Wonderful Ocean

Big and fierce ocean
Sound of waves crashing on land
Blowing in my face

Kaitlyn Joyce, Grade 5
Our Lady of Peace School, IL

Summer/Winter

Summer
Hot, sunny
Playing, bicycling, swimming
Humid, rainy, snowy, cold
Snowing, freezing, icing
Windy, icy
Winter

Tyler Steffen, Grade 5
Adams Central Elementary School, IN

Sports

Baseball
Out, hit
Stealing, sliding, catching
Hands, gloves, feet, cleats
Kicking, substituting, running
Foul, goal
Soccer

Axel C. Doran, Grade 5
GCMS Elementary School, IL

Friend

Friend,
Kind, noble
Caring, loving, helping
Nice, proud, unkind, yelling at you
Pushing, shoving, yelling
Mean, rude
Enemy

Lori Dunham, Grade 5
Adams Central Elementary School, IN

Full of Nothing

I'm full of nothing
Nothing good and nothing bad
I need to do something
Not being excited or sad
But not exactly going mad

Samantha Comerford, Grade 6
Rochester Middle School, IL

My Poems

I am a car poet, driving in the Daytona 500 writing poems.
My poems are speeding past every car in their way.
My poems fly out my window gliding down onto the hot asphalt,
Sometimes sticking to one of my tires.

I am a fire poet, standing in an orange and blue flame.
My poems are gliding through the flame without getting scorched.
The poems that are left get burned to ashes, never to return.

I am a bike poet, writing poems while doing a wheelie.
My poems leave my hands into people's homes and I start writing again.

Patrick Bravo, Grade 6
St Barbara School, IL

Dirty Room

This room is a mess,
It looks like the Loch Ness.
There is peanut butter on the wall,
And odors big and small.
There is pizza stuck to the floor,
And dirty laundry on the door.
There's a creature under the bed,
Hey, there's that book I never read.
Why does the TV in this room and the one in my room look similar?
Oh wait, this is my room I thought it looked familiar.

Tristan Fry, Grade 5
Center Street Elementary School, IL

Door County

In Door County...
going out to eat for every meal
shooting pool, kayaking too

In the restaurants...
pancakes and bacon at Al Johnson's
hamburgers and shakes at Wilson's
having tacos with chips and salsa at J.J's
to top it all off having ice cream at The Ice Cream Factory

In the cabin...
shooting pool and throwing darts
drinking root beer from the keg at the bar while watching football
lying on the couch while watching the sunset
playing Boggle and Mexican Train Dominoes
then staying up till dawn every night of the week

In the lake...
kayaking over the water
racing your siblings in how fast you can swim
diving through the fallen boat that sunk in the water
walking on the beach while skipping rocks along the water

In Door County...I have the best vacation of the year

Scott Milling, Grade 6
Immaculate Conception School, IL

Sky

Looking up at a beautiful sky,
Drifting above me way up high.
With clouds so puffy and sun so bright,
Everything in the world seems just right.
Sometimes it's blue, sometimes it's gray,
When the stars come out in my bed I will lay.
After a storm a rainbow I'll see,
A promise from God for you and me.

Megan Steele, Grade 5
Tri-State Christian School, IL

Brandy

So many words unspoken
So much left to say
Why did you leave me?
I know you wanted to stay
Your smile has faded into dust
Your eyes don't glow anymore
But I'll always remember you
As you soar through those Heavenly doors.

Lindsey Budnik, Grade 6
Laketon Elementary School, IN

Poor Mr. Pete

Mister Pete has a fear of heights
from the ground
to way above the city street lights.

He shivers on airplanes,
and quakes on brick walls.
He fears inch-high carpets
in his house's halls.

He never climbs trees
because he fears he might fall.
Poor Mr. Pete
when he sits in a chair, to stand up he stalls
for when he stands he is 20 feet tall.

Ben Pinkley, Grade 5
Lighted Path Home School Academy, IL

Landscape*

L oves to move the land, to make
A pretty garden by a sidewalk,
N ear a house.
D azzling in the
S un, it
C an't be
A ny better than this
P lants newly planted, the
E nd is finally near, after a long, hard day of work

Cort Lamey, Grade 6
Haubstadt Community School, IN
*Dedicated to my dad, Uncle Brent,
and my landscaping buds

Basketball

Basketball is quite a sport,
As I dribble down the court.
I can dribble between my legs,
The whole time I'm in a gaze.
When we're losing we're usually down,
but our teammates turn us around.
You shoot you "swish,"
The crowd will go wild,
And you feel like you can run a mile.
This is why basketball is such a great sport.
As I dribble down the court.

Ashley N. Coleman, Grade 5
North Intermediate Center of Education, IL

The Beauty of Spring

Flowers bowing with a charm in springtime
Budding since the beginning of time
Flowers, keep on blooming,
For you're the beauty of the world.

Samantha Biggs, Grade 4
Forest Park Elementary School, IN

Violin

When I play the violin the sounds are magical,
When I play the violin the sounds are beautiful,
When I play the violin the sounds are loud,
When I play the violin the sounds are soft,
When I play the violin the music is happy,
When I play the violin the music is sad,
When I play the violin the notes flow from the strings,
When I play the violin I feel free,
When I play the violin I can be powerful,
When I play the violin I can express my feelings,
When I play the violin I can always feel better,
When I play the violin I enjoy myself,
But the most important thing of all,
When I play the violin I can be ME!

Michelle Chin, Grade 5
Beebe Elementary School, IL

The Snowy Mountain

Snowy
snowy
snowy
mountain, a very
beautiful sight. Goats,
gazelle, and Kodiak bear,
a *horrible fright*!!!! See all
the nature, trees, rocks and…
snow. People hiking, hiking, hiking,
climbing, rock climbing, rock climbing,
climbing, climbing, climbing, climbing, climb,
climbing in Colorado, Alaska, New York, Paris,
and Rome; most of all in my D R E A M S !!

Allie Simmons, Grade 4
Marine Elementary School, IL

Secret

The little kids on the
Playground had a lot of private
Business it was a secret for say
It goes into one child's ear
And then goes out the other
But when the child
Says she will keep it
It slips out of her mouth
And it travels through the air
And then the whole world finds out
Barbara Dickmeyer, Grade 6
St Pius X Catholic School, IN

Amazing Spring

Fresh colors and bright skies
Bugs and spring showers
Beautiful butterflies
Smell the sweet flowers
Humming and chirping
All the bells ring
Splash in puddles! Splash in puddles!
This makes spring.
Caitlin Finan, Grade 5
Our Lady of Peace School, IL

Get Ready for Spring

Spring is here!
Get ready to cheer!
Bring your root beer
'Cause we're here!
Easter's near
So get real.
People lose their beard
But don't disappear.
Instead behave
And get ready to play!
Now let's have a parade
And shout hooray!!
Miguel Ruiz, Grade 6
Pickard Elementary School, IL

Forest Night

Wind blows through the night
Causing trees' leaves to rustle
Is truly magic

Elves dance gleefully
Singing to the moving trees
Expressing their love

A secret meeting
Unknown to all but one man
How lucky is he
Megan Hussey, Grade 6
Sacred Heart School, IL

Time to Shine

The game was on the line.
It was my chance to shine.
The fans screamed loud.
The coach felt proud.
Then I woke up, and everything was fine.
Asa Stevenson, Grade 6
ROWVA East Elementary School, IL

Spring Is Here

It's a new time of year,
because spring is here.
There is a noise from outside,
a boy going down the slide.
It is nice outside.
You can hear the ocean's tide.
You can hear it from inside.
It's a new time of year because,
Spring is here.
Jared Grzych, Grade 4
Oak Hill Elementary School, IN

Life Cycle

Egg
Hard, shell
Sitting, waiting, hatching
White, speckled, Blue Jay, Robin
Flying, building, sitting
Peaceful, pretty
Bird
Reed Greenwood, Grade 4
Cynthia Heights Elementary School, IN

Bird of the Night

Flying over buildings
Feeling so free
I pick a perch
In a high-up tree
I sleep till sundown
Then wake up for night
Wind rustling my feathers
I then take flight
Alec Jacquot, Grade 5
Bell-Graham School, IL

Summer and Fall

Summer
Hot, humid
Swimming, playing, sleeping
Ice cream, pools, leaves, pumpkins
Raking, carving, decoration
Colorful, cool
Fall
Kyle Schuett, Grade 6
St Matthew School, IL

I Am a Bull

I am a bull
You know me for my strength
My mother is fast
My father is tough
I was born in a pen
I live in a pen
My best friend is dad
Because we are tough
My enemy is red
Because I hate the color
I fear nothing
Because I am strong
I dream to be free someday
Gabe Harlan, Grade 4
Mentone Elementary School, IN

Christmas

Christmas is like a stoplight
Changing red and green

Christmas is a ball
Whirling around on a tree

Christmas is
White like newly fallen snow

Green like summer grass
Red like a ripe apple

Christmas is cheer
With loving laughs

Christmas is a baby
Born on a wonderful night

Christmas is a plane
Flying children left and right

Christmas is the feeling of
Love.
Cara Rafanelli, Grade 5
St John of the Cross Parish School, IL

My Life

My life is bad. I feel like nothing,
Then I look high in the sky and I see
Something.
It's as little as a dime and as
Bright like a light.
It's a star.
It makes me think how I feel.
Think, think, think how do I really feel.
Alton Cummings, Grade 5
Perry Central Elementary School, IN

The Cardinal

Watch the cardinal as it flies,
Digging tunnels though the skies.

Watch it dive into the trees,
To find tiny bugs on the leaves.

Watch it leap to the ground,
To look for worms all around.

Watch it float up to its nest,
To eat tiny worms before it rests.

But wait, there is something else,
Like little chicks needing to warm themselves.

Now, this is a story of a beautiful bird,
And of her life, you have heard.

Elizabeth Johnson, Grade 5
North Intermediate Center of Education, IL

The House of the Holy

Every Sunday people come in
To put money in the money bin
My bells go bing, bang, bong
All day long

Inside I have priests, pulpits, and pews
And the people have to wear nice shoes
My windows are special and stained
Whoever comes inside me will never be pained

On my roof there is a cross
That you can't miss when you walk across
Won't you come inside to pray
On every Sunday?

Nathan Walloch, Grade 6
Our Lady of Peace School, IL

Spring

Spring
Green, blue
Playing, singing, working
Traveling and loving the warm temperature
Season

Abdallah Hasan, Grade 4
Universal School, IL

South Africa

Penguins roaming the beach
Salty ocean water
Yelp of seagulls
Sand between my toes
Windy air
South African dream

Taylor Katalinic, Grade 5
Frank H Hammond Elementary School, IN

I Wonder

I wonder why there are wars,
I wonder why soldiers have to die,
I wonder why there is life,
I wonder why there are bad leaders,
I wonder why there are dictators,
I wonder why there are school killings,
I wonder why there is a universe,
I wonder why there is no peace in the world,
I wonder why people judge other people,
And I wonder why people have to suffer.

Jaleesa Medina, Grade 6
Norman Bridge Elementary School, IL

My Puppy Loves Me

My puppy loves me
I know this to be true
You can ask me how
When I'm happy, lonely or blue

What other companion would chase their tail in the sun
Panting, wiggling, and barking just to end up where she begun

Her kisses are all wet
Her paws are muddy too
But she still crawls under the blanket
Just to snuggle next to you

She plays ball, retrieving every pass
Pulling on my pant leg to wrestle in the grass

Supper time comes and she finishes all her food
Then when my mother isn't looking, she gets my veggies too

I know my puppy loves me and now you know it too
A puppy loves you always just for being you

Nicholas Bailey, Grade 6
South Spencer Middle School, IN

Running Free

Wild horses running free,
Sometimes I wish that was me.
A stallion at the head of each herd.
Sometimes I just wish I wasn't such a nerd.
Wild horses grazing,
At them I start gazing,
Of all animals the horse is the king,
Even if they stole your wedding ring,
If you take your horse for a swim
He still won't obey your every whim.
Listen to the galloping hooves,
You can hear them on the roofs
Wild horses galloping free
I just wish that was me.

Kaitlyn Parcell, Grade 5
North Intermediate Center of Education, IL

Raindrops

The sky gets grey,
Clouds come out.
Rain in May,
No doubt.
Rain falls on your face,
Falling and falling in a race.
Everything gets wet,
Like they just met.
Once the rain is done,
Once the sun has shown,
A rainbow will sometimes appear!

Anna Shows, Grade 6
St Mary School, IL

Friends

Your friends are like a path,
going this way and that.
Always going the right way,
never going the wrong.

When your friends hit a dead end,
you have to help them through,
to make a decision.
Left or right.

Your friends are like a tree,
with tons of branches.
Spreading this way and that,
all over the place.

The roots stretch far,
holding hands with another,
never letting go,
best friends forever!

Becca Pickenpaugh, Grade 5
Twin Branch Model School, IN

What Are Little Brothers?

What are little brothers?
A pain in my butt
They are annoying
They can be sweet
They hit you
They chase you
Sometimes they make you feel
    sad or happy
Sometimes they make you feel
    like you can pull your hair out
They never stay out of your room
They tell on you
They mess up your stuff
That is little brothers!

Gabrielle Scarpulla, Grade 4
Morgan Elementary School, IN

What Is Singing?

What is singing?
    High notes
    Low notes
    Instruments playing
    Choirs forming
    Fantastic voices
    Boys and girls speaking
    All different languages
    Sad songs
    Happy songs
    Songs that will heal your heart
That is singing!

Haley Zuberbier, Grade 5
Hiawatha Elementary School, IL

The Butterfly

Watch it grow,
coming from the cocoon.
A beautiful sight.
Hovering over the trees,
Watching the children play.

He zooms down, really fast.
And that's when he saw it.

Millions of butterflies
flying so fast.
He thought his kind was
extinct and he was the only one.

He was overjoyed
and flew up in the
sky with them, and
he knew he belonged.

Amy Harenberg, Grade 5
Norman Bridge Elementary School, IL

Moon's Light

The moon is light
It guides you through the night
A flashlight

It shows the way
Through the darkness
Very bright

It lights up the night
A flashlight

The moon lets you see the way
Through the woods or the field
The moon is light

Kortney Schmitt, Grade 6
Haubstadt Community School, IN

Dogs

A dog is my favorite pet
sometimes I have to take him to the vet.

My dog likes to play
and I teach him how to stay.

Dogs like to play catch
and also like to fetch.

A dog is man's best friend
all the way to the end.

Lexie Mallary, Grade 4
Erie Elementary School, IL

My Horse!

I have a horse that loves to play
Outside on a Sunny day.
When she talks to me, it's "Neighhh!"
Her favorite month is May.
She really likes to eat yellow hay.
She sleeps in dry clay!

Katelyn Feldman, Grade 4
Marine Elementary School, IL

Music

Happy, sad,
Singing, writing, reading,
Stories, emotions, friends, characters,
Relaxing, touching, exciting,
Teacher, plot,
Book.

Megan Ellis, Grade 5
Arlington Elementary School, IN

The United States

The United States
Free and exciting
Grows and fights
Enthusiastically
Country

Austin Hornstein, Grade 5
GCMS Elementary School, IL

Waterfalls

Rushing waters,
Sounds like an enormous earthquake
Clear blue water
Like the sky on a beautiful summer day.
Ledges and edges all so big.
So much energy,
Where does it begin?
It's nature!

Francesca Fiermonte, Grade 5
St John of the Cross Parish School, IL

Friends

Friends make you happy like the morning sun,
Friends are like clean, fresh water,
Friends are yellow for happiness,
Friends make you feel happy
Like the sun going across the horizon,
Friends feel smooth like a calm day,
Friends are as shield for the anger to get out.

Michael Donnelly, Grade 5
St John of the Cross Parish School, IL

Dear Person

Dear person said the journal
I looked at it and stared
He said well watcha doing just acting scared
I said but you can't talk that's not normal that can't be

He said well maybe I'm speaking up to say
I hate it when you write in me
I said well fine I'll never write in you again
Well fine he said back to me

After you put me up whey don't you go and climb a tree
I said I change my mind I'll write in you every day
No you can't, don't do that
Aahhhhhᵢ

Sydney Baumann, Grade 5
Floyds Knobs Elementary School, IN

Friendships Are Like Diamonds

Friendships are like diamonds,
Valuable and rare
We love to do each other's nails,
We love to do our hair.

Friendships are like diamonds,
Some are real, some are fake
Sometimes friends make you,
Tremble and quake.

Most times friendships and diamonds are real
When you find that great friend or diamond,
It makes you want to squeal.

Emily Wallace, Grade 6
Haubstadt Community School, IN

Storm

Storm
Thunderous, flashy
Booming, cracking, fearing
Waking me up, scaring me, making me want to hide
Panicking, crying, shivering
Dark, light
Tornado

Jameson Parker, Grade 6
Stanley Clark School, IN

Prisoner

Prisoner
Silent, pressurized
Fighting, resisting, overpowering
Bloodshot eyes, silent communication, trapped inside myself
Sobbing, crying, running
Black, dark
Evil

Edward Alexander, Grade 6
Stanley Clark School, IN

Flowers

F irst take the time to smell some flowers.
L ook at them,
O n top of the table.
W e take our turn to
E ach put one flower in the vase.
R eal colorful flowers.
S uch a beautiful sight.

Rylee Catlin, Grade 4
Liberty Elementary School, IN

Rainbows

Rainbows are so cute
At the other end is loot,
Rainbows are so nice,
But they shine more than ice,
We slide on rainbows everywhere,
The green on it is like the color pear,
I love rainbows how about you?

Candace Burnett, Grade 5
North Intermediate Center of Education, IL

Leaves

Red, gold, yellow, brown,
Colorful leaves all around.
Leaves are beautiful.

Kaity Laumann, Grade 4
McKenney-Harrison Elementary School, IN

Real Skateboarding

Kickflips, heelflips, impossibles, and pop shovits
are all used by pros like Dennis Busentitz

I myself would love to go pro
and probably will
because I know when I skate I put on a show

Why waste your time playing skate video games
and saying, "Oh, I can do that."
and not going outside and skating, how a pro would act

You see, skateboarding isn't a video game,
because skateboarding
is too fun to be in the category of lame

Andreas Komissopoulos, Grade 4
Pritzker Elementary School, IL

Ice Cream

Ice cream is coming
And the best is cookie dough
And it's almost gone.

Maverick Grayer, Grade 5
Floyds Knobs Elementary School, IN

Caribbean Sea

I'm blue, I'm green, I'm aqua too,
I will share my beauty with you.
Yachts, boats, sailors too, come to
Venture these waters of the great blue.

Kendra Alexander, Grade 5
Neil Armstrong Elementary School, IL

Inside the Church

Inside the Church…
lonely minister
looking out
missing her
gazing out
talks to her
loves the stars
talks to me
he's had enough
dies to be
with the love of his life…

Bridget Bankes, Grade 6
Central Jr High School, IL

Puppies

They're soft and very playful.
They make you want to smile.
They make you, oh, so happy,
You may want to run a mile.
If you do, take him with you.
You can't go alone.
He needs his exercise too.
Well now he deserves a bone.
Soon it's time to go to bed,
Your dog who is so cuddly.
Is laying now beside your head.

Katie Seibert, Grade 6
St Mary School, IL

Puppies

Golden furry fuzz balls
Who doesn't love them?
Everybody loves them.
Fat puppies
Furry puppies
Shaggy puppies
Sleepy puppies
But sometimes they are naughty
and chew up my socks!

Jenna Martin, Grade 5
St Anthony's School, IL

Ode to My Black Lab

My dog is great. He likes to run around all day.
My dog's name is Tazz, he likes jazz.
He is as tall as me when he stands on his hind legs.
He used to be very strong, but he is old now and his days will pass on.
I will remember him when he is gone.
As long as I'm here, he will live on in my heart.

Rickey Bowman-Pigg, Grade 5
Morgan Elementary School, IN

A Sorrow Day

I was three years old when my dad had a massive wreck.
My dad broke his back in three places, and he couldn't walk!
My dad was paralyzed. The doctors said he would probably end up dying.
But what came to a surprise is dad's fever went down.
He had pneumonia, but now the doctors can operate. That's how he survived.
But they told us that he would never walk again!
But my mom would get so tired of helping him,
so he would get mad get up and you know what he was walking again!
From now on I keep on thinking
what if my dad had not survived? How would my life be if my dad was gone!

Cassandra Cronin, Grade 5
Perry Central Elementary School, IN

In Summer

Summertime is almost here; hot humid days are dreadful.
I put up hay.
I plant and till the garden.
I can green beans and tomatoes.
One thing I like to do is to mow grass.
When school is out I like to ride my Suzuki four wheelers.
When school is out it is time to drive tractors around the 100 acre field.
When school is out it is time to have some serious fun.
When I stop to think about it…
Summertime is almost here. Hot humid days are wonderful.

Travis Kleaving, Grade 6
Perry Central Elementary School, IN

Fairies

You hear bells in the night
You wish and wish with all your might
You open your eyes to see what you may find
But the lights are out as if you're blind, you hear them again
Your heart goes racing, you get up and start pacing
You hear the bells, your heart swells
You try to figure out what it might be, you try to see
The bells are gone, what are they? The bells will come again but when?
You spend the night wondering what they were, what are they?
Take some time you will see all you have to do is believe, what are they?
The things that twinkle and talk in bells, that make your heart swell
What are they, they twinkle when they fly, making you wish with all your might
They talk in bells, but make sure if you see one that they don't interfere
They can be nice, they can be mean, just don't tell what you have seen
Fairies, do you believe?

Brenna Cameron, Grade 6
South Spencer Middle School, IN

Books

Books are cool, books are fun.
Books are great for everyone.
Reading books will make you smart.
Each book you read is a work of art.
Writing books is also cool.
Being an author would totally rule!
Please don't think reading is a chore.
I love reading books they make your soar!
But, reading school books is such a bore!

Allison Majerczyk, Grade 6
St Daniel the Prophet School, IL

If Hope Could Be…

If hope could be a color
it would be white as soft as a cloud.

If hope could be a taste
it would taste like chocolate fudge brownies.

If hope could be a smell
it would be flowers blooming in the spring.

If hope could be a sound
it would be children's laughter.

If hope could be a feeling
it would be wind blowing in my face.

If hope could be an animal
it would be a puppy playing in the grass.

Briana Navarro, Grade 4
St Agnes School, IL

Spring Time

S pringtime is a wonderful time of year.
P arties of wild flowers bloom in the fields. Animals
R unning through the grassy plains.
I n the air soars the beautiful birds, working on their
N ew nests to live in. Spring is the time when the sun
G leams on our faces.

Like I said, springtime is a wonderful time of year.

Kendra Norman, Grade 6
Harding Grade School, IL

Watching the Farm Animals

Watching the farm animals is neat,
like seeing the cows eat their wheat.
The baby chicks sauntered to the hen,
while the horses neighed to Ben.
The infant stares at the goat,
When the mom is wearing a coat.
Farm animals are excellent to see,
living on a farm is interesting to me.

Nicolas Chavez, Grade 5
North Intermediate Center of Education, IL

Rainbows

The colors are breathtaking in the sky,
A rainbow pops up after a rainstorm.
Some say leprechauns are hiding by them,
Pots of gold lay at the end of it's rays.

You dream of where the rainbow is ending,
I see smiles every time they are there.
Rainbows are beautiful with every glance,
The shiny rainbows make my heart shiver.

Madisen Vales, Grade 6
McHenry Middle School, IL

Tyler

Tyler,
Funny, worker, friendly
Wishes to hold onto a star and float into space.
Dreams of my family living in a castle.
Wants to get a job at Walmart.
Who wonders how the dinosaurs died.
Who fears there are ghosts around.
Who likes to play with his dog, Lucy.
Who believes that Santa is real.
Who loves buttery popcorn.
Who loves playing video games.
Who loves reading about sharks and dinosaurs.
Who plans to help others.
Who plans to get a job at a pet store.
My goal is to have a good life.

Tyler Vela, Grade 5
Staunton Elementary School, IN

Why

Do you know why
People have to die
I won't lie
Sometimes I look at the sky
I think about, the days I pout
Do you remember in December?
When we watched the snow fall
You said you were my best friend
You said we'd be friends until the end
Unfortunately, the end was near
It was something you couldn't see or hear
It was a spirit, you could feel it
So you had to go
It messed up the flow
You were my friend
Together until the end
Unfortunately the end was near
So I am staying here
I miss you
I always think about you
My best friend

Gianna Killingbeck, Grade 6
Rochester Middle School, IL

The Multicolored Dream

If I sleep with my colorful kaleidoscope,
under the warmth of my pillow,
my dreams would be multicolored.
I would be dancing with the birds,
smelling the sweet flowers,
and tasting the tart ones.
It would be a miracle.
The only real person would be me,
just me,
but then I awaken,
my unique dream is over.

Ashley Cooper, Grade 6
Linton-Stockton Elementary School, IN

A Raindrop

A raindrop
swiftly descending
falling from the sky
dripping down the roof
and onto our front lawn
to sit and sit
and never move
for now it has spread
and it is now a puddle.

Anna Huntine, Grade 6
St Pius X Catholic School, IN

Old and Rusty

This is my bike.
It's a two wheel dirt bike.
It is gray, red, and black.
It saves me from a long hike.

This is my bike.
It is my favorite thing to ride
To go around the block,
Even in the cold outside.

This is my bike,
All broken and rusty,
But it's faster than you
Even in the winter when it's dusty.

Rachel Soukup, Grade 5
Our Lady of Peace School, IL

St. Louis

St. Louis
Home sweet home
Home of the St. Louis Cardinals
Where I was born
Nelly's home town
St. Louis

Jake Freytag, Grade 6
Rochester Middle School, IL

Snow

Snow falls from the sky.
It's up so high.
It lands on the ground.
Without a sound.

It's clean and fun to eat.
But it gets dirty under my feet.
It's wet and cold.
And to me it's like gold.

Janelle Miller, Grade 5
Arlington Elementary School, IN

The Little Rain Drop

There once was a little raindrop
who fell from the sky
flying by the birds so blue
soaring by the falling leaves
hitting your head
and slowly burning through
for this is acid rain

Jeff Jorgenson, Grade 6
St Pius X Catholic School, IN

Angel

Angel is my cat,
and she loves to play.
She loves to play
though she is really fat.

She loves to bite
me to and fro.
She is so cute,
and I love her so!

Brady Schaefer, Grade 4
Marine Elementary School, IL

My Pet Hog Married a Dog

My pet hog married a dog
and had an ugly baby.

It had a flat nose
and a tail like a hose.

It was pink and black
and had a round back.

I shaved its head
then it was dead.

And I went to bed
and hit my head
and I felt nauseous.

Bailey Cooper, Grade 5
Gard Elementary School, IL

Grandma

My grandma's name is Mary
She is not even very hairy
She sometimes says yes
She sometimes says no.

My grandma is never scary
Her husband has a friend named Larry
She is very nice
Her house doesn't even have mice.

Sometimes she is sad
Sometimes she is mad
She quit her job
She's no longer part of that mob.

I still love her
Even when problems occur
She is the very best
I think better than all the rest.

Brianna Burelison, Grade 4
Hoagland Elementary School, IN

Moon

Moon
gazed
amazed
moon
cold
shivering
light
moon
half
full
quarter
moon
all things
the dark
dark
night
moon

Amanda Sweeney, Grade 4
Bright Elementary School, IN

Football

Grass and players
Field goals and concession stands
Chalk for the lines
People playing in bands
Tackling and throwing
The field is past the hall
"Fun, Fun, Fun"
This is football.

Michael Fassero, Grade 5
Our Lady of Peace School, IL

Ellie

There once was a dog named Ellie,
Who had a big fat belly.

Whenever she goes outside it's funny,
Because she always chases a bunny.

When she comes inside she wipes her feet,
Then she will beg for a special meat-flavored treat.

She will search around the house with joy,
Until she finds her rubber toy.

She runs around the two-story house,
Like a cat chasing a tiny mouse.

She's my fat, furry, freckled friend,
I hope my dog-sitting job doesn't end.

Joey Zanfardino, Grade 6
St Philip the Apostle School, IL

Loopy Lance

Lance is loopy can't you see
Now he is trying to eat me
He's banging his head on a pole
This kid is out of control!

He got detention twice today
He did not come outside to play
He tried to hijack nineteen cars
He ate too many candy bars

It's like this guy is from Mars
He said he saw five shooting stars
This kid is a wild child
Maybe because the weather is mild

I don't see him anymore because I moved to Ecuador
All of the kids want to move to France
All because of Loopy Lance.

Ian Roets, Grade 6
Thayer J Hill Middle School, IL

Love

I love him
But he doesn't know
He probably doesn't like me
If I asked him out he would probably say no
But…
My heart will follow wherever I go
I will never give up.
I will never back down
'Cause in my heart he'll always be found.

Jessica Meyer, Grade 6
GCMS Middle School, IL

The Jester

There once was a jester
Whose name was Chester.
He told a bad joke.
The poor king had a stroke.
and now he's the yucky food tester.

Skyler Aguilar, Grade 4
Forest Park Elementary School, IN

Worms

I have a bunch of worms,
They've all been here since dawn.
I found some on my porch, in my garage, and on my lawn.
They're all different shapes and sizes,
Big, small, fat, and short.
Some of them can even snort!
I showed some to my mom and she said,
"Ewww, get them out of the house!"
So I let them go,
Next time, I think I'll catch a mouse!!!

Becca Bornac, Grade 5
Central Elementary School, IL

Remembering My Cat

I loved my cat
he looked cute when he played with my hat
we made each other a promise
to remember each other when we left this world
and that we will meet again someday
to be by each other's side

Rianne Doherty, Grade 6
Rochester Middle School, IL

Katie's Poems

I am a beach poet
Sitting on the sand listening the ocean writing peaceful poems.
Slowly, my poems go out with the waves
and are lost in the ocean forever
waiting for someone to find them like buried treasure.

I am a wind poet
Sitting on a cloud writing poems that go with the breeze.
As I write them they fall off the cloud
and get caught in the wind flowing peacefully
and gently land on the ground way below me.

I am a fairy poet
Sitting on flowers writing magical poems.
As I write my poems they disappear quickly
and end up in a far away land for little kids to enjoy.

I am a dance poet
Standing on stage turning on the music
my poems go with the beat.
Gracefully, they go and fill the streets.

Katie Walsh, Grade 6
St Barbara School, IL

I Remember

I remember my friend and I ate fruit
I remember we liked to pick apples
I remember we would pick out the roots
I remember most that she liked grapples

I remember that we went to Lino's
I remember we went on my birthday
I remember we saw the man Gino
I remember my birthday was Thursday

I remember we had a very nice time
I remember we loved being together
I remember we never ate green limes
I remember she looked great in leather

I remember the day she left me here
I remember how she was always dear
Natalie Eckstein, Grade 6
Christian Life Schools, IL

New York City

Have you ever heard of New York City
It's really really pretty
You won't see a horse
Or even a golf course
It's home to the Statue of Liberty
Which is there for all to see
Andrea Vickers, Grade 6
Rochester Middle School, IL

Don't Burst My Bubble

If you burst my bubble
You will see that it
Will pop all over me
If you burst my bubble
I will get mad
If you burst my bubble
I will think you are bad
If you burst my bubble you
Will see that it will not
Pop all over me!
Haley Spencer, Grade 4
John Simatovich Elementary School, IN

The Evening

Loudness, loudness
of the evening,
sunset as bright as
the stars in the night sky.

Crickets chirping
here and there.
Brittany Eldridge, Grade 4
Canaan Elementary School, IN

Baseball

I like to play baseball.
It's played in the fall.

Running around bases in a fast manner,
Causes our team to win a banner.

Hit the ball with all your might.
Watch my team win tonight!
Trevor Hetrick, Grade 5
Staunton Elementary School, IN

Dogs vs Cats

Let me tell you why
I don't mean to make you cry
Dogs are best
Hope you won't protest
You see the cat
Is like a big giant rat
Dogs are true
Through and through
Cats are a fickle
Like a sweet butter pickle
Dogs play with you
That is what cats rarely do
Lovers of kittens
I'm sure you are smitten
But I can tell you true
Dogs are the best pets for me and you…
Teddy Ross, Grade 6
McHenry Middle School, IL

My Favorite Place

My favorite place,
Is where there are people,
Innocent, joyful, and laughing,

My favorite place,
Is where they are qualities,
Serene, quiet, yet strident,

My favorite place,
Is where being truthful,
Just, and legitimate,
Roam people's hearts

My favorite place,
Is where a conscience
Is clean from all invalid actions

My favorite place,
Is a dream, and my dream
Is to make it real
Noorfatema Shamji, Grade 6
Thayer J Hill Middle School, IL

The World

The world is a wonderful place
It has a lot of space
There are bumble bees
And big Oak trees
The world has so much space

The world is a wonderful place
It is not like outer space
It has living things
And they don't have rings
The world is a wonderful place
Abby Clark, Grade 5
Arlington Elementary School, IN

Our Love

I love him so
But he does not know?
He loves me so
That I do know
Though it might not show
Our love for each other will grow
Much more than anyone will ever know
We belong together
That does show
And one day we will be together
Because our love will grow
This I do know!!!
Josie Slaughter, Grade 6
GCMS Middle School, IL

My Brand New Car

If I had a brand new car
It would be orange and partly black
All of my friends would think it's whack
But I wouldn't care
Because it would be my brand new car.
I would put 20-inch wheels on it
And make it look real cool
Then the next day
I would drive it straight to school
I would drive it to the mall
And then to the zoo
I would take my little nephew
And maybe even you
I would take good care of it
And wash it every now and then
I would make sure it didn't get muddy
I may not even lend it to my friend
Getting a brand new car
Would be a great surprise for me
But if I didn't get it
I would still be as happy as can be
Matthew Bitter, Grade 6
St Theresa School, IN

Purple Pain

Purple pain is no fun
Purple pain is like getting burnt by the sun
Purple pain hurts so bad
Purple pain makes me sad
Purple pain is like breaking your knee
Purple pain I don't want to see

Samantha Strack, Grade 6
St Pius X Catholic School, IN

Rainy Days

Man, it's raining!
Whatever shall I do?

Rainy days
I think I have my ways
It's May, I say
Whatever shall I do?

Rainy days
I like to sing
I like to play
I like to drum, play piano, and guitar
Rainy days
Whatever shall I do?

Rainy days
I like to think of flying high in the sky
Playing dress-up with my friends
Rainy days
Whatever shall I do?

Rainy days
Running in the rain, getting soaked from head to toe
I love the rain!

Jena Lutz, Grade 6
St Theresa School, IN

Spent

Today was a boring day,
I don't have time to go out and play.
I had to get to school by eight,
it was so hot outside I wanted to faint.
In school I read and read and read,
but school is now over and piano lessons are where I am at.
Then I had to go to choir,
I had to stay there for three hours.
Finally, I waited for the bus to get me home,
but it didn't come so I called mom on the pay phone.
I had to tell her where I was at,
she came to pick me up but we got stuck in traffic.
We finally got home and the day was now mine,
I looked at the clock, it was a quarter to nine.
I couldn't believe the day came and went,
I wanted to go out to play but my day was spent.

Shavon Watkins, Grade 6
Lombard Middle School, IL

Love

Love is like a fire in the moonlight,
all I see is the angel with great sight.
Your hair blowing gracefully through the breeze,
what starts to tremble, other than my knees.
Your eyes sparkle as good as new,
I would die if I ever lost you.

Joel Glickman, Grade 6
Daniel Wright Jr High School, IL

Summer

The camp is rustling with children enjoying the summer air.
They go to hunt so they can find food to survive on.
It is the day light; the sun is bright in the bright sky.
The sky is where the eagle soars.
The flowers bloom, the butterflies roam.
The animals wake up from their warm homes.
New life starts in the forest.
This is summer.

Christian Wilson, Grade 5
Benjamin Franklin Elementary School, IN

Dream Vacation

Jerry went on a dream vacation,
Jumping and laughing he arrived at the station.
He gets tickets to his favorite show,
He jumps in a cab and away he goes.
He arrives at the stadium in the night,
All the wrestlers are there ready to fight.
Next thing he knew he was in the ring,
Punching and smashing is their main thing.
He went home with bruises and many bumps,
He'll never go back to that dangerous dump.

Alec D'Amico, Grade 5
Tri-State Christian School, IL

Animals

Animals are loved and cared for.
Some animals are mean, and scary,
but they are still sweet and hairy.
You can buy some animals at the store.

Some animals are lovely and nice,
some are ugly and some are cute.
A lot of animals are loud some are mute,
because they are quiet as a mice.

Many animals live in wild places,
some live in our house.
Large animals love to eat meat.
Baby animals love to play with shoelaces,
some like to play with a mouse.
All animals love to play and eat their treat.

Jericho Scott, Grade 6
Christian Life Schools, IL

Colleen's Poems

I am a flower poet
Sitting in the garden.
I watch as my poems
Bloom out to reach the sunshine.

I am an ice cream poet
Sitting in the sugar cone.
I watch as my poems swirl
Above me waiting to be a delicious treat.

I am a volleyball poet
Riding on the game ball
That is soaring over the net.
I watch as my poems ride above me
Having such a fun time.

I am a camp poet
Sitting around the campfire.
I watch my poems flicker in the night
Like little lightning bugs.
Colleen Brown, Grade 6
St Barbara School, IL

Valentine's Day

V ows to marry someone
A lways remember your spouse
L ove is in the air
E nthusiastic kissers
N ever stop hugging
T ime for love
I love you is said
N ever forget me
E veryone remember Cupid
S ome search for love

D ay can't be over yet
A lways remember to buy valentines
Y ou can kiss your true love finally!
Christina Stockman, Grade 5
Adams Central Elementary School, IN

Summer

In the summer it's really hot.
Lemonade really hits the spot.
I have heard a shot from the woods.
When it's breezy I wear my hood.
I almost stepped on a snake.
Cookies I help my mom bake.
I like to run around my house.
My dad killed a mouse.
It's time to end my story.
The day is over and the day is glory.
Zack Blount, Grade 4
Chrisney Elementary School, IN

Life

Night
Unique, mysterious
Darkening, scaring, frightening
Dark, intimidating, bright, welcoming
Coming, going, returning
Fresh, renewing
Day
Hayden Black, Grade 5
Adams Central Elementary School, IN

Best Friends

Sometimes they can be pests
Sometimes they can be the best
They are always at your house
With that dirty little mouse
And they study together on tests
Summer Stow, Grade 4
GCMS Elementary School, IL

Lord of the Rings/Cinderella

Lord of the Rings
Dark, death
Fighting, living, thinking
Sword, bows, dresses, crowns
Dancing, cleaning, ordering
Pink, white
Cinderella
Seth Waring, Grade 6
St Mary Elementary School, IN

A Wild Heart

On the dark and cloudless night,
Other creatures tremble in fright.
An outward call floats on the wind;
A mourning sound from end to end.

While on the hilltop sits a wild heart —
The wolf a creature so apart;
Shall dawn break soon, he'll turn 'round
And silently be homeward bound.
Lindsey Caudle, Grade 6
Cisne Middle School, IL

Peace

No mean wars, no tough battles
Happiness and love
The ground is not shaking.
Only the peaceful dove
No fires and no bombs
No need for police.
No wars. No wars.
This is my idea of peace.
Molly Grasz, Grade 4
St Robert Bellarmine School, IL

Parakeet

P eaceful Parakeets
A re
R esting outside
A round
K ids flying kites
E ating
E xcellent seeds
T ill they pop
Colton Farnsley, Grade 5
Floyds Knobs Elementary School, IN

Illness

Illness
Dizzy, painful
Flowing, traveling, killing
A part of life
Sickness
Esteban Hurtado, Grade 6
San Miguel School, IL

The Sea

Salty water and colorful fish
Whales and waves
Water so cool
Sharks hunting in undersea caves
Swimming and searching
Fish getting to swim free
"Not thinking. Not thinking."
This makes the sea.
Jamie Borkowski, Grade 4
St Robert Bellarmine School, IL

Siblings

Sister
Nice, pretty
Playing, singing, dreaming
Kind, sharing, caring, playful
Play, yell, talk
Eager, helpful
Brother
Hannah Zalaker, Grade 5
GCMS Elementary School, IL

Football

F un sport
O ut of this world experience
O utside sport
T ough sport
B lood sweat and tears
A ll the people playing
L osing sometimes
L ist of teammates
Jake Shubert, Grade 6
GCMS Middle School, IL

Ode to My Mom

My mom is great but never late for a single program. She's always giving lectures but not many fun ones. She's never mean but she sometimes jokes and says I use my head as much as a bean. My mom is my biggest fan even when I'm in big deep trouble. My mom can be nice as ice but I'm dead when I get her mad until I say sorry. I know mom and she know me as well as Einstein knew E=mc2 or something like that. I'm super glad I have the mom I have.

Keith Edward Jones Jr., Grade 5
Morgan Elementary School, IN

Horse

Hair
Their hair is thick, smooth, and shiny. Brush it forever, but after you finish they will go and roll around. Oh, but how beautiful they are.
Outside
They run, eat, breathe, and live outside. What a beautiful, wonderful place to be.
Ride
When you ride them you become one. You feel the air blowing through your hair as your body is moving up and down, faster and faster than the wind.
Saddle
The leather seat and the metal that holds it all together, a saddle, the one thing that makes you ride like a champion.
Everyone
Everyone needs a good friend like a horse, never ever letting you down.

Jessica Pemberton, Grade 5
Lynnville Elementary School, IN

The Hoop Blues

I stand so unsteady in this no one park; on the outskirts of Nobodyville,
Get slammed by a ball by some no one kid star; down my spine runs a bitter chill,
My spine is a little thing, hanging in there; my backboard's a rusty vile red,
My rim is the twig on a tree in the fall; it's surviving by one petty thread,
My name's as thrilling as carnivals to some, dull as a stick to others but still,
To me, I'm just a stack of metal that in this life, there's no reason or will,
Few kids and few more gather into my court; the game's what they really want to play,
The shortest one now hangs on my brittle rim; "Slam Dunk!" all her friends cheerfully say,
And as the ball forcefully falls down my throat; I think about life's own calling for me,
No matter how chilly or lonely out here; I'll never be where I want to be,
I'll always be here in this poor, dirt-paved court; as for all hope, no one cares a bit,
Don't tarry around for a goal to find you; get out there and you will find it,
People today celebrate what I stand for; but I ask for a much better life,
I search day by day for a meaning in this; why all around, all through me is strife,
No place to call home, nowhere I can ever know; no spot to enter or exit,
There's something out there that I never could find; get out there and you will find it,
Swish! The ball falls down my old scratchy throat; it tears so terribly tough on me,
It keeps me longing to get off my feet; leave the balls thrown at me behind, you see,
I want to move on, I want to see others; a thrill that was meant for me to get,
But I waited around and wasted my time; get out there and you will find it.

Kim Gannon, Grade 6
Our Lady of Peace School, IL

Ode to My Potbelly Stove

Dear, potbelly stove u keep me from freezing through the night. From your burning wood to your ashy paper u can help me with only one match. With my blanket and pillow and TV in front u complete my every comforting night. Dear potbelly stove with your bright shiny metal you're like a knight in the 12:00 light, fighting against the Fire Dragon. To my potbelly stove u are dear to me I'm glad u are staying with us. My dad, my mom, and my sister and me, we would be ice-cubes without u. Dear potbelly stove u keep me from freezing through the night. From your burning wood to your ashy paper u help me with only one match.

Olivia Horsley, Grade 5
Morgan Elementary School, IN

Puppies and Kittens
Puppy
playful, mischievous
loving, barking, teething
leash, collar, yarn, balls
playing, purring, leaping
cuddly, sleepy
Kitten
Meghan King, Grade 5
Our Lady of Peace School, IL

April Showers Bring May Flowers
Spring
So bright, so warm so pretty too,
So fun to play in, who knew?
Playing soccer, flying kites,
Oh no, mosquito bites!
Adela Zarzour, Grade 4
Universal School, IL

The Window and Me
Every time I look in the window, it's me,
not always the one I want to see.
There's one who made me so,
hand picked from the rest.
I must be pretty special,
'cause God made me!
Madison Feucht, Grade 5
Tremont Elementary School, IL

Cheetah
Breezes in the wind.
Runs faster than a tiger!
Fastest of them all.
Hannah Windhorst, Grade 5
Floyds Knobs Elementary School, IN

Sunrise and Sunset
The sun rises
On one spot
In the sky.
The rest of the sky,
Is dark and dreary.
But as the sun rises,
The sky lights up like fire
And I watch the world
come to life.

The sun sets
In the west.
As the sky turns colorful.
Purples, and reds, and yellows.
And the sky is alive.
But as the sun sets more,
I watch the world darken.
Chijioke Williams, Grade 4
Lincoln Elementary School, IL

Sisters
My sister and I are very close!
When you add us together we equal dos!
We do a lot together
Even in bad weather!

But, a sister is not just someone to play with:
A sister is someone's hand to hold
A sister is someone to love and adore
A sister is someone close to heart
A sister is someone to tell secrets to
A sister is someone who doesn't make you blue
A sister is someone to walk by your side
A sister is someone to talk to and love
A sister is someone who will never stop loving and will be there when you need them!
Maddie Eggold, Grade 6
Emmanuel-St Michael Lutheran School, IN

The Colors of Fall
Red is the color of leaves, so beautiful,
Tumbling, dancing to the dewy ground below.
Yellow is the color of hayrack rides,
The chilly air blowing in my face, the hay sticking onto my clothes.
Orange is the color of the piping hot fire,
That roasts our gooey marshmallows to perfection.
Gold is the color of these fond memories
carried in my heart, like a treasure.
There is no palette that compares to the colors of fall.
Haley Miller, Grade 5
Tremont Elementary School, IL

The Country
In the country you can be free,
Ponies and horses and all you can see.
Two deer in the forest that are running away,
and the two ducks that are sitting on the pond, are there to stay.
Playing sports like volleyball, and some other like basketball.
Two kids eating their ice-cream cones,
and a playful dog, chewing on his bone,
four-wheeler riding and playing in the creek,
and playing a game of nighttime hide-and-seek.
On hot summer days, we swim in the lake,
In early autumn, leaves fall, and then we rake.
In the winter we sled down our big hill,
then we go inside and have a tasty warm meal.
My cousins and I help Grandpa on the farm,
and pitching hay hurts your arm.
We help Grandma plant their garden and watch the seeds sprout,
then we plant some more seeds, and then we're all out.
Camping is a lot of fun,
And while we're there, we roast hot dogs and eat them on a tasty bun.
The things that you do are always neat,
living in the country is the perfect kind of treat!
Brooke Litherland, Grade 6
Perry Central Elementary School, IN

Mrs. Richison

Mrs. Richison is my teacher.
Her husband is a preacher.
She is always super nice.
Sometimes she has to tell us to do things twice.
Every day she hands out candy.
When it comes to homework she is very handy.
We really drive her crazy.
I'm sure she would appreciate a nice pretty daisy.

Morgan Ewing, Grade 5
North Intermediate Center of Education, IL

Yellow, and Red, and Pink with White

Yellow, and red and pink with white,
Many colors I wear,
All look fabulous and right,
My colors are my pride and joy.

I come beautiful, bountiful, and blooming in spring,
I bloom again in summer,
In fall, bloom I do not bring,
I wither weakly in winter.

I snap suddenly when you squeeze my side,
A dragon, everyone calls me,
I hear that name with tremendous pride,
I'm happily, yellow, and red, and pink with white.

Like a dwarf, I do not grow tall,
My leaves are green and tiny,
If you step on me I rarely fall,
I bounce back enthusiastically to life.

Among all of my many hues,
It's hard to choose which I like the best,
I confess, I have a favorite few,
Yellow, and red, and pink with white.

Lizzie Kramer, Grade 6
Our Lady of Peace School, IL

Cousins

I only have two cousins
But I wish I had dozens.

Boy, they sure are crazy
But that's better than lazy.

Having a dozen cousins would be a lot of fun
Just like playing in the sun
Eating a hot dog on a bun.

At the end of the day
I have two cousins to stay.

Grant Hood, Grade 4
Hoagland Elementary School, IN

Alando Tucker

His team colors are red and white
His number is forty-two,
He is a basketball player, not a teacher,
But he is still able to school you.

Point guard to center
He can play them all,
He can do amazing things
With the basketball.

He can make a basket
As easy as I can clean my plate,
But it's the combination of size, speed, and athleticism,
That makes him great.

He is a senior in college
And will soon have an NBA career,
What a way to go out,
Big Ten Player of the Year!

James Sainsbury, Grade 6
Laketon Elementary School, IN

The Last Day of School

Tests have been taken I'm glad I'm still alive.
The friends I've made I'll see more often,
Plans I've made I'll do more often.
There will be fun in the sun,
And family too.
With all these things going on I have so many things to do.
Summer will be fun but the new school year will be too!
I can't wait to do these things this summer.

Nicole Magnelli, Grade 5
Bell-Graham School, IL

The Big Game

There's ten seconds left in the game
This is my chance to go down in the Hall of Fame
My teammate passes it to me
Quick! My team is down two, I need to hit a three!
Five, four, three, two, one
I nail the three, and the other team's done!

Jonas Cullen, Grade 6
Rochester Middle School, IL

Loving Papaw

Papaw, the smell of freshly cooked baked beans
Papaw, willing to do anything for me
Papaw, the songs we would sing
Papaw, Papaw, the amazing fish we would catch

Papaw, you gently flew away
Papaw, on a blistering summer day
I love you, Papaw
And I know you love me, too

Hayden Flath, Grade 6
Linton-Stockton Elementary School, IN

Stars in the Sky
S hining in dark
T iny from Earth
A lways shining in space
R eady to shine
S hining all the way

I nspiring to me
N ever-ending

T oday still shining
H igh up
E verlasting

S o high up in the sky
K indling in the night
Y ou'll love them too
Alyssa Daugherty, Grade 5
Morgan Elementary School, IN

Best Friends
Who is my best friend?
someone who is always there
someone who is always fair

Who is my best friend?
someone who I spend my summer with
someone who will not tell me a myth

Who is my best friend?
someone who I always call
someone who likes to go to the mall

Who is my best friend?
someone who is my twin
someone who likes to win

Who is my best friend?
someone who has curly hair
someone who will take a dare

This is my best friend.
Amanda Fisher, Grade 6
Rochester Middle School, IL

Water
Water
Cool, pretty
Jumping, diving, boating
Swimming off the boat,
Tubing, driving, skiing,
Amusing, fun
Lake
Emily White, Grade 6
Sacred Heart School, IL

Spring
S pring flowers
P laying softball
R iding my scooter
I n the sun
N ight time walks
G ood night
Courtney Shawver, Grade 6
Elwood C C School, IL

Super Bowl
It's Super Bowl time
It makes me want to rhyme
Peytons' arm is the best
He will put their defense to the test
So the Bears fans sit back
Watch the Colts attack
Braden Robertson, Grade 5
Center Street Elementary School, IL

Big Load
I have a bike,
it's name is Mike.
He is cool.
He is my bike.

He lets me
ride on the road.
he can carry
A very BIG LOAD!!
Noah Radcliffe, Grade 4
Marine Elementary School, IL

Airplane vs Car
Airplane
big, aerodynamic
flying, lifting, landing
computer, wings, roof, wheels
moving, riding, driving
fast, cool
Car
Eric Pimentel, Grade 5
Seton Catholic School, IL

Yellow
Yellow is a pretty color
Yellow is bright
Yellow is the color of the sun
Yellow stands out in the world
Yellow is the color of the safe zone
You won't know when it will appear
Yellow is a big puzzle you
can't find the beginning!
Daphne Valle, Grade 5
Norman Bridge Elementary School, IL

Colors You…
Green —
You really light up a scene.
Blue —
I can always trust you.
Yellow —
You are a handsome fellow.
Brown —
You'll never make me frown.
Orange —
You, WAIT, nothing rhymes with orange.
Jordyne Higginson, Grade 5
Lincoln Trail Elementary School, IN

Myself
I am wonderful.
I am free!
I am wonderful,
lucky me.
I am powerful.
I am good.
I am powerful,
sometimes, misunderstood.
I am powerful.
I am bold.
I always do what
I am told.
I am wonderful.
I am free.
I am lucky to be me!
D'Jane White, Grade 4
Lavizzo Elementary School, IL

My 5th Grade Life
Knit, knit, knit,
We knit during noon
Knit, knit, knit,
It's time to teach you!

Skate, Skate, Skate,
It's all Parker ever does
Skate, Skate, Skate,
Why not go to SCRAP!

Buses, Buses, Buses,
They're all we ever ride
Buses, Buses, Buses,
To and from school!

Birthdays, Birthdays, Birthdays,
Time to get the flag
Birthdays, Birthdays, Birthdays,
Happy birthday to you!
Troy Musillami, Grade 5
Bell-Graham School, IL

Cheerleader

C lap your hands and stomp your feet!
H ey all you Commodore fans stand up and clap your hands.
E verybody stand up and holler!
E lementary cheerleader
R eady?
L et's go green!
E veryone shouting, "Go big green!"
A lways have spirit.
D efense get tough!
E veryone yell, "Go Commodores!"
R -I-M to the rim to the rim!

Laura Wiles, Grade 5
Perry Central Elementary School, IN

Kayley Drake

K ind
A ble to do things
Y aps to much
L oving
E asy
Y ells a lot

D aring
R apper
A ctive
K araoke star
E nergetic

Kayley Drake, Grade 5
Norris City Omaha Elementary School, IL

Traveling the World

I am green and mostly crinkled or folded,
As life goes on I make even more of a crinkle.
Once in a while I see the light,
But get passed to yet another owner.

I have traveled the world.
I have been to everywhere you can think of.
I have nowhere to call home,
I only have my birthplace in Washington D.C.

Sometimes you will find me in a safe,
A safe is a jail, dark, scary, and mysterious,
It's never lonely, like pennies lost in a couch,
But I do not stay in one place for too long.

Noel Fortman, Grade 6
Our Lady of Peace School, IL

The Leprechaun

There once was a leprechaun named Pat,
who rode on the back of a cat.
The cat was so mean,
the worst you have seen,
and that was the end of poor Pat.

Ian Schick, Grade 6
Rochester Middle School, IL

"Sick"arettes

Long, thin, and filled with tobacco and nicotine
Smoking even affects every human being
With the torture of innocent second hand smokers
Their lives are like losing a simple game of poker
It comes down to the sick ending
That cigarette can be quite bending
Rest in peace
Your life is as sturdy as a leaf

Pramod Venkatesh, Grade 6
Thayer J Hill Middle School, IL

Scuba Diving

I stand on the shore,
Sand between my toes,
Watching the waves roll, in,
Like a foaming dog's mouth.
I take a deep breath,
Swim out to the deep,
Let my air out
And start floating down,
And down,
And down,
And down…
The water is busy,
Lots of vibrant colors too.
I have a great feeling,
Exciting and new!
I feel something smooth,
But spiky too,
I feel the horn of a big dolphin's back!
I float up to the surface,
The waves push me in,
They are now like white horses running in!

Jesse Osborne, Grade 4
British School of Chicago, IL

A Beautiful Shore

I am a beautiful shore.
I wonder what it has in store.
I hear the ocean winds.
I see the ocean's high tides.
I want to feel the best in the world.
I am a beautiful shore.
I pretend that the sun is on my back.
I feel the ocean mist hitting my face.
I touch the ocean's cool water.
I worry that someone will pollute me.
I cry about pollution, because it is hurting me.
I am a beautiful shore.
I understand that people try not to pollute me.
I say that people cannot pollute.
I dream that someday I will be fresh and clean again.

Patricia Soto, Grade 6
St Matthias/Transfiguration School, IL

Rainbow

Rainbow
Seven colors
Arching, curving, bending
Look at the sky after a storm
Colors
Cristian Rivera, Grade 4
Norman Bridge Elementary School, IL

Spring

Trees
Big, shelter
Changing, giving, growing
Giving carbon dioxide
Important
Ismaeel Jarad, Grade 4
Universal School, IL

Alarm Clocks

Roaring like a phone
as loud as it can go,
something woke you up
what is it?
Who knows

As loud as a twister ripping through
and it's coming right for you!
The noise will finally stop,
as soon as you hit the button
on the top.
Melissa Willinger, Grade 6
Haubstadt Community School, IN

There Once Was a Boy Named Harry

There once was a boy named Harry
Who didn't like his friend Larry.
They got into a fight
Over a kite
And now they both look scary.
Ted Singleton, Grade 6
St Pius X Catholic School, IN

I Love Computers!

Surfing cyberspace
It is a giant playground
Laughing, chatting, playing
It calms me down
After a bad day
I play games as sweet as sugar
It is like a carnival
It starts to get late
But I don't want to stop
I love computers!
Brooke Donnelly, Grade 5
St John of the Cross Parish School, IL

Flat

Flat
Bright white
Suffocating infuriating blinding
Lost unknown unheard of
Airless meaningless
2 dimensional
Moira Tripp, Grade 6
Stanley Clark School, IN

Fall

I like fall.
The wind blows all
The colorful leaves off the trees.
We take a rake
And then we make
Leaves in a pile
The bigger the pile
The bigger I smile.
Victoria Spires, Grade 5
GCMS Elementary School, IL

Butterflies

I love butterflies.
They fly in so many skies.
Their wings have so much power.
Especially, when they land on a flower.
They eat bugs for food.
They are always in a good mood.
Their biggest fear is hands.
Let's not make them leave their lands.
Shellby Graham, Grade 4
Chrisney Elementary School, IN

Teachers

T ricky teachers.
E legant teachers.
A dvanced teachers.
C ute teachers.
H ilarious teachers.
E verlasting teachers.
R oyal teachers.
S uper teachers.

My teacher is the best!
She is not a pest!
Her name is Mrs. Jones.
She took us to Bones N Cones!
Oh no there is not enough to eat.
Yum but I got keewee!
Oh what A day, made out of clay.
Oh she really didn't do all this!
But she still is the best teacher!
Courtney Fifer, Grade 4
W E Wilson Elementary School, IN

A Hot Air Balloon

A hot air balloon is like a kite
Flying high in the sky
The stripes are a colorful rainbow
Shining in the sun
A hot air balloon is like a cloud
Moving from place to place
It drifts like the shining sun
Covering the whole Earth
A hot air balloon is a sea
Moving calmly
Hot air balloons are as calm
As the night sky
Emily Powers, Grade 5
St John of the Cross Parish School, IL

Red-Tailed Hawk

Powerful, dazzling,
Swooping, diving, devouring
Preying on small animals
Gliding, soaring, hunting
Beautiful, red
Predator
Austin Ross, Grade 4
Dixie Bee Elementary School, IN

Friendship

Friendship is like a
flower that grows and
grows, It could be as big as
a mountain or small as a pin.
Karen Anaya, Grade 6
San Miguel School, IL

Woodpeckers

Woodpeckers
Strong, beautiful,
Flying, pecking, eating
Annoyingly loud in woods
Soaring, tapping, drilling
Busy, distinguished
Holemaker
Jordan Davis, Grade 4
Dixie Bee Elementary School, IN

Ocean/Pool

Ocean
Salty, sandy
Surfing, boating, snorkeling
Fish, seaweed, cement, chlorine
Swimming, floating, diving
Clear, refreshing
Pool
Kristi Brennan, Grade 6
St Mary Elementary School, IN

Turkey

T urkey
U nbelievable
R eally good food
K indness
E nough food
Y ummy

Dylan Huffman, Grade 4
McKenney-Harrison Elementary School, IN

Waiting

I'm lying in his empty desk
waiting…just waiting

I notice the lights of the 6th grade classroom
brighten…it is the guest teacher

I listen quietly to the sound
of the small lockers
loudly opening and closing

Carefully I am lifted
out of his desk

He quickly clicks my head
a couple of times
and he is ready,
to begin the day.

Cole Bradbury, Grade 6
Linton-Stockton Elementary School, IN

Music Is Everything to Me

The beat of your heart,
The rhythm of your soul,
The crisp sound of leaves
Being crushed to the ground
On a cool autumn day,
No matter how the sounds are arranged,
It's music!
Every sound you make, feel, or speak,
There is at least one song being
Played, felt, danced to, sung, made, or thought of
All over the world
Music is everything to me!

The nearly silent splashes of a river,
The impossibly high whistle of a bird in a tree,
The tiger's loud roar,
The crab's claws clicking back and forth,
Everything is music,
Every stomp, clap, scream, or voice,
It's all music and,
Music means everything to me!

Aisha Harris, Grade 6
Laketon Elementary School, IN

Who You'd Be Today

I miss you so much I can hardly breathe
I miss your hugs
Your smile
Your yummy candy
Sometimes I wonder who you'd be today

You shared your love in so many ways
Like a look across the room or a walk down the hall
Sometimes I wonder
Who you'd be today

Time has gone by
Since the day you died
Yet the memories will last forever
Since you've died, the sky has been gray
I miss you so much;
Why couldn't you stay?

I wonder who you'd be today
I will never forget you
Not once in my life
I miss you so much
Though some day I'll see you soon

Emily K Earhart, Grade 6
St Theresa School, IN

True Friends

Friends are true.
Friends make you happy instead of blue.
Friends help you when you fall.
Friends answer when you call.
Friends are there rain or shine.
Friends don't mind if you whine.
Friends appear with care.
Friends don't care if you have bad hair.

Mara Loeb, Grade 5
North Intermediate Center of Education, IL

My Best Friend Paige

There was a girl named Paige.
She stood on the stage,
Reading a story
With a boy named Cory.
She was scored by the judge named Gage.

Haylee Swanson, Grade 6
ROWVA East Elementary School, IL

The Discovery

I was walking in the creek one day.
And there it was, all covered with clay.
The water was filling it as fast as I could dig.
Could I use this pot for just a swig?
Its colors were red, black, and brown.
Gee this thing sure gets around.

Lauren Dean, Grade 5
Freeburg Elementary School, IL

Farm

If you live on a farm,
You either grow things,
Or raise livestock.
If you're a livestock farmer,
Then you have to feed,
And sell your livestock.
You can raise as many animals,
As you want,
If you are a farmer you grow things,
Then you have to hope for good
weather,
And you have to sell your corn and
beans,
If you do both,
Then have to make a profit.
Farming is very fun.
I live on a farm and I love it!

Jessica Miller, Grade 5
Arlington Elementary School, IN

Garden

Tall flowers and small plants
Bees and weeds
The ground so pretty
Gardeners planting seeds
Picking and growing
Yards getting clean
No more mess
It's the nicest garden I ever seen

Taylor Farrell, Grade 4
St Robert Bellarmine School, IL

Tweet, Tweet

Birds
Colorful, fast,
Singing, flying, living,
Always in my business,
Nice

Adam Ahmad, Grade 4
Universal School, IL

Red-shouldered Hawk

Swooping through the air,
while flying so gracefully,
looking for its prey.

Alec Fair, Grade 4
Dixie Bee Elementary School, IN

The Dog

There once was a dog
Who got lost in the fog.
He ran to the light
That very dark night
And tripped over a log.

Alexis Cook, Grade 5
Seton Catholic School, IL

Me

Casey
Athletic, smart, hungry, curious
Brother of John, Emily, and Alex
Friend of Daniel, Brandon, and Ben
Who feels happy, bored, and excited
Who needs food, water, and shelter
Who gives love, money, and friendship
Who fears going broke, late slips, and another poetry assignment
Who wants to see Alaska, Japan, and China
Resident of Moline
DeWitt

Casey DeWitt, Grade 5
Seton Catholic School, IL

My Sister

I have two sisters, one not the type you would expect,
For one main reason, which I'll tell you in a sec.

This sister enjoys a fur coat, the color black,
And this coat goes all over, not just down her back.

She knows only a few words, but don't think that she's slow,
They are very special words, and they get her attention you know.

One word is "treat" and another is "ride,"
When you say either word, she's right by your side.

She loves to run and jump, but is not good at dance,
She never gives up, and always wants a second chance.

My sister spends a lot of time looking out the window at squirrels,
But she never thinks about things like taking a bike out for a whirl.

She gobbles down food, and does not take a break,
It goes quickly from "eat," to the past tense "ate."

Her breath is putrid, but not to her snout,
She doesn't care, for that's not what she's about.

I'm sure you know who my sister is,
And she's not a cow, horse, frog, or pig.

She might have some bad habits, like eating like a hog,
But it doesn't matter to me, because she's my sweet black lab dog.

Kylie Burnham, Grade 6
Daniel Wright Jr High School, IL

Yellow

Yellow
As bright as the morning sun gleaming into the warm souls of our body
Reminds me of sunrise at the crack of dawn
Soaring in the sky.

Valerie Niemiec, Grade 5
Frank H Hammond Elementary School, IN

Glorious Day

I am walking down the street
on a glorious Saturday morning
everything is peaceful
I can hear the snow plopping from the marshmallow trees

the cars trying to go through the street
little children playing in the snow
the magical blue sky making the bushes and trees
seem some kind of incredible dream

friends of mine trudging through the snow
people shoveling their driveways
my dad wiping the snow off his car
the sun shining
the snow making everything around me sparkle
this must be God's gift to the world

Jack Libert, Grade 6
Immaculate Conception School, IL

Main Street

I head outside on Main Street.
I see new people I want to meet.
I wonder if they're weird or not.
Hello, Hi, how are you, no one seems to stop.
Mellow sidewalks busy streets, I'm about to POP!

Brenna Arnold, Grade 5
Lincoln Trail Elementary School, IN

Friends

Friends go,
without saying good-bye,
you have to move on,
It's not as easy as it seems,
but before you know it you get a new friend

Brenda Esparza, Grade 6
San Miguel School, IL

The White Dragon

I see the beaming sun,
The day brings a crisp sky,
A white dragon drifts close,
And she brings shade to my eye.
The day comes where she is a fog,
Spreading across the grass.
I step mysteriously onto it,
And see the wonders that we pass.
The angles leaning over,
To see the people under the clouds.
The sun's golden rays,
Bringing the wealth of light to the ground.
And as she spreads her wings,
We glide down to the earth.
And when I say my goodbyes,
I see what life is worth.

Morgan Spiess, Grade 6
Peotone Jr High School, IL

Caregiver

Caregiver
Loving, caring
Looking, searching, finding
Saves mankind from the man with bloodshot eyes
Reuniting, hugging, telling
Worried, anxious
Hero

Emily Cutcliffe, Grade 6
Stanley Clark School, IN

My Grandfather

My grandfather, Da, died in the past,
So in my mind he is not last.
My grandfather was really fun,
He also was as bright as the sun.
My grandfather was very smart,
In life he always got a good start.
My grandfather was really cool,
He definitely was no fool.
My grandfather was really swell,
He always had a great smell.
My grandfather was always right,
But when it came to being cool he was really tight.
My grandfather was never wrong,
He always lifted my spirits by playing music and singing a song.
My grandfather was a great guy,
He took everything to the next level and sky high,
When Da died I was okay,
Only because I knew he was alive in a new way.
He is in Heaven now as you can see,
And I know he is watching over me.

Michael Hickey, Grade 6
Sacred Heart School, IL

Hope Is…

If hope could be a color
it would be blue as bright as the sky.

If hope could be a taste
it would be a chocolate bar.

If hope could be a smell
it would be a cantaloupe smell when my mom cuts it.

If hope could be a sound
it would be an orchestra.

If hope could be a feeling
it would be a kiss from my mom.

If hope could be an animal
it would be a bird singing in the morning on the top of a tree.

Guadalupe Ibarra, Grade 4
St Agnes School, IL

You and Only You

It's gray outside,
And nasty too,
All I want is to be with you.
You're kind, you're funny,
And heaven knows,
You can be sweeter than a rose.
You don't know this,
That's all right,
I want you to hold me tight.
You're so great,
When I'm by your side,
I always feel some sort of pride.
You hold my hand,
Tell me it's all right,
You always help me win the fight.
I like you a lot,
But I'm in a disguise,
Whenever I'm with you my stomach flies.
You can come over,
Any time you like,
Because when I'm with you I take flight.

Elisa Hoffmann, Grade 6
Benjamin Franklin Middle School, IN

Purple

Purple, is the color of,
A waterfall reflecting the sun's rays.
Purple, is the color of,
A dragonfly flying in the sky
Purple, is the color of,
Violets blossoming in the spring.
I love purple!

Samuel Scherry, Grade 5
Lincoln Trail Elementary School, IN

The Fire

Roasting toasting marshmallows
By the fire
Colors of red, yellow, orange, and blue
Coals and embers
Sparks and flames
Listen to the crackle,
POP.

A fire is like a child
It needs a lot of work
And attention
After you have one
You need to nurse it to be big and strong
When it's weak you help
And guide it to health and
When the time is right it will die.

Morgan Trotter, Grade 5
Indian Creek Elementary School, IN

Penguins in the House

There's penguins in the house,
There's penguins on the lawn,
They've been here since last dusk,
And they'll be here 'till next dawn,

Maybe all these penguins,
Are getting to my head,
'Cause I think I see some penguins,
Sleeping in my bed!

Katie Stinnett, Grade 4
Oak Hill Elementary School, IN

Skating

S kating is fun
K icking the ice is dangerous
A n axel jump is a trick
T ricks are very hard
I ce skating is being athletic
N othing is hard when you practice
G oing ice skating makes me happy.

Tamara Lewis, Grade 4
Norman Bridge Elementary School, IL

Holly

H as a nice room
O pens her sweet perfume
L oves to sing and
L oves Hannah Montana
Y ou're best friends.

Audrey Sanders, Grade 4
Shoals Elementary School, IN

Wishing

Every time you see her
Walking in the hall
You flash a cheesy smile
Wanting to give her a call.

You watch her secretly
While she twirls her hair
You wish that it was you
Being a part of that pair.

You want to be with her
Every second of every day
Loving her personality
But not wanting to say.

You laugh when she laughs
And cry when she cries
Always wishing
Living in sighs.

Kristen Swanson, Grade 6
Belzer Middle School, IN

Spring

Flowers
Pretty, scented
Cutting, smelling, looking
Put them almost anywhere
Beautiful

Adam Gholeh, Grade 4
Universal School, IL

Today

Today my little sister
Swallowed a fly
We rushed her to the hospital
And they asked why?

Today my brother
Got attacked by a pig
Which is kind of funny
Because the pig's not too big

Today the president
Called me on the on the phone
I told him to not bother
Me at home

Today — Wait!
Do you actually believe what I say?
Well, silly you shouldn't,
It's April Fools Day!

Anna Dahms, Grade 5
Bell-Graham School, IL

One Dollar Turns into More

Once I went to a store.
There was a dollar on the floor.
I looked around.
On the ground,
Then I found some more.

David Krans, Grade 6
ROWVA East Elementary School, IL

Snow

I am the sparkling white stuff
That's on the cold gravel
I am as soft as fluff
I fall from the cloudy sky
Above houses, trees and people
In mountains I build up too
But when I melt I start to drip
You will see me near Christmas
But I go away as fast as lightning
Remember I always come back
Sometimes when you least expect me

Joe Kasper, Grade 6
Our Lady of Peace School, IL

Orphaned

She's lonely and hurt
Her life full of misery
Nightmares all the time
Why did her father leave
Her life so very soon?
She cries in despair
Her mother has passed
Her family is unknown.
There's no way to find out
"Why do I exist?" She whispers to the snowflakes
"I just want a home."
She holds a candle to make her icy hands warm
"I can't go on."
She passed, starved and cold
The winter of eighty-six
No one to help her
None to comfort her
Nobody sympathized her
Never fed enough
She made her way to the golden gate
where she saw her Maker and angels

Elizabeth Wu, Grade 6
Gray M Sanborn Elementary School, IL

Ode to Trees

Tree oh tree
how you help me.
Birds that make nests
think you're the best.
When in your branches sitting down
I can see the whole town.
When in your branches with root beer in a mug
I feel like I can give you a hug.
One day where there's a lot of sun
I will bring up a hamburger on a bun.
When I'm famous for art with color
I will hire you a butler.
One day I will bring a girl up there
and we will dive from a branch into a pool.
Tree oh tree I will miss you
sometimes I feel like I can kiss you.

Jason Murner, Grade 4
Morgan Elementary School, IN

Dogs

Dogs
Cute, playful
Playing, running, barking
Shih Tzu, Golden Retriever, Yorkshire Terrier, Welsh Corgi
Catching, licking, drooling
Adorable, sweet
Dogs

Sarah Vavrin, Grade 6
St Matthew School, IL

Outdoor Life

I asked the oak tree, "Why are you tall?"
He gave no response.
I questioned the wind, "Why do you blow?"
She gave no answer
I asked the clouds, "Why do you move?"
But I still got no reply.
I sat on a rock by the river and pondered.
The oak tree is so tall so he can watch every one
in their homes.
The wind blows so we never get hot.
The clouds move so — yes they move so the sun
can shine through.

Samantha Rivera, Grade 6
Alexander G Bell Elementary School, IL

Fairies

Fairies, are they real?
Do they sprinkle miracles?
Pop! And one wish appears in moments
Bringing smiles to the faithful children.
The magic dust settles and then the pixie disappears.

Tiara Cooksey, Grade 4
Forest Park Elementary School, IN

Vacation

O I just can't wait
I really, really can't.
I'm going on vacation
flying across the nation.

Flying to San Juan
to spend the night
next day another flight,
I hope it is bright.

Fun in the sun
this beach bag weighs a ton.
Play in the sand
visiting a mysterious land.

Over the blue sea
Caribbean waits for me.
O no, o no
I have to go!

Molly Martin, Grade 6
Emmanuel-St Michael Lutheran School, IN

Give Me

Give me joy.
Give me hope
And I will give hope to those fighting diseases.
Give me courage.
Give me strength
And I will give it to those who are weak.

Kaylee Sherrod, Grade 6
Norman Bridge Elementary School, IL

Ode to the Graveyard

The graveyard is where ghosts fly.
Goblins and ghouls are very sly.
Witches and warlocks cast their spells.
So they can see what dwells in the wells.
When skeletons cackle
It makes them crackle.
Some things are scary
When others are hairy.
Some ghosts greet you
When others can meet you.

Jedidiah Robson, Grade 4
Morgan Elementary School, IN

Next to Me

Under the stars.
Over the clouds.
Above the trees.
Next to me.

Aboard a ship.
Beneath the sea.
Along the trail.
Next to me.

Across the desert.
Beyond the galaxy.
Within a mile.
Next to me.

Bonnie Buena, Grade 6
St Scholastica School, IL

Life

Life
Short, colorful
Living, loving, dying
It comes and goes
Hourglass

Katie Gilmore, Grade 5
Staunton Elementary School, IN

An Ode to Science

Science oh science
Chemicals of plenty

Science oh science
You make me so messy

If I work with you
You might blow up

That is why I won't work with you
'Til I grow up

Jasmine Jacobi, Grade 4
Morgan Elementary School, IN

Love Is Pure

Why don't we see love
as it's supposed to be
full of excitement
as you can see
do we even know what love is
or how it is used
it should not be tortured
or abused
we don't always find love at first sight
sometimes it takes years
maybe your whole life
we don't always know
if we'd find it at all
but it can't hurt to try
or make a few calls
like it is what we say
love is so pure
but to a broken heart
there is no cure

Angelina Manzuk, Grade 6
McHenry Middle School, IL

Candy

Twizzlers, Starbursts
What's not to like
Snickers, munchy, crunchy
Chocolate, just like Milky Ways
Melts in your mouth
Shockers, tangy, sweet,
Sour, yummy but crunchy
All sugar, bouncing off walls
Candy

Dakota Walter, Grade 6
Rochester Middle School, IL

Lazy Feline

Under the sun, my cat
lies down, bathes her
limp skin, cries out, rests
her head carefully, on
her stomach, looks up
fragilely, runs to the
food bowl, jaws ready to
eat, blinks, stalks the
bowl, gets in a
comfortable spot, sighs,
chows down, comes out
of the room, licking her
fierce chops, ready
again, for another long
all-afternoon nap, in her
loose, limp skin.

Haley DeRaedt, Grade 4
Creekside Elementary School, IL

Carnivals

They have sugary treats
It sure beats those frosted wheats
They have rides that are fun
And they have a raffle I just won
The clowns are funny
When you go there it should be sunny
They have animals like dogs
Some people kiss their frogs
Some people take pictures
They have all sorts of mixtures
They have games that cost a little money
They have foods that are dipped in honey
If you go there you will see
On the big rides you'll go wee

Jacob Arthur Bradford, Grade 5
GCMS Elementary School, IL

What Is a Mom

What is a mom?
A caring loving person
And is fun
And is cool
And makes a good meal
She takes care of me
And my brother
That is my mom.

Taylor Bruderle, Grade 4
Morgan Elementary School, IN

Love

When I saw you my heart
started to flutter I had no
words to say so I started to
stutter each day you pass
by I start to sweat. Your
beautiness shines my life,
my life would be better
if you were mine forever

Cesar Perez, Grade 6
San Miguel School, IL

The Game of Football

The game of football is very brutal,
Yet it is still very fun.
To hear the crunch of bones that creak,
Is to hear the game of the week.
My mind has the dream,
Yet I still eat ice cream.
I love of the game of football,
Oh yes I do.
Do you love the game of football,
It's so cool!

Alex Keller, Grade 6
St Mary School, IL

The Game

It's the ninth inning,
Two outs, and I'm up,
I walk to the plate
Nervous as someone on a tight rope

It's a playoff game.
If I strike out, we lose
Finally, I get walked

The next batter comes up to the dusty plate
One ball flies like a bullet to the backstop
I run as fast as a cheetah to second

I make it
The world is off my shoulders
The batter hits a pop up, and someone catches it
We lose

Then I wake up, relieved
It was just a dream

Dalton Kocher, Grade 6
Linton-Stockton Elementary School, IN

Fish

Down,
Down,
Down in the
Deep sea.

Down,
Down,
Down waiting for me.
I see my wonderful friend,
Looking for me.
I greet him with a grin.
He greets me with a fin. He takes me through
fishy sea to see what's waiting for me.

Brandon Bishop, Grade 4
James R Watson Elementary School, IN

My Beautiful Collection of Colors

A colorful rainbow above my sun
shades from purple to red.
The clouds are above the trees
slowly moving far away.
The light of my sun shines throughout the land,
it gives color to the clouds.
The sun lands on the horizon,
it starts to sink.
The reflection is a gleam of the light.
The palm trees lean from the breeze.
The mountains' shadows bow down to the sky.
My eyes glistened as I stare
at the beautiful collection of the colors.

Madelaine Isobal, Grade 6
St Scholastica School, IL

My Poems

I am a wind poet.
I am standing letting the breezes pass me by.
While the wind blows, my stanzas go with it.

I am a soccer poet.
I am running down a field with the ball in front of me.
My stanzas roll along with the ball.

I am a cloud poet.
I am lying down looking at the clouds.
My stanzas are riding the clouds.

Jonathan Medina, Grade 6
St Barbara School, IL

I Am

I am, a dictionary walking off the shelf
I am, a turtle slowly going with the flow
I am, a caterpillar inching my way through my problems
I am, sadness waiting to get out
      What am I?
I am, a TV constantly flipping through the channels
I am, the candle light glowing with fear
I am, the bubble gum that never loses its flavor
      I am many things
But what I am today I won't be tomorrow.

Sydnie McCormick, Grade 5
Churubusco Elementary School, IN

Charles

Charles is a turtle, who loves to sit all day,
and sometimes I worry that he will fade away.
He is short and pink and lovely, and tiny I might say,
he really cannot cuddle, but I think that's okay.
He is a cute eraser, who writes with me all day,
he says that it gets boring, but also it's okay.
He always says he loves me, and he will always stay,
but I know some day he will be gone just down to a dot,
But I guess I'll give keeping him forever, a very hard shot.

Brooke Cummins, Grade 4
Oak Hill Elementary School, IN

Basketball Season!

Basketball season is so much fun.
Basketball season is number 1!
I run and jump and play hard,
Trying not to give up my guard.
I dribble down the court,
and hope to get a 3-point score.
I turn to listen, what do I hear?
The crowd in the stands giving out a big cheer!
I hope basketball season never ends,
because then I would miss playing with my friends.

Justin Zuniga, Grade 4
Mentone Elementary School, IN

Ducks

Ducks
Yellow, waxy,
Quacking, swimming, flying,
Ducks are very unique.
Birds
Shelby Dupin, Grade 5
Staunton Elementary School, IN

Summer

S un is out;
U nbelievably fun,
M y birthday,
M y favorite season;
E verything is hot;
R ide bikes!
Ivan Fry, Grade 5
First Baptist Christian Academy, IL

Cow and Dog

Cow
White, black
Mooing, grazing, walking
Barn, pasture, dog house, yard
Chewing, barking, scratching
Brown, tan
Dog
Laura Kakert, Grade 5
Seton Catholic School, IL

A Cozy House

In your warm house
You feel cozy…
A soft blanket around you
You glance through the window…
It is storming
You go outside
And feel the cold rain
Touch your warm, pale face
Thinking…
I want to be
Back in my
Cozy house
Kelsie Todd, Grade 6
Linton-Stockton Elementary School, IN

Diabetes

D iabetes hurts your heart,
I t can make you cry,
A ll you can have is sugar free,
B ut that's a real good treat,
E veryone I know,
T akes real good care of me,
E ven when you're feeling down,
S omeone makes me smile!
Kayla Mosley, Grade 5
Perry Central Elementary School, IN

Into the Woods

I remember the forest preserve.
The smell of the cold, fresh wind blowing through the woods
Hiking up the dirty road
Walking across the sturdy wooden bridge
The sound of the raging waters just below my feet
My camera out, looking for a good shot
The tree we love that's center resembles a large belly
Hey!
I catch a glimpse of a graceful deer
Prancing away at high speed
The sound of the animal's tracks in the fallen, crumpling leaves
The distant call of my mother
"Time to go!"
Words I never like to hear there
Passing our discoveries on the way back to the car
The revving of the engine
As we drive away
The cheerless feeling of watching the tress getting smaller in the distance
Wanting to go back
Yet, I still remember.

Eric Goldberg, Grade 6
Alexander G Bell Elementary School, IL

Puck

He started in a fairy forest, looking through it like a tourist.
Looking around the woods for food, always in a joyful mood.
Through the wood he wanders, and he strangely ponders.
How to amuse himself more, like casting spells on the poor.
Oberon sent him out, leaving him without a doubt.
'Oh look, a vulnerable mortal,' thought Puck with a wicked chortle.
Within a flash, there was a crash.
"Hee-Haw!" he cried, as Puck's laughter died.
"Ah hah, young lovers" said Puck when he discovers
He has made a mistake, he has given them a heartache
Woken them in hurtful pain driving them down misery lane
Hypnotizing them to sleep while Oberon would weep and weep
"Sorry, sorry" he chanted loudly until Oberon fixed it proudly
The donkey was in love thinking Titania was from above
They sat and talked all night until Oberon gave her a fright
They changed him back to normal he wasn't very formal
Titania fell out of love and looked at Oberon with a shove
They all married happily they all had a family
This story is now finished or is it unfinished
However Puck still wanders as he strangely ponders
Rebecca Hersbach, Grade 5
British School of Chicago, IL

Inside This School

Inside this school there are so many books it's like a book worm's heaven
Inside this school there are so many computers it's like a techno geek's dream
Inside this school there are so many papers it's a tree hugger's nightmare
Inside this school there are so many shelves it's like a carpenter's workshop
Ben Molenda, Grade 6
St Pius X Catholic School, IN

Parents

My parents are great
They're as nice as a best friend
They love me and I love them, too
They help me as much as a Band-Aid on a cut
I only need two parents
To glide smoothly through my life
Like a soaring kite
I feel I need them
For things like homework
The most important thing I need from them
Is love.

Lizzy Morrissey, Grade 5
St John of the Cross Parish School, IL

Penguins

What slips and slides
In the slushy-slush cold?
What dives in the icy, wet water of a pole?
Can you guess what it is?
Of course! It's a little, chubby penguin!
Penguins have fun every hour of the day,
Even when it's nap time, because they dream about Friday!
They sing and dance to their moms and dads,
And say that they love them, in winter or May.

Olivia Martinez, Grade 4
Oak Hill Elementary School, IN

Laughter

Covering my face, making me look so joyful,
I feel so happy.
It's spreading through the class now,
We feel so happy — we're laughing.

We get a stern look, our teacher's looking mad now,
We are still laughing.
In our classroom laughter slows
I look back down to my notes.

Teacher says to us: I am using the washroom,
Stay in your seats and,
Do your work please finish soon.
Heels click across the floor — slam!

Laughter creeps around, it makes a glorious sound.
Giggles and guffaws,
We truly all love laughter.
Not working never stopping

The handle clicks, and we go back to our work so
Teacher won't get mad.
She comes in and looks all around,
No more laughter for now.

Natalie Stevens, Grade 5
Gray M Sanborn Elementary School, IL

The Beach

Take a day where the sand,
Is so very grand.
As it rolls with the waves
And crabs make their little caves

Watch as the gulls wobble across the shore
As they gobble up snails.
Watch as the surfers
As they catch a wave.

Devan Bader, Grade 5
Bell-Graham School, IL

The Domestic Clay Pot

I like to watch my clay pot in the window.
It is neat, broken, but beautiful.
It has a spirit symbol playing the flute.
I watch it sway in the wind.

Kayla Liefer, Grade 5
Freeburg Elementary School, IL

An Ode to a Special Person

He makes me happy.
He makes me laugh.
He is the special person in my life.
He has passed away, now he is dead.
I wish he was back.
I pray for him from time to time.
Everybody misses him.
I used to go over to his house and talk.
He passed away in a wreck.
He has been gone for at least a year now.

Kiersten Hoehn, Grade 4
Morgan Elementary School, IN

The Big Game

I'm on the court,
In the championship game,
Fans yelling,
At the top of their lungs,
The clock…
Silently ticking down,
We're down 1 point,
With 10 seconds left.

I get the ball at the middle of the court,
My sneakers squeaking,
I fake a pass,
My defender jumps to get it,
I take my shot.

The ball flies through the net,
Teammates and friends swarm around me like bees,
It is the happiest time,
Of my life.

Cody Kocher, Grade 6
Linton-Stockton Elementary School, IN

Adams Central

A wesome school
D rums and music
A midst the country
M y school
S mall children

C enter of Monroe
E lementary
N ice teachers
T all slides
R eal Four Star school
A lot of teachers and children
L oud children

Brad Faurote, Grade 4
Adams Central Elementary School, IN

Shoes

Shoes
Tying, zipping
Running, walking, jogging
Stinky, ripped up, heels, toes
Hurting, stepping, marching
Muddy, ugly
Barefoot

Lane Harrison, Grade 5
Adams Central Elementary School, IN

Rainbows

Rainbow
Colorful sight
Reaching to its top point
The disappearing clouds I see
Prism.

Emily Chapman, Grade 4
Robein Elementary School, IL

Drawing

Inside my head,
   Out on the paper,
   Until I lose the pictures,
   in my head.

Amid the colors, floating
   Across the diameter,
   Of my brain,
   From my imagination,
   down to my hand.

With lots of color,
   From my imagination,
   Out of my heart, my picture is,
   as good as gold.

Dana Lannin, Grade 6
Michael Grimmer Middle School, IN

Why Did You Go?

Why did you go?
When I needed you so?
You're my hero
But without you I'm a zero.
I know it's too late
Because you're in another state
Even when duty calls,
You're farther then Niagara Falls.

Was it something I did or said?
Because it feels like you fled
On a plane
All the way to Maine
Even though it's your job
Why make me sob?
So why did you go?
When I needed you so?

Erin Lindstrom, Grade 6
Rochester Middle School, IL

Lost

I'm looking through the window,
Hoping for him to come.
I'm staring into the rain,
My hopes are getting glum.

I'm waiting in the doorway,
Wishing him home.
I'm standing in the pouring rain,
Picturing where he will roam.

I'm lying in my bed,
Tears on my face,
I'm dreaming in my sleep,
Of my lost Ace.

I wake up and hear barking,
A smile spreads on my face.
I run downstairs to see,
My lost dog Ace!

Erin Ellefsen, Grade 6
Belzer Middle School, IN

Blue

Blue is the sweet taste of
Blueberries on french toast.
It's the sparkle of a new blue car.
Bluebirds singing on a branch.
Blue is the color of a new shirt.
It's the taste of blackberries
In my mouth.
Yum!

Garrett McKenzie, Grade 5
Staunton Elementary School, IN

Family

My brother is lazy,
He can't do anything,
My sister is funner,
She can do stuff,
My mom is the best,
She takes us places,
My dad is the best
He will take us hunting,
My grandma is fun,
She will buy us stuff,
My grandpa is a lot of fun,
He will take us fishing,
My cousin is lazy,
She sleeps all day,
My uncle is fun,
He will let us ride his 4 wheeler,
Miss Ward is the best,
She will give us candy.

Kyle Hewitt, Grade 5
Arlington Elementary School, IN

All I Want Is You

I'll tell it rather simply
I'll say it plain
A single thing is all I want
And all I want is you

There are no other riches
No possessions or treasure
That ever could compare with you
My fondest obsessions

You are the air I breathe
The ration that sustains me
You're all my thoughts tied up as one
The laugh that entertains me

You're all the life I'll ever need
And if I could ask for anything
I'd only ask for you

Quinteo Johnson, Grade 4
Hinton Elementary School, IL

Blackhawk Statue on the Rock River

Staring out across the river
Looking out at all of your land
Seeing gentle humans
Make things by hand
This is your town
These are your women and men
All together happily
Working your land

Elizabeth Goeden, Grade 5
Maplebrook Elementary School, IL

My Best Friend

She is a mall on the way.
She is a nonstop giggle machine.
She is a short mouse shrinking every day.
She is an ant amazing to watch every minute.
She is a talk on the phone.
She is a ride on a bike.
She is a long walk down the street.
She is a big cheese pizza that we eat together.
She is a green pickle.
She is a back handspring ready to flip.
She is the laughter that keeps us together.
She is a bowling ball shooting down the ally.
She is a batter on home plate.
She is a big mouth.
She is a moving piece to a board game.
She is the missing puzzle piece.
She is the talk about anything.
She is a runaway from chores.
She is a sister to my heart.
She is my caring best friend Aleshia.

Amber Mahan, Grade 5
Floyds Knobs Elementary School, IN

Ode to My Dog

My dog is cute, soft, and brown.
When you look at him, you kind of see a frown.
He won't eat your homework or chew on your shoes.
When you go to sleep he'll jump in bed with you.
He stays in our bathroom while we're away,
But when we come back he's still ready to play.

Austin Nolot, Grade 5
Morgan Elementary School, IN

Golf

First you hit the ball.
Then you wait for it to fall.
If you hit it in a lake.
It will get eaten by a snake.
If you hit it in the night,
It will look like star so bright.
If you hit it high.
It will look like an eagle in the sky.
If you hit it in the middle.
It will look like a white skittle.

Chase Witsman, Grade 5
North Intermediate Center of Education, IL

Water Everywhere

Water, water, everywhere and not a drop to drink;
It filled up the bathroom and flooded the kitchen sink.
April showers may devour our crops and stain our shirts;
But if you ever ask me we should all wear diving skirts.
So if you see a dark cloud, over yonder forming;
You'll know my house will be under water by morning.

Lydia Aleman, Grade 5
North Intermediate Center of Education, IL

The Sky

Watching the night sky is the best,
Looking the sky with stars
Makes a great looking car
And when the meteor comes by
As I say "Bye Bye"
As the same time I sigh.
As the branches sway
Back and forth
As if it has a worth
About the meteor
And now I have to say
That I always wonder why the sky is telling me to be shy
Never know why
But some day I'll shine
Like stars in the sky
Looking at them like it's mine
But never know unless I try so always say
"Tell me why!" The sky is always there
Looking at it like it's mine
Never know till I try
Just "Tell me why…"

Kazuki Morita, Grade 5
Fredrick Nerge Elementary School, IL

I Wonder

I wonder how the water falls,
So gently down the rock walls,
How can the water be so clear,
Clear as diamonds on a chandelier,
I wonder how the birds sing,
So sweetly as they flee,
You can hear their songs all trough the day,
I cherish their tunes on the month of May,
I may never find the answers to the questions that I ponder,
But still I wonder I wonder I wonder

Tabitha Bashore, Grade 5
Center Street Elementary School, IL

Extreme Animals

A ll animals	**N** ewt
B lue tongued skink	**O** ctopus
C hinese Firebellied toad	**P** arrot
D inosaurs	**Q** uail
E lephant	**R** ed eyed tree frog
F erret	**S** ugar glider
G reen Anole	**T** adpoles
H edgehog	**U** nicorn
I nsects	**V** eiled chameleon
J ackalope	**W** olf
K angaroo	**X** -ray fish
L eopard gecko	**Y** aks
M adagascar hissing cockroach	**Z** oones

Alexis Young, Grade 4
Shoals Elementary School, IN

A Year

Spring has sprung!
The birds twitter,
The blossoms bloom,
I feel joy in my heart.

Summer has started!
The sun beats down,
The trees give shade,
I feel happiness in my heart.

Autumn has begun!
The leaves blaze,
The trees go bare,
I feel change in my heart.

Winter has settled!
The ground has snow,
The animals hibernate,
I feel stillness in my heart.

Then all over again it goes,
These are the seasons of a year.
Erin Neil, Grade 5
Butterfield School, IL

Snowy Owls

I am an owl. I go hoot,
And also I am really cute.

I also have a beak,
It's by my cheek.

I am pure white,
And I'm up all night.

I have pointy ears,
And have no fears.
Cameron E. Sweeney, Grade 5
Dee Mack Intermediate School, IL

Basketball

You shoot! You swish!
You score! You're in
the lead. Now up
by two. Defense!
Defense! You stole
the ball, six
seconds left.
Go up the court
drive to the
basket. You shoot!
You score!
Sammie Coakley, Grade 5
Cortland Elementary School, IL

Pole Vault

P atience
O utstanding
L unge
E ntertaining

V ery challenging
A erodynamics
U nity
L aunch
T eam
Mark Thompson, Grade 6
Rochester Middle School, IL

Blue

Blue is the strength of mountains
that tower above my head.
Blue is the blueberry
that lingers in my mouth.
Blue is the sky.
Blue is you and me.
Jacob Myers, Grade 5
Staunton Elementary School, IN

I Love You with Everything!!!!

When we are together
You will see,
that we belong together
just you and me.

In my heart,
you hold the key,
I will love you
and be all I can be.

You should take my word
and take my hand,
for with each other
our hearts will band.
Betsey Brimm, Grade 5
Floyds Knobs Elementary School, IN

Quesadillas

I am so yummy
I taste so good
People love to eat me
All of the time.
They say that I look good
With cheese in the middle
If you want to know what
I am it is quesadillas.
That is why people love
That taste of me.
Leslie A. Puentes, Grade 5
Neil Armstrong Elementary School, IL

Love

Love is like a dove
Who flies up above
Oh look how high
It is like a diamond in the sky
And it will never die!
It is like a girl's best friend
Then you know love will never end.

It is like a wish
That might have come from a golden fish
Love is like having a lot of joy
Just like having a Chip's Ahoy
You should never give up to find love
It just might be there from up above.
Emily Janssen, Grade 6
Rochester Middle School, IL

Squirrel

S wift
Q uirky
U nder the ground
I s his greatest prize.
R eady to fight other
R ed squirrels for his trees.
E ating on a
L ow branch.
Clay Travis, Grade 4
James R Watson Elementary School, IN

Springtime

S un getting bigger
P retty woods growing
R aining more lightly
I ntense growing flowers
N ight getting warmer
G rimy mud piles
T oads by the stream
I n gardens butterflies are
M ildest weather
E very tree blooming with buds
Lindsey Thornburg, Grade 5
Tri Elementary School, IN

The Weirdest Farm

On a farm.
there was something wrong.
the cow barked.
the dog moooed.
the pig gobbled.
the turkey oinked.
and the bull talked.
and even the farmer sounded like a bull.
Stephanie Serrano, Grade 5
Gard Elementary School, IL

Ode to My Best Friend Kendra

Kendra is so sweet
She is my best friend
She makes me happy when I'm down
But she sometimes can make me frown
I know she will always be my best friend
She is always fair even when it's hard
I think she lives in a barn
But it doesn't matter she'll always be my best friend!

Kaylee Nordhoff, Grade 5
Morgan Elementary School, IN

Summertime

Summer is a great time of year,
a time to be lazy and play with your friends,
a time to be yourself and do what you want to do,
a time to be free of homework, free of school
a time to swim and go to the park,
a time to have fun and be yourself,
summertime is almost here.

Alexis L. Von Behren, Grade 6
Rochester Middle School, IL

Death

What is death? Do you know?
Is death a horrible nightmare that comes true?
Or is it a relief to know someone is out of this terrible world
Out of pain and suffering
Or is it both, one day you're glad they're gone and the next day
You're wishing you should have died instead of them.

Libby Van Dyke, Grade 6
Rochester Middle School, IL

Peace

Peace
Clouds, silver,
Exciting, rising, flying,
A fun trip turns into a terrifying nightmare —
Terrorizing, descending, falling,
Golden, shadow,
Horror

Robbie Dragani, Grade 6
Stanley Clark School, IN

Ode to My Cat

My cat is big and fat.
He uses my backpack as a nap sack.
My cat likes to climb fences and has good senses.
He likes rats but does not like bats.
He likes cars but does not like bars.
My cat is weird —
He does not like shopping but likes walking.
That is my ode to my cat.

Breana Taylor, Grade 4
Morgan Elementary School, IN

The Crash

I looked around,
all I smelled was the smell of burnt rubber.
The smell of rubber triggered my nose.

I listened closely,
tires squealing in every direction of me.
It's as if I was deaf.

I see darkness everywhere,
as if I was blind.
I couldn't see anything in any direction.

I feel motionless,
because of the big hit from the car,
on the ground feeling like a statue.

I taste blood in my mouth,
as if I got shot with a gun.
BANG!!

The ambulance screams through the streets.
Help was getting closer and closer to me.
I don't know what was going on,
but I felt that my family was terrified.

Sebastian Laszcz, Grade 6
Onahan Elementary School, IL

All About Chips

I am chips.
I wonder if people will eat me.
I hear crunchy sounds.
I see different kinds of chips.
I want to be healthy.
I am chips.
I pretend to be healthy.
I feel other chips.
I touch other bags.
I worry about not being eaten.
I cry about being alone.
I am chips.
I understand about people not eating me.
I say to always eat chips.
I dream about being healthy.

Chris Badion, Grade 6
St Matthias/Transfiguration School, IL

The Road Trip That Didn't Go So Well

As soon as I started the car, it broke down.
I had to push it 300 miles to the nearest gas station
In a far away town.
When I got there I was relieved.
But I realized I had lost my keys.
So I decided not to go,
All the way to Mexico.

Nathan Frelka, Grade 5
Countryside Montessori School, IL

The Wilderness
Creeks and rivers
Rivers and creeks
A place to express my feelings
A place to run
A place to hide
A place to be in the wilderness
And space to see the wildlife
Andrew Bolinger, Grade 6
Laketon Elementary School, IN

Spring
Spring is like a song,
Birds are breaking bits of wood.
And flowers are saying "hello,"
It puts me in a good mood.
Lacey Medlin, Grade 5
Arlington Elementary School, IN

Mamaw and Papaw
M y best friend
A wonderful cook
M agnificent
A lways will be there for me
W arm and pleasant

A bsolutely never yells at me
N ever stops loving me
D efinitely human

P owerful senior citizen
A lways is being funny
P erfect farmer
A lways there for me
W hat the… as he says if it keeps raining
Hayley Elliott, Grade 4
Morgan Elementary School, IN

Shooting Stars
Shooting stars
are like a flying red hot chilly pepper
or maybe a frozen block,
some are red some are blue,
here comes one now,
make a wish
I think it's blue
no it's red
hurry now
hurry now,
make a wish
there it goes
like a rocket
leaving a tail
of little
tiny sparkles.
Jamie Williams, Grade 4
Bright Elementary School, IN

Life
Life is the simple passing of every day;
Everyone's existence intertwining,
Springing anything new into
Our humble sheltered lives.

Happiness is a surprise;
Everyone cooperating and having fun
Doing what you adore, a party is happiness, love is happiness.

Annoyance is a bee buzzing in your ear;
It won't leave unless it is forced.
Annoyance can be a little brother —
But only sometimes.

Anger is thunder booming in the heavens;
Crumpling the weak, frightening the mighty,
Like the sweeping wave of despair, it sinks into your soul, cluttering you forevermore.

Love is a rose blossoming in the spring air;
It appears so fragile, but its roots grow deep.
Love is a family, everything you hoped for,
Your friends, whomever, the people you adore.

Life is bittersweet, the good and the bad;
Smile through your tears; don't show that you're mad.
Every day brings something new — all I want is to share it with you.
Hannah Novak, Grade 5
Ranch View Elementary School, IL

The Cruise
I went on a cruise, and then my brothers sang the blues.
When the thieves stole our money we went to look for clues.
We were in a fright all through the night.
We thought the crime was funky when the crooks turned out to be monkeys.
They wanted bananas, so they tried to steal our dough.
After the crime the monkeys did the time.
We bet on a dime that after they did the time that they would do the same crime.
After the time they did the same crime, and I gave my brother a dime.
Luke Myers, Grade 6
Christian Life Schools, IL

Under the Beautiful Sea
Here I am far from shore in the sea.
In the beautiful sea where open water flows around me.
Waves splashing everywhere I look.
Finally I hold my breath and take a dive into the beautiful sea.
Deeper and deeper I go. Bubbles releasing from my breath.
Many fish many plants, there's so much to see under the beautiful sea.
I wish, I wish to stay longer but my breath is running out I swim back to the air.
If only I could see it longer but my breath is too short.
But I will have it in my memory forever for something
as beautiful as that cannot be forgotten.
Konrad Michalek, Grade 4
Norman Bridge Elementary School, IL

My House
I hear the sizzling steak on the grill
The sweet fragrance of fabric softener
The taste of sweet corn in my mouth
The sun coming through the window makes the room bright
My house

The feel of the chilly hardwood floor beneath my feet
The TV blaring a Pacers' game
The taste of refreshing tea quenching my thirst
The feel of a soft couch after a long school day
My house

Eric Nagy, Grade 6
Linton-Stockton Elementary School, IN

Just Now I…
Just now I heard my mom say we are going to the mall.
Just now I grabbed some cute clothes.
Just now I went to get in the shower.
Just now I got dressed.
Just now I gobbled up breakfast.
Just now I fed my dog.
Just now I brushed my cat.
Just now I take out the trash.
Just now I did the rest of my chores.
Just now I combed my hair.
Just now I scrubbed my teeth.
Just now my mom told me we are going tomorrow!

Bethany Harmon, Grade 4
South Newton Elementary School, IN

My Dream
If I slept with
My shell under my pillow,
My dreams would be
Calm and peaceful like a kitten taking a nap

I would lie at the
Bottom of the clear blue ocean,
And watch all the
Wet creatures swim by.

I would be carried
Back and forth by the crashing waves,
Like a roller coaster.

I would be thrown to shore
There I would sit
Waiting, waiting for someone
To take me home.

If I slept with my
Shell under my pillow,
I would dream
That I was my shell.

Hannah Bough, Grade 6
Linton-Stockton Elementary School, IN

Winter
Winter has swept in,
On glistening silver wings,
Silently blanketing the ground,
In a pristine sheet of snow.
The trees carry a burden of crystals,
Glinting in the weak light,
Dazzling me with their everlasting brightness.
The harsh wind whispers Nature's secrets to the trees,
Nipping slyly at chilly fingers.
The squirrel rests in sheltered hollow,
Bushy tail curled tightly 'round his nose,
Sheltering him from freezing gust,
Slim brown deer, wade weary through the snow
Desperately seeking shelter from the dreaded hunt.
Lumbering bears snatch last pawfuls of honey
Before crawling into covered cave,
Geese flee in haste, with feathers ruffled,
To where the sun still smiles.
As majestically as winter sweeps in,
Its icy magic slowly gives way to new life,
The birth of the new year.

Sanika Bhargaw, Grade 5
Quest Academy, IL

Hot Air Balloon
In a hot air balloon all full of color
Flying in the air like no other
Soaring like a bird, flying like a plane
Flying in a balloon will never be the same
Passing through clouds scattered in the skies
Shooting through the stars as you ask, "Why?"
Going through the air with grace and with glory
This is the end of my balloon story!

Ryan Minik, Grade 5
St John of the Cross Parish School, IL

I Am a Panda
I am a panda.
I wonder why I am black and white.
I hear bamboo rustling in the forest.
I see bamboo waiting to be eaten.
I want to eat bamboo.
I am a panda.
I pretend I am skinny.
I feel very furry.
I touch the green grass.
I worry If I will be hunted.
I cry when I am all alone.
I am a panda.
I understand that I am cute and cuddly.
I say how I love to eat bamboo.
I dream that I were in the zoo so the world can see me.

Jazmine Benitez, Grade 6
St Matthias/Transfiguration School, IL

Winter

A blizzard is coming
I hear the wind humming
Look at all that pretty snow
While I put on my Christmas bow
Santa Claus is coming to town tonight
Dressed in red and white.

Adriane Schoonover, Grade 4
Goodfield Elementary School, IL

Flowers

Flowers can be yellow
They can look like a little fellow.
Some can be so bright
That I might lose my sight.
It might be time to play
And flowers will bloom every day.

Payton Baillie, Grade 5
GCMS Elementary School, IL

My Little Friend

My little friend
Is very, very soft and fluffy
She has four legs
And a stub for a tail
She has two floppy ears
And a wet, wet nose
She goes woof, woof
And gives me lots of kisses
She's my best friend
And watches out for me
I love her more than anything else
Her name is Queen
She's my dog of course!!!

Tori Ihms, Grade 6
Illinois City Elementary School, IL

Knowing Jesus

I am knowing
That I am flowing
With Jesus
On Christmas Day
That's why I obey
On that day.

Seth Rieke, Grade 4
Goodfield Elementary School, IL

The Elephant

There once was an elephant in pajamas.
The zoo gave him bananas.
He ate them up,
Put the peels in a cup,
And changed into a bandana.

Alexis Sutton, Grade 5
Seton Catholic School, IL

Baseball

If you hit a ball up high,
If you don't catch the ball,
It will go up to the sky.
Then you trip and fall.

Andrew Armour, Grade 4
Central Elementary School, IL

Dakota

There once was a pony name Dakota
Who wanted to live in Minnesota
She once had a great owner
Who was an organ donor
Who gave her a kidney and a soda

Olivia Mishler, Grade 5
Adams Central Elementary School, IN

Love

Love is like a flower,
A tulip or a rose
That blooms in a tower,
From your head to toes.

For when you love someone,
So kind and dear,
There just isn't anything
That you should fear.

Blayk Giddens, Grade 6
Laketon Elementary School, IN

Cody

I have a cousin named Cody
Who had a crush on Jody.
One day they had a kiss
That came to be a hissy fit
They had to get a chair to sit
His dad got mad and set him to bed
But in his bed was Ned
And he had to sleep on the floor
And Jody went out the door

Patrik Jones, Grade 5
Center Street Elementary School, IL

School

School is boring,
I find myself snoring.
I feel it's no fun,
And I want to run.

Once it is out,
We all run about.
"Bye," we all say.
No school. Hooray!

Savannah McCafferty, Grade 4
Liberty Elementary School, IN

Western Bluebird

Western Bluebird
Beautiful, delicate,
Swooping, eating, singing
Pretty as a picture
Flying, diving, chirping
Charming, fearless
Unique bird

Nick Truelove, Grade 4
Dixie Bee Elementary School, IN

Music!

Music!
It's an always rhythm,
we always hear.
The rhythm we hear in
every little or big noise.
You can hear it on the street.
Crash,
Vroom,
Beep!
You can hear it by the ocean.
Slish,
Splash,
Sploosh!
You can hear it anywhere,
anytime all the time.
You just have to
Listen!

Eilis Corcoran, Grade 4
Creekside Elementary School, IL

When It's Spring

When it's spring,
you can go to the park.
And play outside
until it gets dark.
Play jump rope in the street.
as you turn,
you listen to the beat.
You hear birds singing,
and many bells ringing.
When it's spring,
you can do lots of things.

Aminat Osibote, Grade 4
Lavizzo Elementary School, IL

The Man in a Log

I once knew a man in a log.
It was located in a bog.
He had good looks.
He always read books,
But why doesn't he just get a dog?

Cody Appell, Grade 6
ROWVA East Elementary School, IL

Basketball

B is for basketball.
A is for adrenaline rush.
S is for stealing the ball.
K is for keeping the ball from your opponent.
E is for excited fan.
T is for three pointer.
B is for best team ever.
A is for being active.
L is for love of the game.
L is for learn the more I play.
    That's my rules for my love of the game.
Demond Davidson, Grade 4
Lincoln Elementary School, IL

The Beach Is My Kind of Place

The sand in my toes.
The water splashing in my face.
The wind blowing my hair.
The beach is my kind of place.

It's hot outside.
The people tanning are lazy.
Little kids running around like crazy!
The beach is my kind of place.

Older kids boogie boarding.
Little kids playing tag.
The big umbrella is the base!
The beach is my kind of place.

I can hear the song.
Of the ice cream truck.
It's not that long.
I'll try to catch it with a good pace.
The beach is my kind of place.

Everybody's gone home.
It's just a big open space.
The beach will always be my kind of place.
Ally Romershausen, Grade 6
St Theresa School, IN

Gold

Gold is the color of the Olympic winner's medal
Gold is the color of the NBA Championship trophy
Gold is the color of the Colt's NFL Super Bowl ring
Gold is the color of the All-Star's game

Gold is the color of a winner's dream
Gold is the color of the Emmy awards
Given to respectable actors
Gold is worth more than green
Keith Fulk, Grade 6
Linton-Stockton Elementary School, IN

Toot! Toot!

A cherry sat on the railroad track,
    Trying to get across the bunch,
The five-fifteen came rushing by —
    Toot! Toot! Fruit punch

A tomato sat on the railroad track,
    Trying to catch up
The five-fifteen came rushing by —
    Toot! Toot! Ketchup.

A million bricks sat on the railroad track,
    Trying to look like a full house
The five-fifteen came rushing by —
    Toot! Toot! Courthouse

A lemon sat on the railroad track
    Trying to waste time
The five-fifteen came rushing by —
    Toot! Toot! Lemon lime!
Malik Issa, Grade 6
Michael Grimmer Middle School, IN

Shopping

I love to shop.
I shop till I drop.
My favorite place to shop is the mall
I always have such a ball.
I love to use my dad's credit card.
Then I have to break it to him, which is hard.
I love to buy lots of things.
Sometimes I even buy myself rings.
Kelly Nohl, Grade 5
North Intermediate Center of Education, IL

Dogs and Cats

Dogs are frolicking through the fresh snow
Cats are meowing, "Go dogs, Go!"
Dogs go chasing after a ball
When dogs come near, cats sprint down an alley

Cats are meowing, "Go dogs, Go!"
It is taking a risk, cats all know
When dogs come near, cats sprint down an alley
Chasing after the darn, stupid ball

It is taking a risk, cats all know
Watching the dogs frolicking in the fresh snow
Chasing after the darn, stupid ball
Causing the cats to sprint down an alley

Watching the dogs frolicking in the fresh snow
None of them care where the ball will go
Causing the cats to sprint down an alley
Dogs are frolicking through the fresh snow
Natalie French, Grade 4
Bell-Graham School, IL

Hanging Around

Ding! Ding! Ding!
I am red like an apple, green as a pear, and yellow like a lemon.
My lights are brighter than the sun.
I squint to see cars' bright lights.

Vroom! Vroom! Vroom!
I tell cars when to go.
You'd better go straight, left, or right.
Make a quick decision when you reach me.
Throughout the day I hear the brakes of cars like the sounds of fierce tornados.

Screech! Screech! Screech!
When you reach me stop, go, or yield.
I work all through the day.
I even work into the late hours of the night.
Always, remember to not make the wrong decision when you reach me.

Christopher Menich, Grade 6
Our Lady of Peace School, IL

The Gates of Heaven

I now fall the third time on this barren wasteland
Then trod my last few steps on Earth
I know not if I shall ever go home to the land beyond the sea
Then I saw a blinding light fall down from up above
The clouds, they shattered like fragile glass
Shards falling down to Earth like inflamed spears
When an angelic figure appeared and quickly grabbed my hand
I noticed just then, tears in my eyes, that I was to die this mournful day
But then suddenly my tears stopped as I gasped in awe at this miraculous sight
The biggest castle ever seen was right before me with every brick made of the finest gold
And tower upon tower of treasure either lost to time or not familiar to our world at all
It was then I realized where I was
I quickly knelt ashamed that I didn't realize sooner
I was in the midst of the Kingdom of the Lord
I looked up at His mystical eyes beckoning me
Then shaking, I started walking down the path of life and death
The path all men fear. Until the path stretched no more
Then I fell into my Father's arms
Cold and weary, yet more spirited than ever before
Then pushed upon the door of everlasting life
I plunged into whatever awaited me in the Kingdom of the Lord

Anthony Pierotti, Grade 6
Immaculate Conception School, IL

Ode to USA Soldiers

You risk your life for us, because freedom doesn't come free. You leave your wife, husband, or your children, and have that empty place in your heart to show you support this country that is under God. God has blessed this country, and God has been good to me and this country. You and I need to bless him too. You risk your life and you know the sacrifice, but you are always ready and standing tall and straight. Even if you have that gap in heart that you and your family have. You support this wonderful country, but yet you are ignored. I don't ignore you brave people but, pray. I support you USA soldiers. God bless you USA soldiers, and you bless him too.

Micah Brumley, Grade 4
Morgan Elementary School, IN

Sweet Things to Eat

Sweets, sweets, and bag of sweets are my kind of things to eat
Salads are not for me
Eating sweets are my kind of things to eat
You can take your vegetables,
But please don't take my sweets from me!

Emmie Johnson, Grade 4
Martin L King Elementary School, IL

Mom-Moo

Mom-moo, a legendary grandma
The sweetest old lady in the world
Sweet memories of brushing her soft, icy-gray hair
Feeding the wild squirrels on steamy summer days
Sitting with her in her wheel chair
Listening to the blue jays sweetly singing in the trees
The delicious warm, creamy taste of
Her homemade chicken pot pies
The soft squishy feeling of
Her Miami Dolphin's slippers
Watching jeopardy with her
On wet soggy days
Mom-moo will always be missed
Sweet memories with Mom-moo is all I have left
Now she's feeding squirrels with Jesus
No longer held back by her wheel chair

Jacie Craft, Grade 6
Linton-Stockton Elementary School, IN

Hail

Hail comes,
starting out like little pieces of glass, falling:
Chink clink kachink click tik tik
Then it gradually builds up,
Pelting houses
and cars
It becomes a roaring lion of a storm,
Although when father cloud sees the damage done
He calls back the hail minions,
and puffs away, as soft as a kitten's purr…

chink clink kachink click tik tik
Oh No!

Kevin Stoffel, Grade 4
Pleasant Hill Elementary School, IL

Sisters

Sisters running everywhere
Getting blisters here and there.
Sisters always reading in books
But never going fishing with hooks.
Sisters can be such a pain
They almost drive us boys insane.
Sisters oh I have two
Someone please tell me what I can do.

Cody Wall, Grade 5
North Intermediate Center of Education, IL

Spring

Spring is a season full of fun
Easter egg hunts, green grass and more sun

Flowers bloom, leaves come out
People fishing, camping, and running all about

Tranquil nights with lots of stars
Exquisite moons, lightning bugs in jars

Birds chirping in the morning light
Leaves me asleep in the night

Garrett Higgins, Grade 5
Tri Elementary School, IN

War

It is what keeps us free
It is what keeps us to be
Many people die
And many people cry
I don't see how anyone can suffer this attack
Without fighting back
We are lucky to live
In a country like this
Free to do whatever we choose
WAR
It is easily criticized
When it keeps us alive

Cole Albers, Grade 6
St Mary School, IL

Black

Black,
Awful, coldness,
Frightening, haunting, hiding,
I'm trapped inside fighting, pounding to get out —
Nothing, something, anything,
Trapped, scary,
Darkness

Makayla Manta, Grade 6
Stanley Clark School, IN

The Cabin

The cabin is where I spend my time
The cabin is where I smell the freshly cut grass
The cabin is where I see the sleek lizards
The cabin is where the hummingbirds sing beautifully
The cabin is the place to be for me

The cabin is where I gobble down delicious marshmallows
The cabin is where I spend time with family
The cabin is where I fish in the shimmering lakes
The cabin is the place to be for me

Mackenzie Kendall, Grade 6
Linton-Stockton Elementary School, IN

I Cannot Write a Poem

I cannot write a poem
It's making me real mad
It always starts out really nice
But it always ends up bad

This poem's due on Monday
It's not even half way done
I've never liked poetry
But my friends all think it's fun

My teacher took it yesterday
Though I made a fuss
Today I got my grade back
And I got an "A+!"

Juliana Trach, Grade 5
Countryside School, IL

Friends

F orever
R eal
I ncredible
E nergetic
N ever let go
D epend on
S afe

Morgan Richardson, Grade 5
Perry Central Elementary School, IN

Crabs

Little tiny crabs.
Crawling in and out of rocks.
Try not to get pinched!

Katie Schnautz, Grade 4
Cynthia Heights Elementary School, IN

Believing Without Seeing

I believe but do not see.
In many ways He has helped me.
And when they say that you believe
I do not grieve
I just nod
I believe in God!
I believe but do not see.

Kayla Carlson, Grade 5
GCMS Elementary School, IL

Buddies

B est friends forever!
U make me smile
D ying of laughter
D on't want to lose each other
I love the way you treat me
E verything about you is great
S weeter than my favorite dessert

Erin Tabor, Grade 4
GCMS Elementary School, IL

Television

Television is like birds chirping in the trees
Like the smell of the ocean surrounding you in every step you take
Television is like watching a radio with a screen
Television can be happy or sad
Television can bring people together or split them apart
You can see joyous or tragic events from near or far
I like television just because I can relax

Robby Helme, Grade 5
St John of the Cross Parish School, IL

Wind

Wind blows through your hair whispering words unheard.
It makes noises that you hear but can't see.
Branches are blown by wind and tap your window.
Wind makes an eerie sound like creaky floorboards in an old house.
It whispers in your ear at night when you're alone.
It pulls at your clothes as if saying, "follow me"
Wind is creepy, exciting, and scary and can give you a chill down your spine.

Summer Buckner, Grade 6
Dakota Elementary School, IL

Soccer

When you shoot people say nice boot.
There is the Maradona, bicycle kick, but most important of all pass the ball.
If you don't win people won't give a hoot.
Defense wins championships, but offense sells tickets.
You better win games or you will hear crickets.
You shoot, you score.
You hear the crowd roar.
Passing, dribbling, and scoring are all keys to winning.
During the game your head is spinning.
You wonder how much time is left.
Then all of a sudden the ball is gone it has been stolen.
Even though the game is over the ball is still rollin.

Rudy Grill, Grade 6
St John Evangelist School, IN

Hatred

Hatred is red
Hatred smells of burning bratwurst and steaming seaweed
Hatred tastes like dried up tofu and crusty cheese
Hatred sounds like a screech of a hawk and a squeal of a dying piglet
Hatred feels like a slap across the face and a kick in the shin

Sarah Monnier, Grade 6
East Elementary School, IN

Down in Tennessee

Tennessee, Tennessee, down in the Tennessee hills my sister lives.
Tennessee, Tennessee, down in the Tennessee hills where my sister is getting married.
Tennessee, Tennessee, down in the Tennessee hills where I'm going to bear the rings.

(I'm the ring bearer.)

Walker Milner Tarr, Grade 4
Churubusco Elementary School, IN

I Am

I am a boy who loves to be funny.
I wonder if I will be like Jamie Foxx.
I hear laughter.
I see money.
I want to make people laugh.
I am a boy who loves to be funny.

I pretend I am JJ on *Good Times*.
I feel delighted.
I touch funny bones.
I worry that my teacher will take my recess.
I cry when I have no more jokes.
I am a boy who loves to be funny.

I understand I am funny.
I say I believe I can fly.
I dream that I will be a comedian.
I try not to make people laugh.
I hope I will always be funny.
I am a boy who loves to be funny.

Shannon Wims-Montgomery, Grade 4
Levan Scott Academy, IN

Spring

I love spring.
It's so pretty when the bluebirds sing.
It's fun even though the bees sting.
The grass is always so very green.
The butterflies flutter over the flowers in a beautiful routine.
I tried to count the birds, I think there were eighteen
The best part is playing with friends on the swing.
I love spring.

Daria Floyd, Grade 6
Delphi Academy of Chicago, IL

Retirement

Memories run through my mind
  About a teacher I used to know.
    Although school was long and tiring,
      She motivated me to go.
Most people think she's wonderful,
  And I thought she was nice,
    Because when she raised her voice,
      It was quieter than mice.
The day that she retired
  It made me want to cry.
    She told me to keep up my good grades,
      And I told her I would try.
    The fact that she retired
      Still brings tears to my eyes.
        If anyone asks,
          Mrs. Ullery deserves number 1 prize.

Jacob Harden, Grade 4
Forest Park Elementary School, IN

Mothers

A mother is wonderful
A mother is kind and loving
A mother is great and true
A mother can also be blue
A mother is a beautiful creation of God
A mother is a person who cares for others
A mother always takes a lot of care for her sick child.
A mother is everything.

Marissa Presnell, Grade 6
First Baptist Christian Academy, IL

Beautiful Green Plant

Are you a weed or a flower,
That an herbivore might soon devour?
How did you survive the April shower,
Still standing tall with such great power?
You haven't been torn or ripped within an hour.
I believe that it is a requirement,
To stand together and help the environment!

Lindsay Efken, Grade 5
Maplebrook Elementary School, IL

Fear Coming to You

Fear coming closer, stopping you in movement.
Fear coming to you know it will freeze you.
Fear coming, coming like the wind,
knowing it will stop right the second it will hit you.
Fear coming, coming closer, and closer.
Not knowing what you want to do.
Fear coming, coming, coming knowing you can't do anything.
Not knowing what to do

Montana M. Martin, Grade 4
Churubusco Elementary School, IN

My Likes

The sights I love,
The loving sunrise as it gently warms my face,
Eryn's sweet little body all tucked in,
My warm bed my thinking place.
Things I love to hear,
The peeps of a brand new baby bird
The crickets chirp on a warm summer's night.
My sister squeaking and grumbling; maybe she's dreaming.

Gabby Savieo, Grade 5
Churubusco Elementary School, IN

The Winter Days

You may like to play outside on a winter day,
but some kids stay inside all day.
They see the snow fall down from the sky
while other kids get snow in their eye,
but when it gets too cold outside,
they come on in and drink
hot chocolate and eat some pie.

Alexandra Mendoza, Grade 4
John Simatovich Elementary School, IN

Silly Things

The silly swan sipped syrup
Betty Bop baked bananas
Cory put cake in the cup
Hundreds of hyenas are in the havana
The pup pleaded for pancakes
Five snakes slithered in the savanna

Gabrielle Davis, Grade 5
GCMS Elementary School, IL

Cold Practice

Ice cold practice,
Shivering…shivering

But still sweating,
Plunging your arms,
Into the pool,
Slicing the frigid water,
With every pull.

You can no longer feel,
Your heavy arms,
You can barely do
The next set.

The coach is yelling at you,
You tell him it is cold,
But he does not care.

One more set left,
You try to swim,
As fast as you can,
You are finally done,
Rushing to the locker room,
To take a steaming, hot shower.

Hammer Parker, Grade 6
Linton-Stockton Elementary School, IN

The Story of Bob and Rob

There was a guy named Bob
he liked corn on the cob.
He had a friend named Rob
who really liked to sob
on Bob's corn on the cob!

Jon Kramer, Grade 5
Gard Elementary School, IL

April Showers

Rain
Clear, wet
Drizzling, raining, pouring
Fun to play in
Showers

Mansour Mohammed, Grade 4
Universal School, IL

Squirrel

Squirrel
Fast, jumpy
Gliding, flying, surprising
Outside and on some trees
Adorable

Sarah Alharsha, Grade 4
Universal School, IL

My Mom

Mom
supportive, smart
cares, loves, helps
very experienced family member
Mother

Trevor Endre, Grade 5
Hiawatha Elementary School, IL

Why My Sister Is a Brat

My sister is a brat
To me she is a fat rat
People think she's nice
To me she's like mice
I should feed her to an owl
But I'll save her for my towel
She thinks she's good at ball
But she can't dress a doll
She wants to be a mother
She shouldn't even bother
For right now
She needs to adopt a cow
She thinks she's pretty
Why won't she just be Judge Judy
She once fell off the stairs
Cause it was a dare
I still love her cause she's my sister

Esthela Ramirez, Grade 5
Gard Elementary School, IL

The Little Green Frog

A little green frog
sat on a log
having some fun
in the sun
until it became night
and there was no light

Molly Jorns, Grade 4
Tallula Elementary School, IL

Summer

Summer is awesome
Summer is extremely hot
Summer is the best

Brittany Cernak, Grade 6
Elwood C C School, IL

The Sun

I am like the sun
So bright and optimistic
Caring for the world

Nick Retherford, Grade 6
GCMS Middle School, IL

Magic

Magic is a cat
He belongs to my brother
He is very fat
Sometimes he's a bother.

He is always there for me
He eats like a pig
He will even drink tea
And eat some figs.

He wishes he was free
We always want to play
But all Magic wants to be
Is sleeping all day.

As you can see
Magic is a little annoying
He wants to be with me
He is a cat we're always enjoying.

Michael Foster, Grade 6
Rochester Middle School, IL

Mountain Peaks

Mountain peaks are cold
There are many mountain peaks
Mountain peaks are high

Mycala Feldman, Grade 5
St Jacob Elementary School, IL

Valentine's Day

Valentine's Day will soon be here
Paper hearts are everywhere
Everybody's wearing red
You better hurry out of bed

Hannah Hirstein, Grade 4
Goodfield Elementary School, IL

Night

Night
Starry, beautiful
Sleep, count, gaze
Dark, gigantic, blinding, gorgeous
Play, school, light
Pretty, bright
Day

Courtney Ringger, Grade 5
Adams Central Elementary School, IN

Tapping

Tapping is my favorite thing to do. I'd tap all day, and I'd tap all night, if only I didn't have school.
Tap, tap, tap, I'll dance, dance, dance, in the night and in the bright. Here are some things I like to do:
I'll do a Cramp Roll to a Figure Eight, I'll do my dance to the Pink Panther and then right before my Maxi Ford,
I do the Broadway Time Step, the Hoofer Time Step and the Rhythm Time Step.
That is a pattern that I have never tried before, but I'll try it once and then do it many times more.

Eliza Mozer, Grade 6
Near North Montessori School, IL

Jessica

Jessica
Happy, funny, kind
Sister of Jordan, daughter of Tim and Stephanie
Who loves the Cardinals, Yankees, Colts, and to read
Who feels bad, sick, and sad when Jordan is sick
Who fears of talking in front of people and failing social studies
Who needs help in social studies, has tons of clothes, and likes for Cardinals, Yankees, and Colts to win.
Who gives time to Jordan, friends, and watching sports on TV
Who would love for everyone to stop littering and hopes everybody will recycle and for me to go to California some day.
Evansville
Miles

Jessica Miles, Grade 6
Haubstadt Community School, IN

Sadness

Sadness is blue like the oceans and also the sky
It sinks into me
It reminds me of the times I would spend my younger days swimming in a lake like a fish
It makes me feel lonely like a sailor out at sea
It makes me want to dive into a pool of hope to find my dreams.

Sarah Allen, Grade 6
St Pius X Catholic School, IN

Shoes

I love these shoes these shoes are totally for me
They shine like the whitest teeth
But I don't have enough money to buy them
Maybe my mom will lend me a few dollars
I'm not sure that she will though
Now what will I do I guess I have to earn the money by babysitting
I put out some flyers and I received a phone call
Just like that I earned the money to buy those awesome shoes
So I go back to the shoe store and I am devastated
The shoes that shine like the whitest teeth are gone
I go and ask the manager if they have any more in the back room
The lady checks if they have any and she tells me that they are all out of the awesome shoes
She tells me that she is sorry and they will have a new shipment in about 2 weeks
I'm crushed on the inside I need these shoes
I go to another shoe store that is supposed to have every shoe that you want
I start looking for the shoes and they don't have them either
The store that I am about to walk into has every shoe imaginable
They have them but I need 2 more dollars
So I call my mom and ask if I can take $2 off my credit card and she says yes
I'm so ecstatic I own the best shoes that none of my friends have
YES!!!!

Caitlynn Kreutzer, Grade 6
McHenry Middle School, IL

The Library

The soft hum of computers
breaks the silence
of the empty library.

Books, decades old
battle for space on the shelves.
One is lifted and motes of dust
swirl faintly in the air.

Magazines' pages turned,
by the breeze's unseen hand.
As if a person is reading them,
yet no one is there.

The silence, the peace,
the sacred quiet,
of the empty library.

Katie Day, Grade 6
British School of Chicago, IL

The Test

I'm taking my science test
But is it H_2O or H_2S?
Or is it CO_2 or CO_4?
I do not like this science test
For it is not the best
Is H_2O water or is H_2S?
Is CO_2 or CO_4 sugar
or carbon dioxide?
But then, what is $C_6H_{12}O_6$?
I do not like this science test

Liam Nelson, Grade 5
Countryside School, IL

Water

Water calmly flows,
while it goes and goes.
In the ocean,
with its unique motion.
It owns
all of the animals and their bones.
With dark things lurking,
and bright things smirking.
Water's old eyes
make it bold and wise.
Which is why,
you could ask anything to try.

Valerie Lewis, Grade 4
Naper Elementary School, IL

Waves

Softly parading
The waves rolling toward land
Its roar echoes on

Chrystal Ragasa, Grade 5
Our Lady of Peace School, IL

The Color of Life

Green is a brave color,
Always ready to defend itself
Green is a quiet, whispering color,
Like the wind

Green gives plants life, and emeralds their color
Green would smell fresh and damp,
Like a fragrant flower

Green would taste minty and juicy, like a newly picked vegetable
Green would feel smooth and waxy,
Like a tree leaf

Green is everywhere, like kind people on this green Earth.

Joel Young, Grade 6
Linton-Stockton Elementary School, IN

The Days I Was a Doorknob

The days I was a doorknob in a ten dollar motel,
I've seen many different things that I would like to tell.
One day walked in a salesman with a suitcase and a hat.
Took off his shoes and watched the news and on the bed he sat.

Then he took out his wallet and counted all he had.
Had enough to stay a week so he was feeling glad.
Three days passed, the salesman left, but he had left his hat.
He left it on his little chair, the chair in which he sat.

One day walked in a writer with a laptop in his case.
He had a very dull expression on his dazed and tired face.
Then he turned on his laptop and he began to type.
He was working on his novel so he stayed up all night.

The next day he grew tired, so he slept for an hour.
Then he drank some coffee though the taste was sort of sour.
Three days passed, the writer left, but he had left his pen.
He left it on the table where he placed his laptop then.

As a doorknob I'm not noticed, and that's what I assume,
'cause all they do is turn me, then enter or leave the room.
As a doorknob, I see many things and people old and new.
If someday you're a doorknob, it's nothing you will rue.

Elliot Bibat, Grade 6
St John the Baptist Elementary School, IN

The Game Boy

There once was a boy who read books all day,
With a single toy he never would play.

His parents put him on drugs yet he was still the same,
So they had him hang out with thugs who thought he was a game.

The thugs showed him a tune that was quite grim,
And soon he was singing, not reading, the robbery hymn.

Cole Griffin, Grade 6
Belzer Middle School, IN

Happy Birthday

I saw happiness clearly,
her yellow party dress bouncing with every step.
Her bright blues eyes sparkled with delight,
while she giggled with her friends.
Tissue streamers and balloons floated around her,
and I had to smile myself.

Kyra Noelle Bell, Grade 6
Alexander G Bell Elementary School, IL

Sadness

Sadness is blue from the tears dripping down your face.
Sadness smells like salt from the water of your tears.
Sadness sounds like drip, drop, drip, drop on the floor.
Sadness tastes sour like the person who made you this way.
Sadness feels mushy, soggy, and is extremely weak.

Hannah Watts, Grade 5
East Elementary School, IN

Basketball

Basketball is the thing for me
I'll be dribbling down the court and pop the three
My dribbling is so crisp; I'll tear you into bits
It's so good you can't handle it
My game is so sick it's like mold
When I'm at the line I'm am good as gold
When I shoot everyone screams
They know it's going in, so does my team
Hey I have the whole package, I could pass too
If you are lucky I'll pass it to you
When my teammates and I beat the other team
We'll celebrate at DQ and eat ice cream

Johnny Taylor, Grade 6
St Philip the Apostle School, IL

Basketball

Dribble, dribble
　　Swish!
　　Two points!
Dribble, dribble
　　Ball!
　　Shoot!
　　Two points!
Time Out!
　　Talk, talk, talk
　　Time in!
Dribble, dribble
　　Ball!
　　Miss!
　　Rebound!
Dribble, dribble
　　Buzz!
　　End of Game
No more dribble, dribble
　　Good game, good game, good game

Ellie Seitzinger, Grade 6
St Mary School, IL

Earth's Power

The ocean waves crashed,
as the rain forest's vines slashed.
Antarctica's frozen tundra snowed,
as the mighty volcanoes blew.
As the sorrow of the Grand Canyon groaned,
also Mount Everest moaned.
The desert heat blazed,
as the animals dazed.
That's the power of the Earth.

Wyatt Cole, Grade 5
Central Elementary School, IL

Waterfall

The mountains touch the sky
and the waterfall falls
from the melting snow.
The gentle mist brushes against my cheek.
It's like a loving mother tucking me into bed
and giving me a kiss goodnight.
The mountain's waterfall
is a mother to all living things.
I feel safe when
I'm around Mother Nature.
The gentle sound is soothing,
different from the city's hustle and bustle
to get from place to place.
Time seems to freeze when
I'm near the waterfall.
This is a peaceful place.

Jenny Bartos, Grade 5
Maplebrook Elementary School, IL

Ge Ge

It is the day to say good-bye.
I had to get use to five bowls
And not six.
I'm going to miss him,
Surely.

Smile!
The camera flashes before our eyes.
Our last moment together captures.

I hug him.
He squeezes me like someone crushes a can.
The dorm is freezing
Yet the warmth of the hug lasts.

I wave
And close the door,
Unready to say,
"Good-bye."

Megan Kung, Grade 6
Onahan Elementary School, IL

I Am

I am kind and respectful.
I wonder about my future.
I hear God's voice.
I see the angels dancing.
I want to go see Haiti.
I am kind and respectful.

I pretend I live in a mansion with streets paved in gold.
I feel the heart of a Christian soul.
I touch God's smiling face.
I worry that I will draw away from the Lord.
I cry for joy because of our adoptions.
I am kind and respectful.

I understand my brother who is deaf
I say I believe Christ died for our sins.
I dream about growing up and having a fabulous family.
I try to play well in basketball games
I hope that I will always love and respect my family.
I am kind and respectful.

Jade Holmes, Grade 5
Tremont Elementary School, IL

Love

Love flies through the air on the wings of a dove
Everyone feels peace and tranquility
The dove brings the sound of a waterfall in a peaceful meadow
Love is the laughter of a child
Love is like falling but never hitting the ground
When you are in love
It is like dying and being reborn
Getting lost in the eyes of another,
Always finding your way back home,
That is love.

Elizabeth Sander, Grade 5
St John of the Cross Parish School, IL

The Shadows Are Coming

The shadows are coming, they are getting near.
The shadows are coming, they're here I fear.
I think they are closing in, I feel them here.
I know they are coming, they are coming I fear.
Nearer and nearer, they come into view.
They take down my toys, and I say, "Stop; they are new."
Closer and closer, they're creeping in.
I see them all around, with all the strength of ten men.
I turn around, I stare them in the eye.
"Get out of here," I say, "you big mean guys."
I go outside, into the night
They disappear and I say, "What a delight."
I walk in the house, I go in the den.
I turn around and say, "Not again."

Cole Freel, Grade 5
Elsie Rogers Elementary School, IN

Oh, What a Whale!

Whales are exciting
They're a treasure in the sea
They're the largest animal in the sea, even larger than me
The largest is the blue whale
No need to have fear
No need to turn pale
It's only a big blue whale
Most whales eat just krill
They are small, if you will
Unless they have razor-sharp teeth
If the squid population goes down
You may see a frown
You'll know that a sperm whale has come to town
Have you come for a song?
With a jump that is long?
Come see the humpback whale
Here comes an orca
Eating many things in the sea
Don't you just love whales
With their big, broad tails?
They're a load of fun in the sea

Adam Kremer, Grade 6
St Theresa School, IN

Things I Hate About You

I hate the way you talk to me
The way you look into my eyes
I hate the way you laugh
The way you make me smile
I hate the way your eyes look
When you make me cry
I hate you so much it's unbearable
But inside I lie

I hate the way your hands feel
I hate it when you smile
I hate the way you sit next to her and flirt
Like there's no tomorrow
I hate it when you lie to me
And talk behind my back
I hate all the qualities you will always lack
I hate you so much and with that I can't lie,
I hate you so much
I have to say goodbye

Justice Skidmore, Grade 6
Linton-Stockton Elementary School, IN

Index

Author Autograph Page

Tara Cecelia Murray
9/6/07

Author Autograph Page

Author Autograph Page

Author Autograph Page

Author Autograph Page

Author Autograph Page